# Formations

## OF FANTASY

# Formations
## OF FANTASY

Edited by
Victor Burgin, James Donald and Cora Kaplan

ROUTLEDGE
London and New York

*First published in 1986 by*
*Methuen & Co. Ltd*
*Reprinted 1989 by*
*Routledge*
*11 New Fetter Lane, London EC4P 4EE*
*29 West 35th Street, New York NY 10001*

*British Library Cataloguing in Publication Data*

*Formations of fantasy.*
  *1. Fantasy      2. Psychoanalysis*
  *I. Burgin, Victor      II. Donald, James*
  *III. Kaplan, Cora*
  *153.3            BF175*
  *ISBN 0-415-05099-5*

*Library of Congress Cataloging in Publication Data*

*Formations of fantasy.*
  *Bibliography: p.*
  *Includes index.*
  *1. Psychoanalysis.    2. Fantasy.    I. Burgin, Victor.*
  *II. Donald, James.    III. Kaplan, Cora.*
  *BV175.F635    1986      154      86-21827*
  *ISBN 0-415-050995*

# CONTENTS

# CONTRIBUTORS

**Jean Laplanche** and **Jean-Bertrand Pontalis** are the co-authors of *The Language of Psychoanalysis* (Hogarth Press, 1973). Jean Laplanche is Professor of Psychoanalysis at the Sorbonne and author of *Hölderlin et la question du père* and *Life and Death in Psychoanalysis* (Johns Hopkins, 1976). Jean-Bertrand Pontalis has been editor of *Nouvelle Revue de Psychanalyse* since it was launched in 1970 and is the author of *Frontiers in Psychoanalysis: Between the Dream and Psychic Pain* (Hogarth Press, 1981). Both have been president of the French Psychoanalytic Association . . . **Stephen Heath** teaches at the University of Cambridge. Among his books are *The Nouveau Roman, Vertige du Deplacement, Questions of Cinema* and *The Sexual Fix* . . . **Francette Pacteau** is currently doing research for a doctoral thesis, on the concept of feminine beauty, at the University of Kent . . . **Victor Burgin** is a Senior Lecturer in the History and Theory of the Visual Arts at the Polytechnic of Central London. His most recent books are *The End of Art Theory: Criticism and Post-Modernity* (Macmillan) and *Between* (Basil Blackwell/ICA) . . . **John Fletcher** lectures in English at Warwick University; he is also involved in the Centre for Research in Philosophy and Literature at Warwick and in Queory, a gay men's theory and literature group . . . **Cora Kaplan** teaches English and American Studies at Sussex University and is author of *Sea Changes: Essays on Culture and Feminism* (Verso, 1986) . . . **Valerie Walkerdine** is a lecturer at the University of London Institute of Education, and is doing research into concepts of gender and education. She is a co-author of *Changing the Subject* (Methuen, 1984) . . . **Erica Carter** and **Chris Turner** work together as translators under the name *Material Word*. Current projects include a collection on Max Weber for Allen & Unwin, and the German feminist text *Frauenformen* for Verso.

# ACKNOWLEDGEMENTS

The editors and publishers would like to thank the following journal editors, organizations and publishers for permission to reproduce copyright material that appears on the pages below. Although every effort has been made to trace copyright holders, they apologise in advance for any unintentional omission or neglect and will be pleased to insert the appropriate acknowledgement in any subsequent edition of this book:
The editors of *The International Journal of Psychoanalysis* for 'Fantasy and the origins of sexuality' by Jean Laplanche and Jean-Bertrand Pontalis on pp. 5–34; Libraire de la Société des Gens de Lettres, Paris, for Alexandre Séon, frontispiece of *L'Androgyne* by Joséphin Péladan on p. 65; Collegiata di San Gimignano (Siena) for Bartolo de Fredi, *The Creation of Eve* on p. 67; Musée Rodin, Paris, for Auguste Rodin, *Paola and Francesca in Clouds* on p. 69; Nationalmuseum, Stockholm, for the Greek hermaphrodite statue on p. 72; Libraire de France, Paris, for *Harlequin Breastfeeds his Son* on p. 75; Gaumont British Films for *First a Girl*, 1935, on pp. 78–9 (stills reproduced by courtesy of the Rank Organization, PLC); Musée Royaux des Beaux Arts de Belgique for Fernand Knopff, *Silence*, on p. 80; the Trustees of The National Gallery, London, for Peter-Paul Rubens, *The Judgment of Paris* on p. 87; The Metropolitan Museum of Art, New York (bequest of William K. Vanderbilt, 1920, 20.155.9), for François Boucher, *The Toilet of Venus* on p. 88; the Trustees of The Wallace Collection, London, for Jean-Baptiste Greuze, *The Broken Mirror*, on p. 89; The Tate Gallery, London, for John Everett Millais, *Ophelia* on p. 102; for the still from *Vertigo* on p. 103 – The National Film Archive, London, Stills Collection. Copyright © by Universal Pictures, a Division of Universal City Studios, Inc. All rights reserved. Courtesy of MCA Publishing Rights, a Division of MCA Inc.; Sylvester Stallone, United Artists and MGM/UA Entertainment Co. for *Rocky II* on p. 170.

# PREFACE

In a recent film about the visit of a Red Cross delegation to a Uraguayan gaol for political prisoners, one of the inmates explains that he has been imprisoned for 'harbouring thoughts likely to disrupt public order'.[1] It is as a defence against this particularly nightmarish form of political inquisition that the liberal tradition has insisted on the distinction between mind and deed, expressed in the English legal maxim, 'the thought of man is not tryable'. The imperative to maintain this particular limit to the jurisdiction of the state has no doubt contributed to that climate of hostility which today prevails, on the democratic left, against *any* consideration of psychology in connection with the political. One consequence (perhaps most conspicuously displayed in the consistent failure of the left to understand nationalism) has been that the mobilizing force of *fantasy* has been effectively ceded to the right.

There is a fundamental objection in common sense to considering fantasy in the context of the social and political. In *Roget's Thesaurus* 'fantasy' is flanked by 'poetry' on one side, and 'visual fallacy' on the other. The distribution of these terms is in agreement with the broad range of everyday uses of the word. On the one hand, the term 'poetry' invokes a more or less intentional act of imagination; on the other hand, 'visual fallacy' signals the unintentional, the hallucinatory. Whatever the case, however, whether the particular sense of 'fantasy' in question is nuanced towards the voluntary caprice or the involuntary delusion, in popular understanding 'fantasy' is always opposed to 'reality'. In this definition fantasy is the *negative* of reality. Here 'reality' is conceived as that which is 'external' to our 'inner' lives. In this common-sense view we simultaneously inhabit two distinct histories: one mental, private; the other physical, public. Political and social considerations are seen as belonging to the latter arena of common empirical realities. Gilbert Ryle, however, noted a fundamental defect of the common-sense view: 'the *transactions* between the episodes of the private history and the public history remain mysterious, since by definition they can only belong to neither series' (our emphasis).[2] It is to this 'mysterious' area of transaction that psychoanalysis allows us access through the theory of the *unconscious* which posits, precisely, '*die Idee einer anderer Lokalität*, the idea of another locality, another space, another scene, *the between perception and consciousness*'.[3] That space in which fantasy stages its *mise-en-scène* of desire.

The widespread resistance, on the left, to the use of psychoanalytic theory[4] (even at the cost of clinging to a tacit uneasy amalgam of behaviourism and psychologism in a social and political environment that is so patently unlawful, unreasonable and irrational) seems further due to a fundamental misrecognition of psychoanalytic method. This is well illustrated in a story told by a psychoanalyst of his encounter with a group of social scientists studying the origins of Nazism:

> I mentioned among other factors ... the failure of German nineteenth-century liberalism, and the subsequent impact of Prussian militarism ... I also mentioned the impact of rapid industrialisation upon a society still almost feudal ... I was then interrupted by my host ... this was not what I had been expected to contribute. As a psychoanalyst I should point out how Nazism had developed from the German form of child rearing. I replied that I did not think that there was any such relationship; in fact, political opinion did not seem to me to be determined in early childhood at all. This view was not accepted and I was told that the way the German mother holds her baby must be different from that of mothers in democracies. When we parted it was clear that my hosts felt that they had wasted their time.[5]

Psychoanalysis does not intend to uncover objective causes *in* reality so much as it seeks to change our very attitudes *to* that reality. This it achieves by effectively deconstructing that positivist dichotomy in which fantasy is simply *opposed* to 'reality', as an epiphenomenon. Psychoanalysis dismantles such a 'logic of the supplement' to reveal the supposedly marginal operations of fantasy at the centre of all our perceptions, beliefs and actions. The object of psychoanalysis is not the 'reality' of common sense, and (in a prevalent view) of empirical science; it is what Freud termed 'psychical reality'. Contrary to psychologism, psychoanalysis recognises no state of totally unambiguous and self-possessed lucidity in which an external world may be seen for, and known as, simply what it *is*. There is no possible 'end to ideologies'. Unconscious wishes, and the fantasies they engender, are as immutable a force in our lives as any material circumstance. The essays collected here all, in their various ways, acknowledge this fact.

We have taken the opportunity to reprint, and thus make more easily available, two essays which in their different ways have become primary points of orientation for some recent cultural theory. The article by

Laplanche and Pontalis on 'Fantasy and the origins of sexuality' (1964) is a brilliant synthesis of Freud's own writings on fantasy, the single most comprehensive account available, which also throws a (Lacanian) light on some of the more shadowy areas of the theory (albeit an illumination which the authors have modulated in their subsequent work, as Professor Laplanche reminds us in his postface to this now 'classic' essay). Demonstrating the extraordinary richness of the Freudian concept of fantasy, this article, by implication, indicates the impoverishment to which the concept has since often been submitted.[6] 'Fantasy and the origins of sexuality' guides us through the labyrinths of the psychical; Joan Riviere's article, 'Womanliness as a masquerade' (1929), conducts us to the promise and the problem of psychoanalysis in the arena of the social. On the one hand, psychoanalytic theory offers an understanding of the *construction* of social subjects in sexual difference – constructed, therefore *mutable*. On the other hand, as Stephen Heath observes in his commentary on Riviere's essay, 'the terms of that understanding give us a pattern of development . . . which seems to fix things for ever in the given, and oppressive, identities, with no connections through to the *social-historical* realities that it also seems accurately to be describing'.

The *articulation* of psychical and social, Heath remarks, is, 'Easier said than done'. What the following articles have in common is simply their recognition of cultural theory's need for such an articulation, one which will not simply collapse the one 'side' into the other in some straining after 'synthesis' (Hegelian desideratum of Freudo–Marxism). 'Easier said than done' perhaps, but though the difficulties remain ineradicable, the necessity rests inescapable.

## Notes

1. *The Eyes of Birds*, Gabriel Auer, France, 1982.
2. G. Ryle, *The Concept of Mind*, Harmondsworth, Penguin, 1963, p.14.
3. J. Lacan, *The Four Fundamental Concepts of Psychoanalysis*, London, Hogarth Press, 1977, p.56.
4. In mitigation it should be recognized that, although Freudian *theory* has been, from the beginning, radical in its social and political implications, the history of the *institution* of psychoanalysis as a professional practice has overwhelmingly tended to elide the socially radical nature of Freud's legacy. See R. Jacoby, *The Repression of Psychoanalysis: Otto Fenichel and the Political Freudians*, New York, Basic Books, 1983.
5. R. Waelder, *Basic Theory of Psychoanalysis*, New York, International Universities Press, 1960, pp.53–4, quoted in P. Roazen, *Freud: Social and Political Thought*, New York, Vintage Books, 1968, pp.15–16.
6. In D.W. Winnicott, for example, where 'an intermediate area of experience . . . (arts, religion, etc.)' is posited as a 'relief' from 'the strain of relating inner and outer reality'. Such functional 'play' being distinguished from dysfunctional 'fantasying', which in its turn is opposed to the dream as being 'a dead end' without symbolic value (D.W. Winnicott, *Playing and Reality*, Harmondsworth, Penguin, 1982, pp.15, 42). For Winnicott, as for the sociologists in the anecdote quoted by Roazen above, 'Child-and-mother was

the theme song' (J. Mitchell, *Psychoanalysis and Feminism*, Harmondsworth, Penguin, 1974, p.228). Today, this refrain has been taken up by a certain 'left-humanist' sector of cultural studies and aesthetic theory. What object-relations theories hold in common is the presupposition of a world of 'objects' preconstituted as always-already 'there' for recognition. What is thereby left out is the *constitutive* role of representations, substantial and psychical, conscious and unconscious, in the cultural production of 'reality'. What results from this 'post-Freudianism' is, effectively, a comforting (indeed, sentimental) *pre-Freudian* positivism. 'Reality' again becomes the privileged, *prior*, term – applied only to the public realm and, along with this realm, segregated from the unconscious. Thus insulated from history, the 'reality' of the mother–child relationship is installed as the transcendental 'biological constant' at the heart of all representations. (For a succinct critique of object-relations theory, particularly in relation to its use in theories of art and literature, see Elizabeth Wright, *Psychoanalytic Criticism*, London, Methuen, 1984, chapter 6, pp.79–98.)

Jean Laplanche and Jean-Bertrand Pontalis

# FANTASY AND THE ORIGINS
# OF SEXUALITY[1]

From its earliest days, psychoanalysis has been concerned with the material of fantasy. In the initial case of Anna O., Breuer was apparently content to plunge into the patient's inner world of imagination, into her 'private theatre', in order to achieve catharsis through verbalization and emotive expression. 'I used to visit her in the evening,' he writes, 'when I knew I should find her in her hypnosis, and I then relieved her of the whole stock of imaginative products which she had accumulated since my last visit.'[2]

It is remarkable to note, when studying this case, how Breuer, unlike Freud, is little concerned to recover the elements of experience which might underlie these daydreams. The event which provoked the trauma is considered to contain an imaginary element, a hallucination leading to trauma. There is a circular relationship between the fantasy and the dissociation of consciousness which leads to the formation of an unconscious nucleus: fantasy becomes trauma when it arises from a special hypnoid state but, equally, the panic states it induces help to create this fundamental state by a process of auto-hypnosis.

If Breuer worked from within the world of imagination and tried to reduce its pathogenic force without reference to extrinsic factors, the same can be said of the methods of certain contemporary analysts, notably the followers of Melanie Klein. First, the imaginary dramas underlying the verbal or behavioural material produced by the patient during the session – for instance, introjection or projection of the breast or penis, intrusions, conflicts or compromises with good or bad objects and so on – are made explicit and verbalized (no doubt in this case by the analyst).[3] A successful outcome to the treatment, if it does lead eventually to a better adaptation to reality, is not expected from any corrective initiative, but from the dialectic 'integration' of the fantasies as they emerge. Ultimately the introjection of the good object (no less imaginary than the bad) permits a fusion of the instincts in an equilibrium based on the predominance of the libido over the death instinct.

Fantasy, in German 'Phantasie', is the term used to denote the imagination, and not so much the faculty of imagining (the philosophers'

*Einbildungskraft*) as the imaginary world and its contents, the imaginings or fantasies into which the poet or the neurotic so willingly withdraws. In the scenes which the patient describes, or which are described to him by the analyst, the fantastic element is unmistakable. It is difficult therefore to avoid defining this world in terms of what it is not, the world of reality. This opposition antedates psychoanalysis by many centuries, but is liable to prove restrictive both to psychoanalytic theory and practice.

Psychoanalysts have fared rather badly with the theory itself, all too often basing it on a very elementary theory of knowledge.

Analysts such as Melanie Klein, with techniques devoid of any therapeutic intention, are, more than others, careful to distinguish between the contingent imagery of daydreams and the structural function and permanence of what they call 'unconscious phantasies'. (We shall discuss this distinction later.) Yet in the last resort they maintain that the latter are 'false perceptions'. The 'good' and 'bad' object should, for *us*, always be framed in quotation marks,[4] even though the whole evolution of the patient will occur within this framework.

Turning to Freud, we shall find a marked ambiguity of his conceptions as new avenues open out to him with each new stage in his ideas. If we start with the most accepted formulation of his doctrine, the world of fantasy seems to be located exclusively within the domain of opposition between subjective and objective, between an inner world, where satisfaction is obtained through illusion, and an external world, which gradually, through the medium of perception, asserts the supremacy of the reality principle. The unconscious thus appears to inherit the patient's original world which was solely subject to the pleasure principle. The fantasy world is not unlike the nature reserves which are set up to preserve the original natural state of the country:

> With the introduction of the reality principle one species of thought-activity was split off; it was kept free from reality-testing and remained subject to the pleasure principle alone. This activity is *'fantasying'*.[5]

> The strangest characteristic of unconscious processes is due to their entire disregard of reality testing; they equate reality of thought with external actuality, and wishes with their fulfilment.[6]

This absence of the 'standards of reality' in the unconscious may lead to its being depreciated as a lesser being, a less differentiated state.

In psychoanalytic practice any inadequacy of the conceptual background cannot fail to make itself felt. It is no purely formal necessity to recall how many techniques are founded on this opposition between the real and the imaginary, and which envisage the integration of the pleasure principle into the reality principle, a process which the neurotic is supposed to have only partially achieved. No doubt any analyst would find it incorrect to invoke 'realities' external to the treatment, since the material must be developed in the context of the analyst–patient relationship, the transference. But, unless we are careful, any interpretation of the transference 'You are treating me as if I . . .' will imply the underlying '. . . and you know very well that I am not really what you think I am'.

Fortunately we are saved by the technique: we do not actually make this underlying comment.[7] Speaking more fundamentally, the analytical rule should be understood as a Greek $\epsilon\pi o\chi\pi$, an absolute suspension of all reality judgements. This places us on the same level as the unconscious, which knows no such judgements. A patient tells us that he is an adopted child, and relates fantasies in which, while searching for his true mother, he perceives that she is a society woman turned prostitute. Here we recognize the banal theme of the 'family romance', which might equally well have been composed by a child who had not been adopted. In the course of our 'phenomenological reduction' we should no longer make any distinction, except to interpret, as a 'defence by reality', the documents which the patient brings to prove his adoption.[8]

Preoccupied, understandably, by the urge to discover at what level he was working, Freud does not come out so well when he has to justify the suspension of reality judgements in the course of treatment. At first he feels it almost his duty to show the patient what is under the counter. But, caught like the patient himself between the alternatives real–imaginary, he runs the double risk of either seeing the patient lose all interest in the analysis, if he is told that the material produced is nothing but imagination (*Einbildung*), or incurring his reproaches later for having encouraged him to take his fantasies for realities.[9] Freud has recourse here to the notion of 'psychical reality', a new dimension not immediately accessible to the analysand. But what does Freud mean by this term?

Frequently it means nothing more than the reality of our thoughts, of our personal world, a reality at least as valid as that of the material world and, in the case of neurotic phenomena, decisive. If we mean by this that we contrast the reality of psychological phenomena with 'material reality',[10] the reality of thought with 'external actuality',[11] we are in fact just saying that we are dealing with what is imaginary, with the subjective, but that this subjective is our object: the object of psychology is as valid as that of the sciences of material nature. And even the term itself, 'psychical reality', shows that Freud felt he could confer the dignity of object on psychological phenomena only by reference to material reality, for he asserts that 'they too possess a reality of a sort'.[12] In the absence of any *new* category, the suspension of reality judgements leads us once more into the 'reality' of the purely subjective.

Yet this is not Freud's last word. When he introduces this concept of 'psychical reality', in the last lines of the *Interpretation of Dreams*, which sums up his thesis that a dream is not a fantasmagoria, but a text to be deciphered, Freud does not define it as constituting the *whole* of the subjective, like the psychological field, but as a heterogeneous nucleus within this field, a resistant element, alone truly real, in contrast with the majority of psychological phenomena:

> Whether we are to attribute *reality* to unconscious wishes, I cannot say. It must be denied, of course, to any transitional or intermediate thoughts. If we look at unconscious wishes reduced to their most fundamental and truest shape, we shall have to conclude, no doubt, that *psychical* reality is a particular form of existence which is not to be confused with *material* reality.[13]

There are therefore three kinds of phenomena (or of realities, in the widest sense of the word): material reality, the reality of intermediate thoughts or of the psychological field, and the reality of unconscious wishes and their 'truest shape': fantasy. If Freud, again and again, finds and then loses the notion of psychical reality, this is not due to any inadequacy of his conceptual apparatus: the difficulty and ambiguity lie in the very nature of its relationship, to the real and to the imaginary, as is shown in the central domain of fantasy.[14]

The years 1895–9 which completed the discovery of psychoanalysis are significant not only because of the dubious battle taking place but also because of the oversimplified way in which its history is written.

If we read, for instance, Kris's introduction to the *Origins of Psychoanalysis*,[15] the evolution of Freud's views seems perfectly clear: the facts, and more especially Freud's own self-analysis, apparently led him to abandon his theory of seduction by an adult. The scene of seduction which until then represented for him the typical form of psychological trauma is not a real event but a fantasy which is itself only the product of, and a mask for, the spontaneous manifestations of infantile sexual activity. In his 'History of the psychoanalytic movement' Freud thus traces the development of his theory from his experience:

> If hysterical subjects trace back their symptoms to traumas that are fictitious, then the new fact which emerges is precisely that they create such scenes in *fantasy*, and this psychical reality requires to be taken into account alongside practical reality. This reflection was soon followed by the discovery that these fantasies were intended to

cover up the autoerotic activity of the first years of childhood, to embellish it and raise it to a higher plane. And now, from behind the fantasies, the whole range of a child's sexual life came to light.[16]

Freud would, in these lines, be admitting his error in imputing to the 'outside' something that concerns the 'inside'.

The very words, '*theory* of sexual seduction', should arrest our attention: the elaboration of a schema to explain the aetiology of neuroses, and not the purely clinical *observation* of the frequency of the seduction of children by adults, nor even a simple *hypothesis* that such occurrences would preponderate among the different kinds of traumas. Freud was concerned theoretically to justify the connection he had discovered between sexuality, trauma and defence: to show that it is in the very nature of sexuality to have a traumatic effect and, inversely, that one cannot finally speak of trauma as the origin of neurosis except to the extent that sexual seduction has occurred. As this thesis becomes established (1895–7), the role of the defensive conflict in the genesis of hysteria, and of the defence in general, is fully recognized, although the aetiological function of trauma is not thereby reduced. The notions of defence and trauma are closely articulated one to the other: the theory of seduction, by showing how only a sexual trauma has the power to activate a 'pathological defence' (repression) is an attempt to do justice to a clinically established fact (*Studies on Hysteria*), that repression concerns specifically sexuality.

We should consider a moment the schema propounded by Freud. The action of the trauma can be broken down into various time sequences and always implies the existence of *at least two events*. In the first scene, called 'seduction scene', the child is subjected to a sexual approach from the adult ('attempt' or simply advances), without arousing any sexual excitation in himself. To try to describe such a scene as traumatic would be to abandon the somatic model of trauma, since there is neither an afflux of external excitation nor an overflow of the defences. If it can be described as sexual, it is only from the point of view of the external agent, the adult. But the child has neither the somatic requisites of excitation nor the representations to enable him to integrate the event: although sexual in terms of objectivity, it has no sexual connotation for the subject, it is 'pre-sexually sexual'.[17] As for the second scene, which occurs after puberty, it is, one might say, even less traumatic than the first: being non-violent, and apparently of no particular significance, its only power lies in being able to evoke the first event, retroactively, by means of association. It is then the recall of the first scene which sets off the upsurge of sexual excitation, catching the ego in reverse, and leaving it disarmed, incapable of using the normally outward-directed defences, and thus falling back on a pathological defence, or 'posthumous primary process'; the recollection is repressed.

If we dwell on concepts which might, at first sight, appear only of historic interest since they seem to presuppose an innocent child, without sexuality, thus contradicting undeniable later findings, it is not solely to outline the various stages of a discovery.

This explanatory schema, which Freud described as *proton pseudos*, is of remarkable value in considering the significance of human sexuality. In fact, it introduces two major propositions. On the one hand, in the first stage, sexuality literally breaks in from outside, intruding forcibly into the world of childhood, presumed to be innocent, where it is encysted as a simple happening without provoking any defence reaction – not in itself a pathogenic event. On the other hand, in the second stage, the pressure of puberty having stimulated the physiological awakening of sexuality, there is a sense of unpleasure, and the origin of this unpleasure is traced to the recollection of the first event, an external event which has become an inner event, an inner 'foreign body', which now breaks out from within the subject.[18]

This is a surprising way to settle the question of trauma. The question often arises, whether it is an afflux of external excitation which creates the trauma or whether, on the contrary, it is the internal excitation, the drive, which, lacking an outlet, creates a 'state of helplessness'[19] in the subject.

However, with the theory of seduction, we may say that the whole of the trauma comes *both* from within and without: from without, since sexuality reaches the subject from *the other*;[20] from within, since it springs from this internalized exteriority, this *'reminiscence* suffered by hysterics' (according to the Freudian formula), reminiscence in which we already discern what will be later named fantasy. This is an attractive solution, but it is liable to collapse when the meaning of each term deviates: the external towards the event, the internal towards the endogenous and biological.

Let us look at the seduction theory more positively and try to salvage its deeper meaning. It is Freud's first and sole attempt to establish an intrinsic relationship between repression and sexuality.[21] He finds the mainspring of this relationship, not in any 'content', but in the temporal characteristics of human sexuality, which make it a privileged battlefield between both too much and too little excitation, both too early and too late occurrence of the event: 'Here we have the one possibility of a memory subsequently producing a more powerful release than that produced by the corresponding experience itself' (Draft K). Hence the repartition of the trauma into two stages, as the psychological trauma can be conceived only as arising from something *already there*, the reminiscence of the first scene.

But how can we conceive the formation of this 'already there', and how can this first scene, which is 'pre-sexually sexual', acquire a meaning for the subject? Given a perspective which tends to reduce temporal dimensions to chronology, one must either embark on an infinite regression in which each scene acquires sexual quality solely through the evocation of an earlier scene without which it would have no meaning for the subject or, on the other hand, one must stop short arbitrarily at a 'first' scene, however inconceivable it may be.

No doubt the doctrine of an innocent world of childhood into which sexuality is introduced by perverse adults is pure illusion: illusion, or rather a myth, whose very contradictions betray the nature. We must conceive of the child both as outside time, a *bon sauvage*, and as one already endowed with sexuality, at least in germ, which is ready to be awakened; we must accept the idea of an intrusion from without into an interior which perhaps did not exist as such before this intrusion: we must reconcile the passivity which is implied by merely receiving meaning from outside with the minimum of activity necessary for the experience even to be acknowledged, and the indifference of innocence with the disgust which the seduction is assumed to provoke. To sum up, we have a subject who is pre-subjectal, who receives his existence, his sexual existence, from without, before a distinction between within and without is achieved.

Forty years later Ferenczi was to take up the theory of seduction and give it analogous importance.[22] His formulations are no doubt less rigorous than Freud's, but they have the advantage of filling out the myth with two essential ingredients: behind the facts, and through their mediation, it is a new *language*, that of passion, which is introduced by the adult into the infantile 'language' of tenderness. On the other hand, this language of passion is the language of desire, necessarily marked by prohibition, a language of guilt and hatred, including the sense of annihilation linked with orgastic pleasure.[23] The fantasy of the primal scene with its character of violence shows the child's introjection of adult erotism.

Like Freud in 1895, Ferenczi is led to assign a chronological location to this intrusion, and to presuppose a real nature of the child before seduction. One might, on the other hand, be tempted to close the discussion once and for all by introducing the concept of myth: the seduction would become the myth of the origin of sexuality by the introjection of adult desire, fantasy and 'language'. The relationship of the myth to the time factor (the event) is present and, as it were, embedded in the myth itself. But we cannot rest there. This myth (or fantasy) of the intrusion of the fantasy (or myth) into the subject, cannot but occur to the organism, the little human being, at a point in time, by virtue of certain characteristics of his biological evolution, in which we can already distinguish what is too much or too little, too early (birth) and too late (puberty).

In 1897 Freud abandoned his theory of seduction. On 21 September he wrote to Fliess: 'I will confide in you at once the great secret that has been slowly dawning on me in the last few months: I no longer believe in my *neurotica* . . .'. He adduces a number of arguments. Some were factual: the impossibility of conducting analyses to their conclusion, that is, back to the first pathogenic event; even in the deepest psychosis – where the unconscious seems the most accessible – the key to the enigma is not available. Others were of a logical nature: one would have to generalize the father's perversity even beyond the cases of hysteria, since when hysteria supervenes it entails the intervention of other factors. On the other hand, and this is the point that interests us, 'there are no indications of reality in the unconscious, so that one cannot distinguish between the truth and fiction that is cathected with affect'. Two solutions are mentioned by Freud, either to consider fantasies of childhood as only the retroactive effect of a reconstruction performed by the adult (which would amount to the Jungian concept of retrospective fantasies [*Zurückphanta-sieren*] which Freud rejected), or to revert to the idea of hereditary predisposition. If this second possibility – which Freud admitted he had always 'repressed' – returns to favour, it is because the search for the first scene has led to an impasse. But it is also because Freud, momentarily at a loss, did not succeed in isolating the positive element, lying beyond the realistic chronological approach, in the seduction theory. If the event evades us, then the alternative factor, constitution, is rehabilitated. Since reality, in one of its forms, is absent, and proves to be only fiction, then we must seek elsewhere for a reality on which this fiction is based.

When the historians of psychoanalysis tell us, picking up Freud's own version of his evolution, that the abandonment of the seduction theory in the face of facts cleared the ground for the discovery of infantile sexuality, they oversimplify a much more involved process. To a contemporary psychoanalyst, to Kris as to us, infantile sexuality is inseparable from the Oedipus complex. And in effect, at the very moment of the 'abandonment' of seduction, we find three themes predominant in the correspondence with Fliess: infantile sexuality, fantasy, and the Oedipus complex. But the real problem lies in their interrelation. And we find that inasmuch as real trauma and the seduction scene have been effectively swept away,[24] they have not been replaced by the Oedipus complex but by the description of a spontaneous infantile sexuality, basically endogenous in development. Libidinal stages succeeding each other in a natural and regular evolution, fixation considered as an inhibition of development, genetic regression, form at least one of the perspectives suggested in the *Three Essays on Sexuality* (1905). In this direction, we must notice that the second essay, on infantile sexuality, discusses neither the Oedipus complex nor fantasy. An article which appeared at the same time as the *Three Essays* is typical of this point of view: in it Freud is able to discuss his 'Views on the part played by sexuality in the aetiology of the neuroses' (1906) without a single word about the Oedipus complex. The sexual development of the child is here defined as endogenous, and determined by the sexual constitution:

> Accidental influences derived from experience having thus receded into the background, the factors of constitution and heredity necessarily gained the upper hand once more; but there was this difference between my views and those prevailing in other quarters, that on my theory the 'sexual constitution' took the place of a 'general neuropathic disposition'.

It may however be objected that it was also in 1897, at the very moment when he abandoned the seduction theory, that Freud in his self-analysis discovered the Oedipus complex. We should emphasize, though, that in spite of Freud's immediate recognition of its importance, the Oedipus complex was, for twenty years, to lead a marginal existence alongside his theoretical syntheses. It was deliberately set apart in a section devoted to 'the choice of objects at puberty' (in the *Three Essays*), or to studies of 'typical dreams' (in *The Interpretation of Dreams*). In our opinion the discovery of the Oedipus complex in 1897 was neither the cause of the abandonment of the seduction theory, nor clearly indicated as its successor. It seems much more probable that, being encountered in a 'wild' form in the seduction theory, the Oedipus complex nearly suffered the same fate of being replaced by biological realism.

Freud himself recognized, much later, all that was positive and foreboding in the seduction theory: 'here I had stumbled for the first time upon the Oedipus complex'[25] or again,

> I came to understand that hysterical symptoms are derived from fantasies and not from real occurrences. It was only later that I was able to recognize in this fantasy of being seduced by the father the expression of the typical Oedipus complex . . .[26]

At that time (1897) Freud had discarded on the one hand the idea, contained in the seduction theory, of a foreign body which introduces human sexuality into the subject from without, and, on the other hand, discovered that the sexual drive becomes active before puberty. But for some time he was not able to articulate the Oedipus complex with infantile sexuality. If the latter existed, as clinical observation undoubtedly proved, it could henceforward only be *conceived* as biological reality, fantasy being no more than the secondary expression of this reality. The scene in which the subject describes his seduction by an older companion is, in fact, a double disguise: pure fantasy is converted into real memory, and spontaneous sexual activity into passivity.[27] One is no longer justified in attributing psychical reality – in the stricter sense sometimes employed by Freud – to the fantasy, since reality is now totally attributed to an endogenous sexuality, and since fantasies are only considered to be a purely imaginary efflorescence of this sexuality.

Something was lost with the discarding of the seduction theory: beneath the conjunction and the temporal interplay of the two 'scenes' there lay a pre-subjective structure, beyond both the strict happening and the internal imagery. The prisoner of a series of theoretical alternatives, subject–object, constitution–event, internal–external, imaginary–real, Freud was for a time led to stress the first terms of these 'pairs of opposites'.

This would suggest the following paradox: at the very moment when fantasy, the fundamental object of psychoanalysis, is discovered, it is in danger of seeing its true nature obscured by the emphasis on an endogenous reality, sexuality, which is itself supposed to be in conflict with a normative, prohibitory external reality, which imposes on it various disguises. We have indeed the fantasy, in the sense of a product of the imagination, but we have lost the structure. Inversely, with the seduction theory we had, if not the theory, at least an *intuition* of the structure (seduction appearing as an almost universal datum, which in any case transcended both the event and, so to speak, its protagonists). The ability to elaborate the fantasy was, however, if not unknown, at least underestimated.

It would be taking a very limited view to describe as follows the evolution of Freud's ideas during the period around 1897: from historical foundation of the symptoms to the establishment of an ultimately biological theory, to the causal sequence, sexual constitution→fantasy→symptom. Freud never makes the theory entirely his own until he is obliged to present his aetiological views in systematic fashion. If we intended, which we do not, to present a step-by-step account of the development of his thought, we should have to distinguish at least two other currents in this central period.

The one derives from the fresh understanding of fantasy which is effective from 1896 onwards: fantasy is not merely material to be analysed, whether appearing as fiction from the very start (as in daydreaming) or whether it remains to be shown that it is a construction contrary to appearances (as in screen-memory), it is also the result of analysis, an end-product, a latent content to be revealed behind the symptom. From *mnesic symbol* of trauma, the symptom has become the *stage-setting of fantasies* (thus a fantasy of prostitution, of street-walking, might be discovered beneath the symptom of agoraphobia).

Freud now starts to explore the field of these fantasies, to make an inventory, and to describe their most typical forms. Fantasies are now approached from two aspects at once, both as manifest data and latent content; and, located thus at the crossroads, they acquire in due course the consistency of an object, the specific object of psychoanalysis. Henceforward analysis will continue to treat fantasy as 'psychical reality', whilst exploring its variants and above all analysing its processes and structure. Between 1897 and 1906 appear all the great works which explore the mechanisms of the unconscious, that is to say, the transformations (in the geometric sense of the word) of fantasy, namely, *The Interpretation of Dreams* (1900), *The Psychopathology of Everyday Life* (1901), *Jokes and their Relation to the Unconscious* (1905).

But, and here is the third current, the development of Freudian research and psychoanalytic treatment display at the outset a regressive tendency towards the origin, the foundation of the symptom and the neurotic organization of the personality. If fantasy is shown to be an autonomous, consistent and explorable field, it leaves untouched the question of its own origin, not only with regard to structure, but also to content and to its most concrete details. In this sense nothing has changed, and the search for chronology, going backwards into time towards the first real, verifiable *elements*, is still the guiding principle of Freud's practice.

Speaking of one of his patients, he writes in 1899: 'Buried deep beneath all his fantasies we found a scene from his primal period (before twenty-two months) which meets all requirements and into which all the surviving puzzles flow (Letter 126).' A little later we come across these lines, eloquent of his passion for investigation, pursued ever deeper and with certainty of success, and the resort to a third person, if necessary, to verify the accuracy of his enquiry:

> In the evenings I read *prehistory, etc., without any serious purpose* [our italics], and otherwise my only concern is to lead my cases calmly towards solution. . . . In E's case the second real scene is coming up after years of preparation, and it is one that it may *perhaps* be possible to confirm objectively by asking his elder sister. Behind it there is a third, long-suspected scene . . . (Letter 127).

Freud defines these scenes from earliest infancy, these *true* scenes, as *Urszenen* (original or primal scenes). Later, as we know, the term will be reserved for the child's observation of parental coitus. The reference is to the discussion in *From the History of a Childhood Neurosis* (1918) of the relationship between the pathogenic dream and the primal scene on which it is based. When reading the first draft of the clinical account composed during 'the winter of 1914/15, shortly after the end of treatment', one is struck by the passionate conviction which urges Freud, like a detective on the watch, to establish the reality of the scene down to its smallest details. If such concern is apparent so long after the abandonment of the seduction theory, it is surely a proof that Freud had never entirely resigned himself to accepting such scenes as *purely imaginary* creations. Although discarded as concerns the seduction scene, the question re-emerges in identical terms twenty years later, in the case of the observation of parental coitus by the Wolf Man. The discovery of infantile sexuality has not invalidated in Freud's mind the fundamental schema underlying the seduction theory: the same deferred action (*Nachträglichkeit*) is constantly invoked; we meet once more the two events (here the scene and the dream), separated in the temporal series, the first remaining un-understood and, as it were, excluded within the subject, to be taken up later in the elaboration of the second occasion.[28] The fact that the whole process develops in the first years of infancy affects nothing essential in the theoretical model.

It is well known that before publishing his manuscript Freud added, in 1917, two long discussions which showed that he was disturbed by the Jungian theory of retrospective fantasy (*Zurückphantasieren*). He admits that since the scene is, in analysis, the culmination of a reconstruction, it might indeed have been constructed by the subject himself, but he nevertheless insists that perception has at least furnished some indications, even if it were only the copulation of dogs. . . .

But, more particularly, just at the moment when Freud appears to lose hope of support from the *ground of reality* – ground so shifting on further enquiry – he introduces a new concept, that of the *Urphantasien*, primal (or original) fantasy. The need for a theoretical foundation has now undergone a veritable transmutation. Since it has proved impossible to determine whether the primal scene is something truly experienced by the subject, or a fiction, we must in the last resort seek a foundation in something which transcends both individual experience and what is imagined.

For us too it is only at a deferred date (*nachträglich*) that the full meaning of this new direction of Freud's thought becomes apparent. Nothing appears to be changed: there is the same pursuit of an ultimate truth, the same schema is used once more, the dialectic of the two successive historical events, the same disappointment – as if Freud had learned nothing – as the ultimate event, the 'scene', disappears over the horizon. But simultaneously, thanks to what we have described as the second current, there is the discovery of the unconscious as a structural field, which can be reconstructed, since it handles, decomposes and recomposes its elements according to certain laws. This will henceforward permit the quest for origins to take on a new dimension.

In the concept of original fantasy,[29] there is a continuation of what we might call Freud's desire to reach the bedrock of the event (and if this disappears by refraction or reduction, then one must look further back still), and the need to establish the structure of the fantasy itself by something other than the event.

The original fantasies constitute this 'store of unconscious fantasies of all neurotics, and probably of all human beings'.[30] These words alone suggest that it is not solely the empirical fact of frequency, nor even generality, which characterizes them. If 'the same fantasies with the same content are created on every occasion',[31] if, beneath the diversity of individual fables we can recover some 'typical' fantasies,[32] it is because the historical life of the subject is not the prime mover, but rather something antecedent, which is capable of operating as an organizer.

Freud saw only one possible explanation of this antecedence, and that was phylogenesis:

> It seems to me quite possible that all the things that are told to us in analysis as fantasy . . . were once real occurrences in the primaeval times of the human family [what was factual reality would, in this case, have become psychological reality] and that children in their fantasies are simply filling in the gaps in individual truth with prehistoric truths.

Thus once again a reality is postulated beneath the elaborations of fantasy, but a reality which, as Freud insists, has an autonomous and structural status with regard to the subject who is totally dependent on it. He pursues this some considerable way, since he admits the possibility of discordance between the schema and individual experiences, which would lead to psychological conflict.[33]

It is tempting to accept the 'reality' which inspires the work of imagination according to its own laws, as a prefiguration of the 'symbolic order' defined by Lévi-Strauss and Lacan in the ethnological and psychoanalytical fields respectively. These scenes, which Freud traces back in *Totem and Taboo* to the prehistory of man, are attributed by him to primeval man (*Urmensch*), to the primal father (*Urvater*). He invokes them, less in order to provide a reality which escapes him in individual history, than to assign limits to the 'imaginary' which cannot contain its own principle of organization.

Beneath the pseudo-scientific mask of phylogenesis, or the recourse to 'inherited memory-traces', we should have to admit that Freud finds it necessary to postulate an organization made of signifiers anteceding the effect of the event and the signified as a whole. In this mythical prehistory of the species we see the need to create a pre-structure inaccessible to the subject, evading his grasp, his initiatives, his inner 'cooking pot', in spite of all the rich ingredients our modern sorceresses seem to find there. But Freud is in fact caught in the trap of his own concepts; in this false synthesis by which the past of the human species is preserved in hereditarily transmitted patterns, he is vainly trying to overcome the opposition between event and constitution.

However we should not be in a hurry to replace the phylogenic explanation by a structural type of explanation. The original fantasy is first and foremost fantasy – it lies beyond the history of the subject but nevertheless in history – a kind of language and a symbolic sequence, but loaded with elements of imagination; a structure, but activated by contingent elements. As such it is characterized by certain traits which make it difficult to assimilate to a purely transcendental schema, even if it provides the possibility of experience.[34]

The text in which Freud first mentions primal fantasies leaves no doubt in this respect.[35] In it he describes the case of a woman patient who declared that she had been watched and photographed while lying with her lover. She claimed to have heard a 'noise', the click of the camera. Behind this delirium Freud saw the primal scene: the sound is the noise of the parents who awaken the child; it is also the sound the child is afraid to make lest it betray her listening. It is difficult to estimate its role in the fantasy. In one sense, says Freud, it is only a provocation, an accidental cause, whose role is solely to activate 'the typical fantasy of overhearing, which is a component of the parental complex', but he immediately corrects himself by saying: 'It is doubtful whether we can rightly call the noise "accidental". . . . Such fantasies are on the contrary an indispensable part of the fantasy of listening.' In fact, the sound alleged by the patient[36] reproduces in actuality the indication of the primal scene, the element which is the starting point for all ulterior elaboration of the fantasy. In other words, *the origin of the fantasy is integrated in the very structure of the original fantasy*.

In his first theoretical sketches on the subject of fantasy, Freud stresses, in a way which may intrigue his readers, the role of aural perception.[37] Without placing too much importance on these fragmentary texts, in which Freud seems to be thinking more particularly of paranoid fantasies, one must consider why such a privileged position was accorded to hearing. We suggest there are two reasons. One relates to the *sensorium* in question: hearing, when it occurs, breaks the continuity of an undifferentiated perceptual field and at the same time is a sign (the noise waited for and heard in the night) which puts the subject in the position of having to answer to something. To this extent the prototype of the signifier lies in the aural sphere, even if there are correspondences in the other perceptual registers. But hearing is also – and this is the second reason to which Freud alludes explicitly in the passage – the history or the legends of parents, grandparents and the ancestors: the family *sounds* or *sayings*, this spoken or secret discourse, going on prior to the subject's arrival, within which he must find his way. In so far as it can serve retroactively to summon up the discourse, the noise – or any other discrete sensorial element that has meaning – can acquire this value.

In this content, in their theme (primal scene, castration, seduction . . .), the original fantasies also indicate this postulate of retroactivity: they relate to the origins. Like myths, they claim to provide a representation of, and a solution to, the major enigmas which confront the child. Whatever appears to the subject as something needing an explanation or theory, is dramatized as a moment of emergence, the beginning of a history.

Fantasies of origins: the primal scene pictures the origin of the individual; fantasies of seduction, the origin and upsurge of sexuality; fantasies of castration, the origin of the difference between the sexes.[38] Their themes therefore display, with redoubled significance, that original fantasies justify their status of being already there.

There is convergence of theme, of structure, and no doubt also of function: through the indications furnished by the perceptual field, through the scenarios constructed, the varied quest for origins, we are offered in the field of fantasy, the origin of the subject himself.

Since we encounter fantasy as given, interpreted, reconstructed or postulated, at the most diverse levels of psychoanalytic experience, we have obviously to face the difficult problem of its metapsychological status, and first of all, of its topography within the framework of the distinction between the unconscious, preconscious and conscious systems.

There are certain tendencies in contemporary psychoanalysis to settle the question by making a theoretical transposition, which seems inevitable in practice, between the fantasy as it presents itself for interpretation and the fantasy which is the conclusion of the work of analytic interpretation.[39] Freud would thus have been in error in describing by the same term, *Phantasie*, two totally distinct realities. On the one hand there is the unconscious *Phantasie*, 'the primary content of unconscious mental processes' (Isaacs), and on the other, the conscious or subliminal imaginings, of which the daydream is the typical example. The latter would be only a manifest content, like the others, and would have no more privileged relationship to unconscious *Phantasie* than dreams, behaviour, or whatever is generally described as 'material'. Like all manifest data, it would require interpretations in terms of unconscious fantasy.[40]

Freud's inspiration is shown by his persistent employment of the term *Phantasie* up to the end, in spite of the very early discovery that these *Phantasien* might be either conscious or unconscious. He wishes thereby to assert a profound kinship:

> The contents of the clearly conscious fantasies of perverts (which in favourable circumstances can be transformed into manifest behaviour), of the delusional fears of paranoiacs (which are projected in a hostile sense on to other people), and of the unconscious fantasies of hysterics (which psychoanalysis reveals behind their symptoms) – all these coincide with one another even down to their details.[41]

That is to say, that the same content, the same activation can be revealed in imaginary formations and psychopathological structures as diverse as those described by Freud, whether conscious or unconscious, acted out or represented, and whether or not there is a change of sign or permutation of persons.

Such an affirmation (1905) does not come from any so-called proto-Freud. It is of cardinal importance, particularly in the period 1906–9, when much research was devoted to the subject (in *'Gradiva'*, 'Creative writers and day-dreaming', 'Hysterical fantasies and their relation to bisexuality', 'On the sexual theories of children', 'Some general remarks on hysterical attacks', 'Family romances'). At this time the unconscious efficacy of fantasy was fully recognized as, for instance, underlying the hysterical attack which symbolizes it. Freud however takes the conscious fantasy, the daydream, not only as paradigm, but as source. The hysterical fantasies which 'have important connections with the causation of the neurotic symptoms' (we must be dealing with unconscious fantasies) have as 'common source and normal prototype what are called the daydreams of youth'.[42] In fact it is conscious fantasy itself which may be repressed and thus become pathogenic. Freud even considers fantasy as the privileged point where one may catch in the raw the process of transition from one system to another, repression, or the return of repressed material.[43] It is indeed the same mixed entity, the same 'mixed blood' which, being so close to the limits of the unconscious, can pass from one side to the other, particularly as the result of a variation of cathexis.[44] It may be objected that Freud is not here taking fantasy at its deepest level, and that we are not dealing with a true fantasy, but simply with a subliminal reverie. But Freud does describe the process of dismissal as repression and the frontier of which he speaks is indeed that of the unconscious in the strict, topographical, sense of the term.

We do not, of course, deny that there are different levels of unconscious fantasy, but it is remarkable to note how Freud, when studying the metapsychology of dreams, discovers the same relationship between the deepest unconscious fantasy and the daydream: the fantasy is present at both extremities of the process of dreaming. On the one hand it is linked with the ultimate unconscious desire, the 'capitalist' of the dream, and as such it is at the basis of that 'zigzag' path which is supposed to follow excitation through a succession of psychological systems: 'The first portion [of this path] was a progressive one, leading from the unconscious scenes of fantasies to the preconscious',[45] where it collects 'the day residues' or transference thoughts. But fantasy is also present at the other extremity of the dream, in the secondary elaboration which, Freud insists, is not part of the unconscious work of the dream, but must be identified 'with the work of our waking thought'. The secondary elaboration is an *a posteriori* reworking which takes place in the successive transformations which we impose on the story of the dream once we are awake. This consists essentially in restoring a minimum of order and coherence to the raw material handed over by the unconscious mechanism of displacement, condensation and symbolism, and in imposing on this heterogeneous assortment a façade, a scenario, which gives it relative coherence and continuity. In a word, it is a question of making the final version relatively similar to a daydream. Thus the secondary elaboration will utilize those ready-made scenarios, the fantasies or daydreams with which the subject has provided himself in the course of the day before the dream.

This is not necessarily to say that there is no privileged relationship between the fantasy which lies at the heart of the dream, and the fantasy which serves to make it acceptable to consciousness. Preoccupied by his discovery of the dream as the fulfilment of unconscious desire, it was no doubt natural for Freud to devalue anything close to consciousness which might appear to be defence and camouflage, in fact, the secondary elaboration.[46] But he quickly returns to a different appreciation:

> It would be a mistake, however, to suppose that these dream-façades are nothing other than mistaken and somewhat arbitrary revisions of the dream-content by the conscious agency of our mental life. . . . The wishful fantasies revealed by analysis in night-dreams often turn out to be repetitions or modified versions of scenes from infancy; thus in some cases the façade of the dream directly reveals the dream's actual nucleus, distorted by an admixture of other material.[47]

Thus the extremities of the dream, and the two forms of fantasy which are found there, seem, if not to link up, at least to communicate from within and, as it were, to be symbolic of each other.

We have spoken of a progression of Freud's thought with regard to the metapsychological status of fantasy. It does, of course, move towards differentiation, but we believe we have already shown that this goes without suppression of the homology between different levels of fantasy, and above all there is no attempt to make the line of major differentiation coincide with the topographical barrier (censorship), which separates the conscious and preconscious systems from the unconscious. The difference occurs within the unconscious: 'Unconscious fantasies have either been unconscious all along or – as is more often the case – they were once conscious fantasies, daydreams, and have since been purposely forgotten and have become unconscious through "repression".'[48] This distinction is later, in Freudian terminology, to coincide with that between original fantasies and others, those that one might call secondary, whether conscious or unconscious.[49]

Apart from this fundamental difference, the unity of the fantasy whole depends, however, on their mixed nature, in which both the structural and the imaginary can be found, although to different degrees. It is with this in mind that Freud always held the model fantasy to be the reverie, that form of novelette, both stereotyped and infinitely variable, which the subject composes and relates to himself in a waking state.

The daydream is a shadow play, utilizing its kaleidoscopic material drawn from all quarters of human experience, but also involving the original fantasy, whose *dramatis personae*, the court cards, receive their notation from a family legend which is mutilated, disordered and misunderstood. Its structure is the primal fantasy in which the Oedipus configuration can be easily distinguished, but also the daydream – if we accept that analysis discovers typical and repetitive scenarios beneath the varying clusters of fable.

However, we cannot classify or differentiate different forms of fantasy[50] as they shift between the poles of reverie or primal fantasy, simply, or even essentially, by the variability or inversion of the ratios between imaginary ingredient and structural link. Even the structure seems variable. In terms of daydream, the scenario is basically in the first person, and the subject's place clear and invariable. The organization is stabilized by the secondary process, weighted by the ego: the subject, it is said, lives out his reverie. But the original fantasy, on the other hand, is characterized by the absence of subjectivization, and the subject is present *in* the scene: the child, for instance, is one character amongst many in the fantasy 'a child is beaten'. Freud insisted on this visualization of the subject on the same level as the other protagonists, and in this sense the screen memory would have a profound structural relationship with original fantasies.[51]

'A father seduces a daughter' might perhaps be the summarized version of the seduction fantasy. The indication here of the primary process is not the absence of organization, as is sometimes suggested, but the peculiar character of the structure, in that it is a scenario with multiple entries, in which nothing shows whether the subject will be immediately located as *daughter*; it can as well be fixed as *father*, or even in the term *seduces*.

When Freud asked himself whether there was anything in man comparable to the 'instinct in animals', he found the equivalent not in the drives (*Triebe*), but in primal fantasies.[52] It is a valuable clue, since it demonstrates indirectly his unwillingness to explain fantasy on biological grounds: far from deriving fantasy from the drives, he preferred to make them dependent on earlier fantasy structures. It is also valuable in clarifying the position of certain contemporary concepts. Finally, it leads us to investigate the close relationship between desire and fantasy involved in the term *Wunschphantasie* (wish-fantasy).

Isaacs, for instance, considered unconscious fantasies to be 'an activity parallel to the drives from which they emerge'. She sees them as the 'psychological expression' of experience, which is itself defined by the field of force set up by libidinal and aggressive drives and the defences they arouse. Finally she is concerned to establish a close link between the specific forms of fantasy life and the bodily zones which are the seat of the drives, though this leads her to underestimate one part of the Freudian contribution to the theory both of fantasy and drives. In her view, fantasy is only the imagined transcription of the first objective of any drive, which is a specific object: the 'instinctual urge' is necessarily experienced as a fantasy which, whatever its content (desire to suck, in a baby), will be expressed, as soon as verbalization is possible,[53] by a phrase consisting of three parts: subject (I), verb (swallow, bite, reject), object (breast, mother).[54] Of course, in so far as the drives are, for the Kleinians, in the first place in the nature of relationships, Isaacs shows how such a fantasy of incorporation is also experienced in the other sense, the active becoming passive. Furthermore, this fear of a return to sender is a constituent element of the fantasy itself. But it is hardly enough to recognize the equivalence of eating and being eaten in the fantasy of incorporation. So long as there is some idea of a subject, even if playing a passive role, are we sure to reach the structure of deepest fantasy?

For Isaacs, fantasy is the direct expression of a drive, and almost consubstantial with it, and can, in the last resort, be reduced to the relationship which links subject to object by a verb of action (in the sense of the omnipotent wish). This is because, for her, the structure of the drive is that of a subjective intentionality and inseparable from its object: the drive 'intuits' or 'knows' the object which will satisfy it. As the fantasy, which at first expresses libidinal and destructive drives, quickly transforms itself into a form of defence, so finally it is the whole of the subject's internal dynamic which is deployed in accordance with this unique type of organization. Such a concept postulates, in agreement with certain

Freudian formulations, that 'all that is conscious has passed through a preliminary unconscious stage', and that the ego is 'a differentiated part of the id'. One is therefore obliged to provide every mental operation with an underlying fantasy which can itself be reduced on principle to an instinctual aim. The biological subject is in a direct line of continuity with the subject of fantasy, the sexual, human subject, in accordance with the series: soma → id → fantasy (of desire, of defence) → ego mechanism: the action of repression is difficult to grasp, since 'fantasy life' is more implicit than repressed, and contains its own conflicts by virtue of the co-existence within the psyche of contradictory aims. There is, in fact, a profusion of fantasy, in which it is impossible to recognize the special type of structure which Freud tried to distinguish and where the elusive but elective relationship which he established between fantasy and sexuality also dissolves.

It is a little surprising that Freud, at a time when he fully recognized the existence and extent of sexuality and fantasy in the child, should have continued, as for instance in a footnote to the *Three Essays* in 1920,[55] to consider the period of maximum fantasying activity to occur in the period of pubertal and pre-pubertal masturbation.[56] It is perhaps because to him there was a close correlation between fantasy and auto-erotism, which was not sufficiently accounted for by the belief that the second is camouflaged by the first. In fact he seems to be sharing the common belief that in the absence of real objects the subject seeks and creates for himself an imaginary satisfaction.

   Freud himself did much to authorize this viewpoint when he tried to establish a theoretical model of desire, both in its object and purpose.[57] The origin of fantasy would lie in the hallucinatory satisfaction of desire; in the absence of a real object, the infant reproduces the *experience* of the original satisfaction in a hallucinated form. In this view the most fundamental fantasies would be those which tend to recover the hallucinated objects linked with the very earliest experiences of the rise and the resolution of desire.[58]

   But before we try to discover what the Freudian fiction (*Fiktion*) is really intended to cover, we must be clear about its meaning, more particularly since it is rarely formulated in detail, but always presupposed in Freud's concept of the primary process. One might consider it a myth of origin: by this figurative expression Freud claims to have recovered the very first upsurgings of desire. It is an analytic 'construction', or fantasy, which tries to cover the moment of *separation* between *before* and *after*, whilst still containing both: a mythical moment of disjunction between the pacification of need (*Befriedigung*) and the fulfilment of desire (*Wunscherfüllung*), between the two stages represented by real experience and its hallucinatory revival, between the object that satisfies and the sign[59] which describes both the object and its absence: a mythical moment at which hunger and sexuality meet in a common origin.

If, caught in our own turn by the fantasy of origins, we were to claim to have located the emergence of fantasy, we should start from the standpoint of the real course of infantile history, and the development of infantile sexuality (seen from the viewpoint of Chapter 2 of *Three Essays*), and we should relate it to the appearance of auto-erotism, to the moment of what Freud calls the 'pleasure premium'. This is not a pleasure in the fulfilment of function, or the resolution of tension created by needs, but a marginal product, emerging from the world of needs, these vitally important functions whose aims and mechanisms are assured and whose objects are pre-formed.

But in speaking of the appearance of auto-erotism, even when taking care not to transform it into a stage of libidinal development, and even stressing its permanence and presence in all adult sexual behaviour, one is liable to lose sight of all that gives the notion its true meaning, and all that can illuminate the *function* as well as the *structure* of fantasy.

If the notion of auto-erotism is frequently criticized in psychoanalysis, this is because it is incorrectly understood, in the object-directed sense, as a first stage, enclosed within itself, from which the subject has to rejoin the world of objects. It is then easy to demonstrate, with much clinical detail, the variety and complexity of the links which, from the beginning, relate the infant to the outer world and, particularly, to its mother. But when Freud, principally in the *Three Essays*, speaks of auto-erotism, he has no intention of denying the existence of a primary object relationship. On the contrary, he shows that the drive *becomes* auto-erotic, only after the loss of the object.[60] If it can be said of auto-erotism that it is objectless, it is in no sense because it may appear before any object relationship,[61] nor because on its arrival no object will remain in the search for satisfaction, but simply because the natural method of apprehending an object is split in two: the sexual drive separated from the non-sexual functions, such as feeding, which are its support (*Anlehnung*[62]) and which indicate its aim and object.

The 'origin' of auto-erotism would therefore be the moment when sexuality, disengaged from any natural object, moves into the field of fantasy and by that very fact becomes sexuality. The moment is more abstract than definable in time, since it is always renewed, and must have been preceded by erotic excitation, otherwise it would be impossible for such excitation to be sought out. But one could equally state the inverse proposition, that it is the breaking in of fantasy which occasions the disjunction of sexuality and need.[63] The answer to the question of whether this is a case of circular causality or simultaneous appearance is that, however far back one may go, they originate from the same point.

Auto-erotic satisfaction, in so far as it can be found in an autonomous state, is defined by one very precise characteristic: it is the product of the anarchic activity of partial drives, closely linked with the excitation of specific erogenous zones, an excitation which arises and is stilled on the spot. It is not a global, functional pleasure, but a fragmented pleasure, an organ pleasure (*Organlust*) and strictly localized.

It is known that erogeneity can be attached to predestined zones of the body (thus, in the activity of sucking, the oral zone is destined by its very physiology to acquire an erogenous value), but it is also available to any organ (even internal organs), and to any region or function of the body. In every case the function serves only as support, the taking of food serving, for instance, as a model for fantasies of incorporation. Though modelled on the function, sexuality lies in its difference from the function: in this sense its prototype is not the act of sucking, but the enjoyment of going through the motions of sucking (*Ludeln*), the moment when the external object is abandoned, when the aim and the source assume an autonomous existence with regard to feeding and the digestive system. The ideal, one might say, of auto-erotism is 'lips that kiss themselves'.[64] Here, in this apparently self-centred enjoyment, as in the deepest fantasy, in this discourse no longer addressed to anyone, all distinction between subject and object has been lost.

If we add that Freud constantly insisted on the seductive role of the mother (or of others), when she washes, dresses or caresses her child,[65] and if we note also that the naturally erogenous zones (oral, anal, uro-genital, skin), are not only those which most attract the mother's attention, but also those which have an obvious exchange value (orifices or skin covering) we can understand how certain chosen parts of the body itself may not only serve to sustain a local pleasure, but also be a meeting place with maternal desire and fantasy, and thus with one form of original fantasy.

By locating the origin of fantasy in the auto-erotism, we have shown the connection between fantasy and desire. Fantasy, however, is not the object of desire, but its setting. In fantasy the subject does not pursue the object or its sign: he appears caught up himself in the sequence of images. He forms no representation of the desired object, but is himself represented as participating in the scene although, in the earliest forms of fantasy, he cannot be assigned any fixed place in it (hence the danger, in treatment, of interpretations which claim to do so). As a result, the subject, although always present in the fantasy, may be so in a desubjectivized form, that is to say, in the very syntax of the sequence in question. On the other hand, to the extent that desire is not purely an upsurge of the drives, but is articulated into the fantasy, the latter is a favoured spot for the most primitive defensive reactions, such as turning against oneself, or into an opposite, projection, negation: these defences are even indissolubly linked with the primary function of fantasy, to be a setting for desire, in so far as desire itself originates as prohibition, and the conflict may be an original conflict.

But as for knowing who is responsible for the setting, it is not enough for the psychoanalyst to rely on the resources of his science, nor on the support of myth. He must also become a philosopher.

## Summary

1 The status of fantasy cannot be found within the framework of the opposition reality–illusion (imaginary). The notion of *psychical reality* introduces a third category, that of structure.

2 Freud's theory of seduction (1895–7) is re-examined from the point of view of its pioneering and demonstrative value: it permits the analysis of the dialectic relationship between fantasy productions, the underlying structures, and the reality of the scene. This 'reality' is to be sought in an ever more remote or hypothetical past (of the individual or of the species) which is postulated on the horizon of the imaginary and implied in the very structure of the fantasy.

3 Freud's so-called abandonment of the reality of infantile traumatic memories, in favour of fantasies which would be based only on a biological, quasi-endogenous evolution of sexuality, is only a transitional stage in the search for the foundation of neurosis. On the one hand seduction will continue to appear as one of the data of the relationship between child and adult (Freud, Ferenczi); on the other hand, the notion of *primal* (or *original*) *fantasies* (*Urphantasien*), of 'inherited memory traces' of prehistoric events, will in turn provide support for individual fantasies.

The authors propose an interpretation of this notion: such a prehistory, located by Freud in phylogenesis, can be understood as a prestructure which is actualized and transmitted by the parental fantasies.

4 Original fantasies are limited in their thematic scope. They relate to problems of origin which present themselves to all human beings (*Menschenkinder*): the origin of the individual (primal scene), the origin of sexuality (seduction), and the origin of the difference between the sexes (castration).

5 The origin of fantasy cannot be isolated from the origin of the drive (*Trieb*) itself. The authors, reinterpreting the Freudian concept of the *experience of satisfaction,* locate this origin in the auto-erotism, which they define not as a stage of evolution but as the moment of a repeated disjunction of sexual desire and non-sexual functions: sexuality is

detached from any natural object, and is handed over to fantasy, and, by this very fact, starts existing as sexuality.

6 The *metapsychological* status of this mixed entity, the fantasy, is finally established. The authors refuse to accept the main line of separation between conscious and unconscious fantasies (Isaacs). They place this division between the original and the secondary fantasies (whether repressed or conscious) and demonstrate the relationship and the profound continuity between the various fantasy scenarios – the stage-setting of desire – ranging from the daydream to the fantasies recovered or reconstructed by analytic investigation.

### RETROSPECT, 1986

Written alongside *The Language of Psychoanalysis*, this essay may be considered as belonging to the genre of exegesis, if one understands by that the fact of allowing one's thinking to be fertilized by another thought, sovereign yet enigmatic, and not the further exploitation of an over-exploited resource.

In the discovery of a treasure there is a time of wonder, then a time of inventory, followed by an unavoidable dilapidation. The wealth of the Freudian thesaurus, let us remember, was hardly suspected by those who, at the time, were content to live off the interest it generated, unless they handed over the responsibility of pronouncing its Truth to a single Other.

It was first necessary to bring back to light completely forgotten concepts (forgotten *from the beginning*, by the Freudians, and even by Freud himself), such as 'propping' and 'primal fantasy'. It was necessary to restore to their full value, founding if not transcendental, such banalized notions as 'auto-erotism', such disparaged and misunderstood notions as 'seduction'.

But the task soon became more arduous, torn between two necessities. On one hand, neither to falsify nor to schematize Freud's thought, but to try to restore to it its exigencies, its repressions and returns, its ambiguities, perhaps its 'naïveties' (the phylogenetic hypothesis). But, on the other hand, to progress in a personal attempt at drawing, between the rediscovered notions, a configuration more explicit, more coherent, more stimulating.

This is to say that the reader – and we ourselves on re-reading our essay – will uncover many strata in this text: a necessary and salubrious archaeology of the concepts, which aims to be at once faithful and critical; an attempt at interpretation of the problematic of the originary (*originaire*), where a certain structuralist inspiration remains perceptible, in spite of the denegations;[1] the onset, at least, of new developments where each of the authors will subsequently engage himself more freely, asserting his choice within the field of experience which Freud delimited and ploughed.

To question oneself today, *after Freud*, about the primal fantasies (*fantasmes originaires*),[2] their topographical situation, their efficacy, their transmission and, first and foremost, their type of reality, is an obligation of which it is impossible to divest oneself, if one wants to advance, at the same pace, as a psychoanalyst *and* as a philosopher.

## Notes

1. Translated from the French, 'Fantasme originaire, fantasmes des origines, origine du fantasme', translators in *Les Temps Modernes*, 1964, 19, no.215. This translation first published in *The International Journal of Psychoanalysis (IJPA)*, vol.49 (1968), part 1; reprinted with permission.
2. J. Breuer and S. Freud, *Studies on Hysteria* [1895], in *The Standard Edition of the Complete Psychological Works of Sigmund Freud*, ed. J. Strachey, London, Hogarth Press, 1953–74, (SE), vol.I.
3. See M. Klein, *Narrative of a Child Analysis*, London, Hogarth, 1960.
4. 'Good' and 'bad' objects are 'imagos which are a phantastically distorted picture of the real objects upon which they are based' (M. Klein, 'A contribution to the psychogenesis of manic-depressive states' [1934], in *Contributions to Psychoanalysis*, London, Hogarth Press, 1949).
5. S. Freud, 'Formulations on the two principles of mental functioning' [1911], SE, vol.XII, p.222.
6. ibid, p.225.
7. It is fascinating to observe how Melanie Klein, who provides an uninterrupted interpretation of the transference relationship, never brings in any 'in reality', or even an 'as if'.
8. However, we have found, in the case of actual adoption to which we are referring, clinical manifestations quite obviously different from those encountered in adoption fantasies: an actualization, quickly blurred, of fantasies of the recovery of the mother, episodes where the attempts to rejoin the *true* mother, are worked out symbolically in a kind of secondary state, etc. Even in treatment, from the very beginning, many elements such as dream contents, the repeated occurrence of sleep during the session, showing a massive working out of a far-reaching tendency, demonstrated the disjunction between crude reality and verbalization.
9. S. Freud, *Introductory Lectures* [1916–17], SE, vol.XIV, p.368.
10. ibid, p.369.
11. S. Freud [1911], SE, vol.XII, p.225.
12. S. Freud [1916–17], SE, vol XV–XVI, p.368.
13. S. Freud, *The Interpretation of Dreams*, SE, vol.IV–V, p.620. The successive reformulations of this principle in the various editions of the *Traumdeutung* show both Freud's concern to define accurately the concept of psychical reality, and the difficulties he experienced in so doing – cf. Strachey's note to this passage.
14. One further word about the suspension of judgement in the analytic rule: 'Verbalize everything, but do no more than verbalize.' This is not suspension of the reality of external events for the *benefit* of subjective reality. It creates a new field, that of verbalization, where the difference between the real and the imaginary may retain its value (cf. the case of the patient referred to above). The homology between the analytic and the unconscious field, whose emergence it stimulates, is not due to their common subjectivity, but to the deep kinship between the unconscious and the field of speech. So it is not 'It is *you* who say so', but 'It is you who *say* so'.
15. Introduction to S. Freud, *The Origins of Psychoanalysis* [1950], London, Imago, 1954,

especially the section entitled 'Infantile sexuality and self-analysis'.

16. S. Freud, 'On the history of the psychoanalytic movement' [1914], *SE*, vol.XIV.

17. S. Freud, [1950], letter 30.

18. In *Studies on Hysteria* we already find the idea that psychological trauma cannot be reduced to the once-and-for-all effect on an organism of some external event. 'The causal relation between the determining psychical trauma and the hysterical phenomenon is not of a kind implying that the trauma merely acts like an *agent provocateur*, in releasing the symptom which thereafter leads an independent existence. We must presume rather that the psychical trauma – or more precisely the memory of the trauma – acts like a foreign body which long after its entry must be regarded as an agent that is still at work' (*SE*, vol.II, p.6).

19. The problem is constantly present in these terms in such works as Freud's *Beyond the Pleasure Principle, Inhibitions, Symptoms and Anxiety* and Rank's *Trauma of Birth*.

20. 'It seems to me more and more that the essential point of hysteria is that it results from *perversion* on the part of the seducer, and *more and more* that heredity is seduction by the father' (Letter 52).

21. He never ceased to assert this relationship (cf. *An Outline of Psychoanalysis, SE*, vol.XXIII, pp.185–6), but without stating the theory.

22. S. Ferenczi, 'Confusion of tongues between the adult and the child' [1933], in *Final Contributions to the Problems and Methods of Psychoanalysis*, London, Hogarth Press, 1955.

23. From the beginning Freud rejected the banal thesis which attributed the unpleasure provoked by sexuality to a purely external prohibition. Whether they are of internal or external origin, desire and prohibition go hand in hand. 'We shall be plunged deep into the riddles of psychology if we enquire into the origin of the unpleasure which is released by premature sexual stimulation and without which the occurrence of a repression cannot be explained. The most plausible answer will recall the fact that shame and morality are the repressing forces and that the neighbourhood in which nature has placed the sexual organs must inevitably arouse disgust at the same time as sexual experiences . . . I cannot think that the release of unpleasure during sexual experiences is the consequence of a chance admixture of certain unpleasurable factors. . . . In my opinion there must be some independent source for the release of unpleasure in sexual life; if that source is present, it can activate sensations of disgust, lend force to morality, and so on' (Draft K).

24. It would be easy to demonstrate that Freud, throughout his life, continued to insist on the reality of the fact of seduction.

25. S. Freud, 'An autobiographical study' [1925], *SE*, vol.XX.

26. And no longer the expression of the child's spontaneous, biological sexual activity. S. Freud, 'Femininity' [1933], *SE*, vol.XXII.

27. 'I have learned to explain a number of fantasies of seduction as attempts at fending off the subject's *own* sexual activity (infantile masturbation)' (S. Freud, 'My views on the part played by sexuality in the neuroses' [1906], *SE*, vol.VII).

28. There is an obvious similarity between the Freudian schema of *Nachträglichkeit* and the psychotic mechanism of 'repudiation' (*forclusion*) described by Lacan: that which has not been admitted to symbolic expression ('repudiated') reappears in reality in the form of hallucination. This non-symbolization corresponds precisely to the earliest time described by Freud. As Lacan and Freud illustrate their theory by the case of the Wolf Man, it may be asked whether Lacan may not have treated as specifically psychotic what is really a very general process, or whether Freud has not taken the exception to be the rule, when basing his demonstration on a case of psychosis.

Freud's demonstration is strengthened by the fact that in this particular case the primal scene is very probably authentic. But one might conceive of such absence of subjective elaboration or of symbolization, normally characteristic of the first stage, as not a prerogative of a truly experienced scene. This 'foreign body', which is to be internally excluded, is usually brought to the subject, not by the perception of a scene, but by parental desire and its supporting fantasy. Such would be the typically neurotic case: in the first stage (not locatable in time, since it is fragmented into the series of transitions to autoeroticism), a pre-symbolic symbolic, to paraphrase Freud, is isolated within the subject who will, at a later stage, recover and symbolize it. In psychosis the first stage would consist of naked reality and is evidently not symbolized by the subject, but will offer an irreducible nucleus for any later attempt at symbolization. Hence, in such cases, the failure, even the catastrophe, of the second stage.

This offers an approach to a distinction between repression (original) and the psychotic mechanism which Freud tried to delimit throughout his work (more particularly by describing it as *Verleugnung*: denial), and which Lacan called 'forclusion'.

29. We might be accused of exaggeration in speaking of concept. 'Original fantasy' does not, of course, form part of the classical psychoanalytic concepts. Freud uses it marginally in his very precise study of the question whose development we have traced. The phrase therefore has the value of an 'index' and requires clarification.

30. S. Freud, 'A case of paranoia running counter to the psychoanalytic theory of the disease' [1915], *SE*, vol.XIV.

31. S. Freud, 'The paths to the formation of symptoms' [1916], *SE*, vol.XVI.

32. An ever present concern of Freud's (cf. Draft M): 'One of our brightest hopes is that we may be able to define the number and species of fantasies as well as we can those of the "scenes".'

33. 'Wherever experiences fail to fit in with the hereditary schema, they become remodelled in the imagination. . . . It is precisely such cases that are calculated to convince us of the independent existence of the schema. We are often able to see the schema triumphing over the experience of the individual; as when in our present case, the boy's father became the castrator and the menace of his infantile sexuality in spite of what was in other respects an inverted Oedipus complex. . . . The contradictions between experience and the schema seem to supply the conflicts of childhood with an abundance of material' (S. Freud, 'From the history of an infantile neurosis' [1918], *SE*, vol.XVII).

34. We are not here trying to develop a coherent psychoanalytic theory which would involve the relationship between the level of the Oedipus structure and that of the original fantasies. One would first have to define what was meant by the Oedipus structure. Indeed the structural aspect of the Oedipus complex – considered both in its basic function and its triangular form – was worked out much later by Freud: it does not appear at all, for instance, in the *Three Essays on the Theory of Sexuality* [1905], *SE*, vol.VII. The so-called generalized formulation of the complex appeared first in *The Ego and the Id* [1923], *SE*, vol.XIX, and the generalization in question cannot be taken in any formal sense: it describes a limited series of concrete positions within the interpsychological field created by the father–mother–child triangle. From the point of view of structural anthropology, one might see this as *one of the forms* of the law governing human interchanges, a law which in other cultures might be incarnated in other persons and in other forms. The prohibitory function of the law might, for instance, be expressed by an agency other than the father. By adopting this solution the analyst would feel he had lost an essential dimension of his experience: the subject is, admittedly, located in a structure of interrelationship, but the latter is transmitted by the parental unconscious. It is therefore less easy to assimilate it to a language system than to the complexities of a particular speech.

Freud's concept of the Oedipus complex is, in fact, remarkable for its realism: whether it is represented as an inner conflict (nuclear complex) or as a social institution, the complex remains a given fact; the subject is *confronted* by it: 'every new arrival on this planet is faced by the task of mastering it' (*Three Essays on the Theory of Sexuality* [1905], *SE*, vol.VII, p.226, footnote).

Perhaps it was the realism of the concept which lead Freud to allow the notion of original fantasy to co-exist alongside the Oedipus complex, without being concerned to articulate them: here the subject does not encounter the structure, but is carried along by it.

35. S. Freud, 'A case of paranoia . . .' [1915] *SE*, vol.XIV.

36. According to Freud it is incidentally a projection, the projection of a beat in her clitoris, in the form of a noise. There would be a new, circular relationship between the pulsation

which actualizes the fantasy, and the drive which arouses it.

37. 'Built up out of things that have been heard about and then *subsequently* turned to account, they combine things that have been experienced and things that have been heard about past events (from the history of parents and ancestors) and things seen by the subject himself. They are related to things heard in the same way as dreams are related to things seen' (Draft L). And again: 'Fantasies arise from an unconscious combination of things experienced and heard' (Draft M).

38. If we ask what these fantasies mean to *us*, we are embarking on a different level of interpretation. We then see that they are not only symbolic, but represent the insertion, mediated by an imagined scenario, of the most radically formative symbolism, into corporeal reality. The primal scene represents for us the conjunction of the biological fact of conception and birth with the symbolic act of filiation: it unites the 'savage Act' of coitus and the existence of a mother–child–father triad. In the fantasies of castration the conjunction of real and symbolic is even more apparent. With regard to seduction, we should add that it was not only, as we believe we have shown, because Freud had come across numerous actual cases, that he was able to use fantasy as a scientific theory and thus, by a roundabout way, hit on the true function of fantasy. It was also because he was trying to account, in terms of origins, for the advent of sexuality to human beings.

39. See S. Isaacs, 'The nature and function of phantasy', *IJPA*, vol.29 (1948).

40. The proposal to eliminate the unfortunate confusion by the graphological device of using 'ph' for unconscious fantasies and 'f' for the daydream type has been declared at times to be real progress, the result of half a century of psychoanalysis. Whether or not this distinction is in fact justified, it seems undesirable to use it in translations of Freud's work. It betrays little respect for the text to render words such as *Phantasie* or *Phantasieren*, which Freud invariably employed, by different terms according to the context. Our opposition to this terminological and conceptual innovation rests on three grounds: (i) the distinction should not be introduced into translations of Freud's work, even if this interpretation of his thought were correct; (ii) this interpretation of Freud's thought is incorrect; (iii) this distinction contributes less to the study of the problem than Freud's concept.

41. S. Freud [1905], *SE*, vol.VII, pp.165–6.

42. S. Freud, 'Hysterical phantasies and their relation to bisexuality' [1908], *SE*, vol.IX.

43. 'In favourable circumstances, the subject can still capture an unconscious fantasy of this sort in consciousness. After I had drawn the attention of one of my patients to her fantasies, she told me that on one occasion she had suddenly found herself in tears in the street and that, rapidly considering what it was she was actually crying about, she had got hold of a fantasy to the following effect. In her imagination she had formed a tender attachment to a pianist who was well known in the town (though she was not personally acquainted with him); she had had a child by him (she was in fact childless); and he had then deserted her and left them in poverty. It was at this point in her romance that she had burst into tears' (Freud [1908], *SE*, vol.IX).

44. 'They draw near to consciousness and remain undisturbed so long as they do not have an intense cathexis, but as soon as they exceed a certain height of cathexis they are thrust back' (Freud, 'The unconscious' [1915], *SE*, vol.XIV, p.191).

45. S. Freud, *The Interpretation of Dreams*, *SE*, vol.IV–V, p.574.

46. There must of course be a dismantling of the secondary elaboration in order to be able to take the dream element by element. But Freud does not forget that by *setting everything on the same level*, which is one of the aspects of psychoanalytic listening, the structure, the scenario, becomes itself an element, just as much, for instance, as the global reaction of the subject to his own dream.

47. S. Freud, 'On dreams' [1901], *SE*, vol.V, p.667. Freud seems also to have indicated that, generally speaking, desire can be more readily discovered in the *structure* of the fantasy than in the dream, unless the dream has been much restructured by the fantasy, as is particularly the case in 'typical dreams'. 'If we examine the structure [of fantasies] we shall perceive the way in which the wishful purpose that is at work in their production, has mixed up the material of which they are built, has re-arranged it and has formed it

into a new whole' (*SE*, vol.V, p.492).
48. S. Freud [1908], *SE*, vol.IX, p.161.
49. We suggest the following schema:

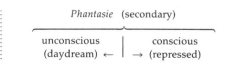

*Urphantasie*
(original unconscious)

*Phantasie* (secondary)

unconscious | conscious
(daydream) ← | → (repressed)

The repression which returns secondary fantasies to the unconscious would be that described by Freud as 'secondary repression' or 'after-pressure'. A further type of repression, more mythical and obscure, which Freud called 'primal repression' (*Urverdrängung*) corresponds to the constitution of the primal fantasies or their reception by the individual. We attempt later to indicate an approach to this subject. Cf. also J. Laplanche and S. Leclaire, 'The unconscious: a psychoanalytic study' [1961], *Yale French Studies*, no.48, 1972.
50. Amongst which we should obviously include screen memories and infantile sexual theories.
51. Freud saw in this characteristic of screen-memories that they were not true memories, yet of all conscious fantasies, they are the only ones to claim reality. They are *true* scenes, the screens of primal fantasies or scenes.
52. S. Freud, 'The unconscious' [1915], *SE*, vol.XIV, p.195; 'From the history of an infantile neurosis' [1918], *SE*, vol.XVII, p.120, footnote.
53. According to Isaacs, 'primary phantasies are . . . dealt with by mental processes far removed from words'. It is only through practical necessity that we express them in words, but we thereby introduce a 'foreign element'. Isaacs, using one of Freud's expressions, speaks of 'the language of drives', and it is true that it is not its verbal or non-verbal character which defines the nature of language. But if Isaacs confuses language and the power of expression, perhaps this leads her to a failure to appreciate the originality of Melanie Klein's concepts; her attempt to describe a language which is non-verbal, but nonetheless structured, on the basis of pairs of opposites (good–bad, inner–outer). The audacity of the techniques does at least assume a reference, not to the mobile expression of instinctual life, but to some fundamental oppositions.
54. Cf. the variants formulated by Isaacs: 'I want to eat her all up', 'I want to keep her inside me', 'I want to throw her out of me', 'I want to bring her back', 'I must have her *now*', etc.
55. S. Freud [1905], *SE*, vol.VII, p.226.
56. More often than not masturbation implies, of course, an imaginary relationship with an object: thus it can only be described as auto-erotic from an external standpoint, to the extent that the subject obtains satisfaction by resorting solely to his own body. But an infantile auto-erotic activity, such as sucking the thumb, in no sense implies the absence of any object. What makes it eventually auto-erotic is, as we shall show later, a special mode of satisfaction, specific to the 'birth' of sexuality, which lingers on into pubertal masturbation.
57. 'The first wishing (*Wünschen*) seems to have been a hallucinatory cathecting of the memory of satisfaction' (S. Freud [1900], *SE*, vol.IV–V, p.598).
58. Cf., for instance, Isaacs's interpretation of Freud's hypothesis of the first hallucination: 'It seems probable that hallucination works best at times of less instinctual tension, perhaps when the infant half-awakes and begins to be hungry. . . . The pain of frustration then stirs up a still stronger desire, viz. the wish to take the whole breast into himself and keep it there as a source of satisfaction; and this in its turn will for a time omnipotently fulfil itself in belief, in hallucination. . . . This hallucination of the internal satisfying breast may, however, break down altogether if frustration continues, and hunger is not satisfied, the instinct-tension proving too strong to be denied.'

    It is obvious that the author is in difficulty about reconciling a hallucinated satisfaction with the demands of a frustrated instinct. How indeed can an infant *feed itself* on wind alone? The Freudian model is incomprehensible unless one understands that it is not the real object, but the lost object; not the milk, but the breast as a signifier, which is the object of the primal hallucination.

59. The breast, wrongly named 'object of desire' by psychoanalysts.

60. 'At a time at which the first beginnings of sexual satisfaction are still linked with the taking of nourishment, the sexual instinct has a sexual object outside the infant's own body in the shape of the mother's breast. It is only later that the instinct loses that object, just at the time perhaps when the child is able to form a total idea of the person to whom the organ that is giving him satisfaction belongs' (S. Freud [1905], *SE*, vol.VII, p.222). The passage is also invaluable as a further indication that the very constitution of the auto-erotic fantasy implies not only the partial object (breast, thumb or substitute), but the mother as a total person, withdrawing as she becomes total. This 'totalization' is not to be understood as in the nature of a *Gestalt*, but by reference to the child's demand, which may be granted or refused by the mother.

61. Described by some psychoanalysts as an 'objectless' stage, on a genetic basis, which one might call totalitarian, since it confuses the constitution of the libidinal object with that of objectivity in the external world, and claims to establish stages in the development of the ego as 'organ of reality', stages which they also hold to be correlative with those of the libido.

62. Elsewhere (in *The Language of Psychoanalysis*, London, Hogarth Press, 1973) we develop this notion which is fundamental to the Freudian theory of instincts.

63. In one of his first reflections on fantasy Freud notes that the *Impulse* could perhaps emanate from fantasy (Draft N).

64. Cf. also, in S. Freud, 'Instincts and their vicissitudes' [1915], *SE*, vol. XIV, the analysis of the pairs of opposites, sadism–masochism, voyeurism–exhibitionism. Beneath the active or passive form of the phrase (seeing, being seen, for instance), we must assume a reflexive form (seeing oneself) which, according to Freud, would be primordial. No doubt this primordial degree is to be found when the subject no longer places himself in one of the different terms of the fantasy.

65. '. . . a child's intercourse with anyone responsible for his care affords him an unending source of sexual excitation and satisfaction from his erotogenic zones. This is especially so since the person in charge of him, who, after all, is as a rule his mother, herself regards him with feelings that are derived from her own sexual life, and quite clearly treats him as a substitute for a complete sexual object' (S. Freud [1905], *SE*, vol.VII, p.223). It is, however, customary to say that Freud took a long time to recognize the link with the mother.

## Retrospect 1986

1. In a letter to the editors, Professor Laplanche writes: 'I have, in fact, taken a certain distance in relation to this text which, on numerous points, reflects rather the point of view of Freud, or a certain structuralist Freud, than my personal point of view. This is inevitable in a work which is at the same time historical and theoretical.'

2. Professor Laplanche has expressed a preference that the term *originaire* be translated, 'as far as possible', by the English word 'original'. It was, however, never the editors' intention to undertake a new translation of 'Fantasme originaire, fantasmes des origines, origines du fantasme'; they have sought simply to make the existing translation more readily available. (A translator who took account of this preference would need to know if Freud's '*Urphantasien*', the usual French translation of which is '*fantasmes originaires*', should now be rendered as 'original fantasies', rather than the 'primal phantasies' of the Standard Edition – with the danger of loss of precision this would incur).

Joan Riviere

# WOMANLINESS AS A MASQUERADE[1]

Every direction in which psychoanalytic research has pointed seems in its
turn to have attracted the interest of Ernest Jones, and now that of recent
years investigation has slowly spread to the development of the sexual life
of women, we find as a matter of course one by him among the most
important contributions to the subject. As always, he throws great light on
his material, with his peculiar gift of both clarifying the knowledge we
had already and also adding to it fresh observations of his own.

In his paper on 'The early development of female sexuality'[2] he
sketches out a rough scheme of types of female development which he first
divides into heterosexual and homosexual, subsequently subdividing the
latter homosexual group into two types. He acknowledges the roughly
schematic nature of his classification and postulates a number of
intermediate types. It is with one of these intermediate types that I am
today concerned. In daily life types of men and women are constantly met
with who, while mainly heterosexual in their development, plainly
display strong features of the other sex. This has been judged to be an
expression of the bisexually inherent in us all; and analysis has shown that
what appears as homosexual or heterosexual character-traits, or sexual
manifestations, is the end-result of the interplay of conflicts and not
necessarily evidence of a radical or fundamental tendency. The difference
between homosexual and heterosexual development results from differences in the degree of anxiety, with the corresponding effect this has on
development. Ferenczi pointed out a similar reaction in behaviour,[3]
namely, that homosexual men exaggerate their heterosexuality as a
'defence' against their homosexuality. I shall attempt to show that women
who wish for masculinity may put on a mask of womanliness to avert
anxiety and the retribution feared from men.

It is with a particular type of intellectual woman that I have to deal.
Not long ago intellectual pursuits for women were associated almost
exclusively with an overtly masculine type of woman, who in pronounced
cases made no secret of her wish or claim to be a man. This has now
changed. Of all the women engaged in professional work today, it would
be hard to say whether the greater number are more feminine than
masculine in their mode of life and character. In university life, in
scientific professions and in business, one constantly meets women who

seem to fulfil every criterion of complete feminine development. They are excellent wives and mothers, capable housewives; they maintain social life and assist culture; they have no lack of feminine interests, e.g. in their personal appearance, and when called upon they can still find time to play the part of devoted and disinterested mother-substitutes among a wide circle of relatives and friends. At the same time they fulfil the duties of their profession at least as well as the average man. It is really a puzzle to know how to classify this type psychologically.

Some time ago, in the course of an analysis of a woman of this kind, I came upon some interesting discoveries. She conformed in almost every particular to the description just given; her excellent relations with her husband included a very intimate affectionate attachment between them and full and frequent sexual enjoyment; she prided herself on her proficiency as a housewife. She had followed her profession with marked success all her life. She had a high degree of adaptation to reality and managed to sustain good and appropriate relations with almost everyone with whom she came in contact.

Certain reactions in her life showed, however, that her stability was not as flawless at it appeared; one of these will illustrate my theme. She was an American woman engaged in work of a propagandist nature, which consisted principally in speaking and writing. All her life a certain degree of anxiety, sometimes very severe, was experienced after every public performance, such as speaking to an audience. In spite of her unquestionable success and ability, both intellectual and practical, and her capacity for managing an audience and dealing with discussions, etc., she would be excited and apprehensive all night after, with misgivings whether she had done anything inappropriate, and obsessed by a need for reassurance. This need for reassurance led her compulsively on any such occasion to seek some attention or complimentary notice from a man or men at the close of the proceedings in which she had taken part or been the principal figure; and it soon became evident that the men chosen for the purpose were always unmistakable father-figures, although often not persons whose judgement on her performance would in reality carry much weight. There were clearly two types of reassurance sought from these father-figures: first, direct reassurance of the nature of compliments about her performance; secondly, and more important, indirect reassurance of the nature of sexual attentions from these men. To speak broadly, analysis of her behaviour after her performance showed that she was attempting to obtain sexual advances from the particular type of men by means of flirting and coquetting with them in a more or less veiled manner. The extraordinary incongruity of this attitude with her highly impersonal and objective attitude during her intellectual performance, which it succeeded so rapidly in time, was a problem.

Analysis showed that the Oedipus situation of rivalry with the mother was extremely acute and had never been satisfactorily solved. I shall come back to this later. But beside the conflict in regard to the mother, the rivalry with the father was also very great. Her intellectual work, which took the form of speaking and writing, was based on an evident identification with her father, who had first been a literary man and later had taken to political life; her adolescence had been characterized by conscious revolt against him, with rivalry and contempt of him. Dreams and phantasies* of this nature, castrating the husband, were frequently uncovered by analysis. She had quite conscious feelings of rivalry and claims to superiority over many of the 'father-figures' whose favour she would then woo after her own performances! She bitterly resented any assumption that she was not equal to them, and (in private) would reject the idea of being subject to their judgement or criticism. In this she corresponded clearly to one type Ernest Jones has sketched: his first group of homosexual women who, while taking no interest in the other women, wish for 'recognition' of their masculinity from men and claim to be the equals of men, or in other words, to be men themselves. Her resentment, however, was not openly expressed; publicly she acknowledged her condition of womanhood.

Analysis then revealed that the explanation of her compulsive ogling and coquetting – which actually she was herself hardly aware of till analysis made it manifest – was as follows: it was an unconscious attempt to ward off the anxiety which would ensue on account of the reprisals she anticipated from the father-figures after her intellectual performance. The exhibition in public of her intellectual proficiency, which was in itself carried through successfully, signified an exhibition of herself in possession of the father's penis, having castrated him. The display once over, she was seized by horrible dread of the retribution the father would then exact. Obviously it was a step towards propitiating the avenger to endeavour to offer herself to him sexually. This phantasy, it then appeared, had been very common in her childhood and youth, which had been spent in the Southern States of America; if a negro came to attack her, she planned to defend herself by making him kiss her and make love to her (ultimately so that she could then deliver him over to justice). But there was a further determinant of the obsessive behaviour. In a dream which had a rather similar content to this childhood phantasy, she was in terror alone in the house; then a negro came in and found her washing clothes, with her sleeves rolled up and arms exposed. She resisted him, with the secret intention of attracting him sexually, and he began to admire her arms and caress them and her breasts. The meaning was that she had

*[Editors' note: author follows Kleinian practice of spelling 'phantasy' thus.]

killed father and mother and obtained everything for herself (alone in the house), became terrified of their retribution (expected shots through the window), and defended herself by taking on a menial rôle (washing clothes) and by *washing off* dirt and sweat, guilt and blood, everything she had obtained by the deed, and 'disguising herself' as merely a castrated woman. In that guise the man found no stolen property on her which he need attack her to recover and, further, found her attractive as an object of love. Thus the aim of the compulsion was not merely to secure reassurance by evoking friendly feelings towards her in the man; it was chiefly to make sure of safety by masquerading as guiltless and innocent. It was a compulsive reversal of her intellectual performance; and the two together formed the 'double-action' of an obsessive act, just as her life as a whole consisted alternately of masculine and feminine activities.

Before this dream she had had dreams of people putting masks on their faces in order to avert disaster. One of these dreams was of a high tower on a hill being pushed over and falling down on the inhabitants of a village below, but the people put on masks and escaped injury!

Womanliness therefore could be assumed and worn as a mask, both to hide the possession of masculinity and to avert the reprisals expected if she was found to possess it – much as a thief will turn out his pockets and ask to be searched to prove that he has not the stolen goods. The reader may now ask how I define womanliness or where I draw the line between genuine womanliness and the 'masquerade'. My suggestion is not, however, that there is any such difference; whether radical or superficial, they are the same thing. The capacity for womanliness was there in this woman – and one might even say it exists in the most completely homosexual woman – but owing to her conflicts it did not represent her main development and was used far more as a device for avoiding anxiety than as a primary mode of sexual enjoyment.

I will give some brief particulars to illustrate this. She had married late, at 29; she had had great anxiety about defloration and had had the hymen stretched or slit before the wedding by a woman doctor. Her attitude to sexual intercourse before marriage was a set determination to obtain and experience the enjoyment and pleasure which she knew some women have in it, and the orgasm. She was afraid of impotence in exactly the same way as a man. This was partly a determination to surpass certain mother-figures who were frigid, but on deeper levels it was a determination not to be beaten by the man.[4] In effect, sexual enjoyment was full and frequent, with complete orgasm; but the fact emerged that the gratification it brought was of the nature of a reassurance and restitution of something lost, and not ultimately pure enjoyment. The man's love gave her back her self-esteem. During analysis, while the hostile castrating impulses towards the husband were in process of coming to light, the desire for intercourse very much abated, and she became for periods relatively frigid. The mask of womanliness was being peeled away, and she was revealed either as castrated (lifeless, incapable of pleasure), or as wishing to castrate (therefore afraid to receive the penis or welcome it by gratification). Once, while for a period her husband had had a love-affair with another woman, she had detected a very intense identification with him in regard to the rival woman. It is striking that she had had no homosexual experiences (since before puberty with a younger sister); but it appeared during analysis that this lack was compensated for by frequent homosexual dreams with intense orgasm.

In everyday life one may observe the mask of femininity taking curious forms. One capable housewife of my acquaintance is a woman of great ability, and can herself attend to typically masculine matters. But when, e.g. any builder or upholsterer is called in, she has a compulsion to hide all her technical knowledge from him and show deference to the workman, making her suggestions in an innocent and artless manner, as if they were 'lucky guesses'. She has confessed to me that even with the butcher and baker, whom she rules in reality with a rod of iron, she cannot openly take up a firm straightforward stand; she feels herself as it were 'acting a part', she puts on the semblance of a rather uneducated, foolish and bewildered woman, yet in the end always making her point. In all other relations in life this woman is a gracious, cultured lady, competent and well-informed, and can manage her affairs by sensible rational behaviour without any subterfuges. This woman is now aged 50, but she tells me that as a young woman she had great anxiety in dealings with men such as porters, waiters, cabmen, tradesmen, or any other potentially hostile father-figures, such as doctors, builders and lawyers; moreover, she often quarrelled with such men and had altercations with them, accusing them of defrauding her and so forth.

Another case from everyday observation is that of a clever woman, wife and mother, a university lecturer in an abstruse subject which seldom attracts women. When lecturing, not to students but to colleagues, she chooses particularly feminine clothes. Her behaviour on these occasions is also marked by an inappropriate feature: she becomes flippant and joking, so much so that it has caused comment and rebuke. She has to treat the situation of displaying her masculinity to men as a 'game', as something *not real*, as a 'joke'. She cannot treat herself and her subject seriously, cannot seriously contemplate herself as on equal terms with men; moreover, the flippant attitude enables some of her sadism to escape, hence the offence it causes.

Many other instances could be quoted, and I have met with a similar mechanism in the analysis of manifest homosexual men. In one such man with severe inhibition and anxiety, homosexual activities really took second place, the source of greatest sexual gratification being actually masturbation under special conditions, namely, while looking at himself in the mirror dressed in a particular way. The excitation was produced by the sight of himself with hair parted in the centre, wearing a bow tie. These extraordinary 'fetishes' turned out to represent a *disguise of himself* as his sister; the hair and bow were taken from her. His conscious attitude was a desire to *be* a woman, but his manifest relations with men had never been stable. Unconsciously the homosexual relation proved to be entirely sadistic and based on masculine rivalry. Phantasies of sadism and '*possession of a penis*' could be indulged only while reassurance against anxiety was being obtained from the mirror that he was safely 'disguised as a woman'.

To return to the case I first described. Underneath her apparently satisfactory heterosexuality it is clear that this woman displayed well-known manifestations of the castration complex. Horney was the first among others to point out the sources of that complex in the Oedipus situation; my belief is that the fact that womanliness may be assumed as a mask may contribute further in this direction to the analysis of female development. With that in view I will now sketch the early libido-development in this case.

But before this I must give some account of her relations with women. She was conscious of rivalry of almost any woman who had either good looks or intellectual pretensions. She was conscious of flashes of hatred against almost any woman with whom she had much to do, but where permanent or close relations with women were concerned she was none the less able to establish a very satisfactory footing. Unconsciously she did this almost entirely by means of feeling herself superior in some way to them (her relations with her inferiors were uniformly excellent). Her proficiency as a housewife largely had its root in this. By it she surpassed her mother, won her approval and proved her superiority among rival 'feminine' women. Her intellectual attainments undoubtedly had in part the same object. They too proved her superiority to her mother; it seemed probable that since she reached womanhood her rivalry with women had been more acute in regard to intellectual things than in regard to beauty, since she could usually take refuge in her superior brains where beauty was concerned.

The analysis showed that the origin of all these reactions, both to men and women, lay in the reaction to the parents during the oral-biting sadistic phase. These reactions took the form of the phantasies sketched by Melanie Klein[5] in her Congress paper, 1927. In consequence of disappointment or frustration during sucking or weaning, coupled with experiences during the primal scene which is intepreted in oral terms, extremely intense sadism develops towards both parents.[6] The desire to

bite off the nipple shifts, and desires to destroy, penetrate and dis-
embowel the mother and devour her and the contents of her body succeed
it. These contents include the father's penis, her fæces and her children –
all her possessions and love-objects, imagined as within her body.[7] The
desire to bite off the nipple is also shifted, as we know, on to the desire to
castrate the father by biting off his penis. Both parents are rivals in this
stage, both possess desired objects; the sadism is directed against both
and the revenge of both is feared. But, as always with girls, the mother is
the more hated, and consequently the more feared. She will execute the
punishment that fits the crime – destroy the girl's body, her beauty, her
children, her capacity for having children, mutilate her, devour her,
torture her and kill her. In this appalling predicament the girl's only safety
lies in placating the mother and atoning for her crime. She must retire
from rivalry with the mother and, if she can, endeavour to restore to her
what she has stolen. As we know, she identifies herself with the father;
and then she uses the masculinity she thus obtains by *putting it at the
service of the mother*. She becomes the father and takes his place; so she can
'restore' him to the mother. This position was very clear in many typical
situations in my patient's life. She delighted in using her great practical
ability to aid or assist weaker and more helpless women, and could
maintain this attitude successfully so long as rivalry did not emerge too
strongly. But this restitution could be made on one condition only; it must
procure her a lavish return in the form of gratitude and 'recognition'. The
recognition desired was supposed by her to be owing for her self-
sacrifices; more unconsciously what she claimed was recognition of her
*supremacy* in *having* the penis to give back. If her supremacy were not
acknowledged, the rivalry became at once acute; if gratitude and
recognition were withheld, her sadism broke out in full force and she
would be subject (in private) to paroxysms of oral-sadistic fury, exactly
like a raging infant.

In regard to the father, resentment against him arose in two ways: (1)
during the primal scene he took from the mother the milk, etc., which the
child missed; (2) at the same time he gave to the mother the penis or
children instead of to her. Therefore all that he had or took should be taken
from him by her; he was castrated and reduced to nothingness, like the
mother. Fear of him, though never so acute as of the mother, remained;
partly, too, because his vengeance for the death and destruction of the
mother was expected. So he too must be placated and appeased. This was
done by masquerading in a feminine guise for him, thus showing him her
'love' and guiltlessness towards him. It is significant that this woman's
mask, though transparent to other women, was successful with men, and
served its purpose very well. Many men were attracted in this way, and
gave her reassurance by showing her favour. Closer examination showed

that these men were of the type who themselves fear the ultra-womanly woman. They prefer a woman who herself has male attributes, for to them her claims on them are less.

As the primal scene the talisman which both parents possess and which she lacks is the father's penis; hence her rage, also her dread and helplessness.[8] By depriving the father of it and possessing it herself she obtains the talisman – the invincible sword, the 'organ of sadism'; he becomes powerless and helpless (her gentle husband), but she still guards herself from attack by wearing towards him the mask of womanly subservience, and under that screen, performing many of his masculine functions herself – 'for him' – (her practical ability and management). Likewise with the mother: having robbed her of the penis, destroyed her and reduced her to pitiful inferiority, she triumphs over her, but again secretly; outwardly she acknowledges and admires the virtues of 'feminine' women. But the task of guarding herself against the woman's retribution is harder than with the man; her efforts to placate and make reparation by restoring and using the penis in the mother's service were never enough; this device was worked to death, and sometimes it almost worked her to death.

It appeared, therefore, that this woman had saved herself from the intolerable anxiety resulting from her sadistic fury against both parents by creating in phantasy a situation in which she became supreme and no harm could be done to her. The essence of the phantasy was her *supremacy* over the parent-objects; by it her sadism was gratified, she triumphed over them. By this same supremacy she also succeeded in averting their revenges; the means she adopted for this were reaction-formations and concealment of her hostility. Thus she could gratify her id-impulses, her narcissistic ego and her super-ego at one and the same time. The phantasy was the mainspring of her whole life and character, and she came within a narrow margin of carrying it through to complete perfection. But its weak point was the megalomanic character, under all the disguises, of the necessity for supremacy. When this supremacy was seriously disturbed during analysis, she fell into an abyss of anxiety, rage and abject depression; before the analysis, into illness.

I should like to say a word about Ernest Jones' type of homosexual woman whose aim is to obtain 'recognition' of her masculinity from men. The question arises whether the need for recognition in this type is connected with the mechanism of the same need, operating differently (recognition for services performed), in the case I have described. In my case direct recognition of the possession of the penis was not claimed openly; it was claimed for the reaction-formations, though only the possession of the penis made them possible. Indirectly, therefore, recognition was none the less claimed for the penis. This indirectness was due to apprehension lest her possession of a penis *should be* 'recognized', in other words 'found out'. One can see that with less anxiety my patient too would have openly claimed recognition from men for her possession of a penis, and in private she did in fact, like Ernest Jones' cases, bitterly resent any lack of this direct recognition. It is clear that in his cases the primary sadism obtains more gratification; the father has been castrated and shall even acknowledge his defeat. But how then is the anxiety averted by these women? In regard to the mother, this is done of course by denying her existence. To judge from indications in analyses I have carried out, I conclude that, first, as Jones implies, this claim is simply a displacement of the original sadistic claim that the desired object, nipple, milk, penis, should be instantly surrendered; secondarily, the need for recognition is largely a need for absolution. Now the mother has been relegated to limbo; no relations with her are possible. Her existence appears to be denied, though in truth it is only too much feared. So the guilt of having triumphed over both can be absolved only by the father; if he sanctions her possession of the penis by acknowledging it, she is safe. By *giving* her recognition, he *gives* her the penis and to her instead of to the mother; then she has it, and she may have it, and all is well. 'Recognition' is always in part reassurance, sanction, love; further, it renders her supreme again. Little as he may know it, to her the man has admitted his defeat. Thus in its content such a woman's phantasy-relation to the father is similar to the normal Oedipus one; the difference is that it rests on a basis of sadism. The mother she has indeed killed, but she is thereby excluded from enjoying much that the mother had, and what she does obtain from the father she has still in great measure to extort and extract.

These conclusions compel one once more to face the question: what is the essential nature of fully developed femininity? What is *das ewig Weibliche*? The conception of womanliness as a mask, behind which man suspects some hidden danger, throws a little light on the enigma. Fully developed heterosexual womanhood is founded, as Helene Deutsch and Ernest Jones have stated, on the oral-sucking stage. The sole gratification of a primary order in it is that of receiving the (nipple, milk) penis, semen, child from the father. For the rest it depends upon reaction-formations. The acceptance of 'castration', the humility, the admiration of men, come partly from the overestimation of the object on the oral-sucking plane; but chiefly from the renunciation (less intensity) of sadistic castration-wishes deriving from the later oral-biting level. 'I must not take, I must not even ask; it must be *given* me'. The capacity for self-sacrifice, devotion, self-abnegation expresses efforts to restore and make good, whether to mother- or to father-figures, what has been taken from them. It is also what Radó has called a 'narcissistic insurance' of the highest value.

It becomes clear how the attainment of full heterosexuality coincides with that of genitality. And once more we see, as Abraham first stated, that genitality implies attainment of a *post-ambivalent* state. Both the 'normal' woman and the homosexual desire the father's penis and rebel against frustration (or castration); but one of the differences between them lies in the difference in the degree of sadism and of the power of dealing both with it and with the anxiety it gives rise to in the two types of women.

## Notes

1. This article was first published in *The International Journal of Psychoanalysis (IJPA)*, vol. 10 (1929).
2. E. Jones, 'The early development of female sexuality', *IJPA*, vol. 8 (1927).
3. S. Ferenczi, 'The nosology of male homosexuality', in *Contributions to Psychoanalysis*, 1916.
4. I have found this attitude in several woman analysands and the self-ordained defloration in nearly all of them (five cases). In the light of Freud's 'Taboo of virginity', this latter symptomatic act is instructive.
5. M. Klein, 'Early stages of the Oedipus conflict', *IJPA*, vol. 9 (1928).
6. E. Jones, op. cit, p. 469, regards an intensification of the oral-sadistic stage as the central feature of homosexual development in women.
7. As it was not essential to my argument, I have omitted all reference to the further development of the relation to children.
8. Cf. M.N. Searl, 'Danger situations of the immature ego', Oxford Congress, 1929.

Stephen Heath

# JOAN RIVIERE AND
# THE MASQUERADE

Joan Riviere was born Joan Verrall in 1883. Her education was later to be described by James Strachey, the general editor of the *Standard Edition* of Freud's works, as 'a little irregular'[1] but two things in it may be noted as of particular importance for her subsequent career: first, at the age of 17 she was sent off for a year to Gotha where she gained fluency in German; second, she was the niece of A.W. Verrall, the classical scholar, and spent a good deal of time mixing in Cambridge intellectual circles on her frequent visits to her uncle's home (where Strachey indeed would like to think he first met her). Through the Cambridge Verralls she was connected with the Society for Psychical Research and she may have arrived at Freud by the same path (Freud was made a corresponding member of the Society in 1911 and a year later provided a 'Note on the unconscious in psycho-analysis' for publication in its *Proceedings*). From 1916 to 1920 she was in analysis with Ernest Jones and by 1919 had patients of her own. The relationship with Jones was intense and fraught, a result certainly of strong transference and counter-transference and possibly too of an actual love-affair. She writes to Jones in 1918 of 'the long tragedy of my relationship with you'; he describes her as a patient as 'the worst failure I ever had'.[2]

That description is in a letter to Freud to whom Jones recommends Riviere for analysis in 1921 (she had already met Freud in 1920 at the first post-war International Congress of Psychoanalysis, held at The Hague):

> It is a case of typical hysteria, almost the only symptoms being sexual anaesthesia and unorganised Angst, with a few inhibitions of a general nature. . . . She has a most colossal narcissism imaginable, to a great extent secondary to the refusal of her father to give her a baby and her subsequent masculine identification with him.[3]

The situation thus created is common enough in the early years of psychoanalysis, with Freud and a forceful male disciple exchanging a woman for analysis in a complex erotic imbroglio; and exchanging her for analysis too in the sense that the woman is seen as a potential gain for the cause, 'a valuable translator and member of the society', as Jones puts it in Riviere's case[4] (the most striking example of such a triangle is no doubt that involving Freud, Jung and Sabina Spielrein[5]). In 1922 Jones is assuring Freud that his relationship with Riviere has never been a sexual one: 'She is not the type that attracts me erotically though I certainly have the admiration for her intelligence that I would have with a man.'[6] Which is just what Jones will then say in his *Sigmund Freud: Life and Work* of Freud's attraction to Riviere, will say in a brief paragraph sandwiched between mention of the famous question *Was will das Weib?* and comment on Freud's actual 'type of sexual object', 'a gentle feminine one':

> Freud was also interested in another type of woman, of a more intellectual and perhaps masculine cast. Such women several times played a part in his life, accessory to his men friends though of a finer calibre, but they had no erotic attraction for him. The most important of them were first of all his sister-in-law Minna Bernays, then in chronological order: Emma Eckstein, Loe Kann, Lou Andreas-Salomé, Joan Riviere, Marie Bonaparte.[7]

(It is worth noting in this list that Loe Kann, despite classification as being of this 'more intellectual and perhaps masculine cast', had a passionate affair with Jones who recommended her too for analysis with Freud). Nothing else of the Jones–Freud–Riviere triangle gets into *Sigmund Freud: Life and Work*, only this quick reference to her and her type; as well as, in a different vein, quotation of 'an intimate impression' of Freud written by Riviere for *The Lancet* at the time of Freud's death.[8]

Subsequent to her analysis with Freud, Riviere was analysed by Melanie Klein with whom she worked closely in London, helping in the development of child analysis and practising generally as a lay analyst. Her major intellectual work was in translating Freud (most notably the four volumes of *Collected Papers*, 1924–5) and in overseeing translations for the *International Journal of Psychoanalysis*, many of which she did herself. To her we owe many of the English Freudian terms, many of our now familiar phrases – 'civilization and its discontents', for example (where Freud himself had proposed 'man's discomforts in civilization'). She died in 1962.

Her life remains to be written but reading the letter in which Jones presents her to Freud – 'typical hysteria', 'sexual anaesthesia', 'masculine identification' – is to find oneself at once in the world of her 'Masquerade' paper, just as Jones's discourse of types – the intellectual and the gentle feminine – gives us immediately the context of the masquerade as defence, defence in this system of male identities and consequent identifications. Relations between the paper and the life are doubtless strong, more than strong. What did it mean to be an intellectual and a woman, an intellectual woman? The question for Riviere's patient in the paper can hardly but have been a question for her too (as it was so widely in the writing of the period, the question of identity as a woman explored, for instance, in those novels contemporary with and contiguous to Riviere's life that make up Dorothy Richardson's *Pilgrimage*). Reminiscences by those who knew her bring up fragments, touches of her existence that seem to make a pattern here: a visual memory of her at an evening party, 'tall, strikingly handsome, distinguished-looking and somehow impressive'; the inter-ruption of a work-session at lunchtime one Sunday when, her husband at home, 'Joan became the hostess . . . a delicious meal at a beautifully laid table'; her liking for cosmetics which she enjoyed 'in a quite weighty manner'; her taste in and knowledge of dresses (for a time she worked as a professional dressmaker).[9] If the pattern is that of the masquerade, however, we would then have to know what that means – defence against the implications of her intellectual and perhaps masculine cast? expression of genuine womanliness? subjection to the male régime of 'the woman'? derision of that régime? an ambiguous mixture of all or some of these things? Perhaps the one account to quote above all others is Katherine West's childhood memory, which gets the right feel, sets Riviere and the masquerade: the scene, the period, the assumptions, the identities, the recognition of the woman and the masculine equal and the problem of that, she 'of all things' a psychoanalyst:

> I still . . . cherish the vision of a friend of my mother's – a tall, Edwardian beauty with a picture hat and scarlet parasol – walking up and down the seashell path in lively conversation with a gentleman. Perhaps they were discussing theatres or the Post-Impressionists. Or perhaps they were talking about Freud – since this chic and decorative creature Joan Riviere was, of all things, Freud's first translator and a pioneer lay analyst.[10]

Published in the *International Journal of Psychoanalysis* in 1929, 'Womanli-ness as a masquerade' is now no doubt Riviere's best-known and most important piece of analytic writing. Its immediate context is that of the work done by analysts in the 1920s on sexual difference and, in particular, on female sexuality; including, of course, most crucially for Riviere, the work of Ernest Jones himself (Riviere refers at the outset to Jones's paper on 'The early development of female sexuality' and he in turn will use her paper in his 'The phallic phase'[11]). Freud's own writings respond to this whole debate but never specifically to 'Womanliness as a masquerade': Riviere has no entry in the index to the *Standard Edition* and the term 'masquerade' appears only twice in its twenty-four volumes, both times in the translation of texts written before Riviere's paper and with no connection whatsoever to the discussion of women and feminity.[12] It is not until more recent years that the idea of the masquerade has received significant attention and gained a certain currency, this with the renewal of the debate around female sexuality and its understanding at once through psychoanalysis and through feminist critique of psychoanalysis (the key moment is Lacan's commentary on Jones and the phallic phase in 1958, which then also retrieves Riviere and the masquerade[13]). The idea has subsequently known a wider cultural extension and found a place in thinking about questions of representation and sexual difference, notably in connection with film and cinema.

The paper itself is straightforward, up to a point. Its concern is with 'women who wish for masculinity' and who may then put on 'a mask of womanliness' as a defence, 'to avert anxiety and the retribution feared from men' (p.35); given which, it can be seen immediately as a contribution to discussion of the evolution of the Oedipus complex in women (the title, in fact, of a paper by Jeanne Lampl-de Groot published in the *International Journal* in the previous year[14]). The case from which Riviere develops her argument involves a successful intellectual woman who seeks reassurance from men after her public engagements, reassurance above all in the form of sexual attentions: 'To speak broadly, analysis of her behaviour after her performances showed that she was attempting to obtain sexual advances from the particular type of men by means of flirting and coquetting with them in a more or less veiled manner. The extraordinary incongruity of this attitude with her highly impersonal and objective attitude during her intellectual performance, which it succeeded so rapidly in time, was a problem' (p.36). The problem can be solved by reference to Oedipal rivalry: in her successful professional career, the woman rivals and takes the place of the father; in her acknowledgement nevertheless of womanliness, the flirting and coquetting, she placates him: 'it was an unconscious attempt to ward off the anxiety which would ensue on account of the reprisals she anticipated from the father-figures after her intellectual performance' (p.37). Having exhibited herself in possession of the father's penis, having thus castrated him, she then seeks protection from his expected anger, offering herself now as the castrated woman to the particular type of men, 'unmistakable father-figures' (p.36). Hence her life as a whole, which 'consisted alternately of masculine and feminine activities' (p.38).

Riviere then extends her discussion and proposes a fuller explanation in terms of the castration complex and its sources in the Oedipal situation. Both her parents, father and mother, are the patient's rivals, objects of her sadistic fury: 'In consequence of disappointment or frustration during sucking or weaning, coupled with experience during the primal scene which is interpreted in oral terms, extremely intense sadism develops towards both parents' (p.40). The primal scene confronts her with her lack of the father's penis – 'the talisman which both parents possess' (p.42) – and produces rage and dread. The masquerading woman becomes the father through her masculine success, dominating him (her gentle husband), but conciliating him all the same (her mask of womanliness); equally, she robs the mother of the penis, taken from the father, but guards against retaliation of her victory by the self-sacrifice she makes for weaker women: 'The essence of the phantasy was her *supremacy* over the parent-objects; by it her sadism was gratified, she triumphed over them. By this same supremacy she also succeeded in averting their revenges; the means she adopted for this were reaction-formations and concealment of her hostility. Thus she could gratify her id-impulses, her narcissistic ego and her super-ego at one and the same time' (p.42).

So we have Riviere's masquerade – the 'mask of womanliness' (p.38), '"disguising herself" as merely a castrated woman' (p.38), 'masquerading as guiltless and innocent' (p.38), 'masquerading in a feminine guise' (p.41). A woman identifies as a man – takes on masculine identity – and then identifies herself after all as a woman – takes up a feminine identity. What could be more simple? Except that at the centre of Riviere's paper is the *question* of the feminine identity:

> The reader may now ask how I define womanliness or where I draw the line between genuine womanliness and the 'masquerade'. My suggestion is not, however, that there is any such difference; whether radical or superficial, they are the same thing. The capacity for womanliness was there in this woman – and one might even say it exists in the most completely homosexual woman – but owing to her conflicts it did not represent her main development and was used far more as a device for avoiding anxiety than as a primary mode of sexual enjoyment. (p.38)

In the masquerade the woman mimics an authentic – genuine – womanliness but then authentic womanliness is such a mimicry, *is* the masquerade ('they are the same thing'); to be a woman is to dissimulate a fundamental masculinity, feminity is that dissimulation. At times Riviere seems critical of the masquerade, both as travesty of womanliness ('compulsive ogling and coquetting', p.37) and as inappropriate betrayal of true ability (as with the university lecturer who 'cannot treat herself and her subject seriously', p.39); at others she seems to see it as answering to 'the essential nature of fully developed femininity' (p.43). But then again, that femininity – 'I must not take, I must not even ask; it must be *given* me' (p.43) – is a masquerade, a way of dealing with 'sadistic castration wishes' (p.43).

The attainment of full heterosexuality, which coincides with genitality, is at that price, the price of the masquerade that is the woman. Or that is 'the woman', the male fiction, construction, condition. Jones and Freud (according to Jones) will deny erotic attraction to Riviere in these terms, she is masculine not feminine, at the same time as the erotic attraction is there; she is after all of the same type as Loe Kann. Riviere is admirable and disturbing and so disturbed: the letter in which Jones presents her to Freud is premonitory of the 'Masquerade' paper, right down to the characterization of her as despising 'all the rest of us, especially the women.'[15] The problem is not the mask but its assumption or not, its fit or misfit, with the latter pointing to it as mask, womanliness as a mask, 'behind which man suspects some hidden danger' (p.43). As indeed he would: if there is a mask, then there is a behind-the-mask and we need to know what is behind, to be *sure*. Man's suspicion is the old question, *Was will das Weib?*, *das ewig Weibliche*, all the others, always the same. Riviere's position in her paper is difficult: the masquerade is the woman's thing, hers, but is also exactly *for* the man, a male presentation, as he would have her (and, Riviere will say, as the mother would have her, making up the woman over again, not the stealer but the receiver of the penis). Which leaves Riviere where? 'What is *das ewig Weibliche?* The conception of womanliness as a mask, behind which man suspects some hidden danger, throws a little light on the enigma' (p.43). Whose enigma? What light? Collapsing genuine womanliness and the masquerade together, Riviere undermines the integrity of the former with the artifice of the latter. That she then concludes, provides the psychoanalytic explanation, changes nothing, on the contrary: the identity of the woman – the assumption of 'the woman' – slips; which is then enigma, danger, darkness needing light, and that identity here becomes struggle, rebellion 'against frustration (or castration)' (p.44), the contradiction of her identification in the world, of being 'the woman'. Riviere's paper knows that contradiction, in its writing as in its thesis.

The strongest commentator on and respondent to the masquerade is no doubt Nietzsche, troubled with woman and truth and masks and veils and feminism. He writes, in *Beyond Good and Evil*: 'Comparing man and woman in general one may say: woman would not have the genius for finery [*das Genie des Putzes*] if she did not have the instinct for the *secondary* role.'[16] The finery goes with the secondary – 'the acceptance of "castration", the humility, the admiration of men', as Riviere will have it (p.43). Woman is secondary and so supplementary and so an act: 'her great art is the lie, her supreme concern is appearance and beauty'; which is after all, 'let us confess it', what we men 'love and honour'.[17] But then, meanwhile, 'female voices are raised which . . . make one tremble': 'there are threatening and medically explicit statements of what woman *wants* of man.'[18] Nietzsche is already caught on the *Was will das Weib?* and the problem is, of course, that woman wants, that she makes a difference to man and that men, Nietzsche first and foremost, feel something wanted of them, which is fear, threat, the medically explicit, as Nietzsche says, conflating along with his time feminism, hysteria and sexuality. Better if she did not want; Nietzsche, hopefully, doubts she can, doubts whether woman 'really *wants* or *can* want', and specifically not 'enlightenment about herself', her pretence to which is just another '*adornment* for herself [*einen neuen Putz für sich*]' – 'self-adornment [*das Sich-Putzen*] pertains to the eternal-womanly, does it not?'[19] The intellectual woman, the feminist (the two are synonymous for Nietzsche), is a lie, a self-adorner, but then woman is a lie, adornment is her truth.

Is her sexual truth; hence the enigma (who is she, how can we know her, what does she want?): woman in the sexual act is just that, in an *act*. In *The Gay Science* Nietzsche spells it out:

> Finally, *women*. Reflect on the whole history of women: do they not *have* to be first of all and above all else actresses? Listen to physicians who have hypnotized women; finally, love them – let yourself be 'hypnotized by them'! What is always the end result? That they 'put on something' even when they take off everything [*dass sie 'sich geben', selbst noch wenn sie – sich geben*]. Woman is so artistic.[20]

The German is clear: even when they give themselves, women only '"give themselves"'. Truth goes into quotation marks, with women everything is mask, masquerade; which is essence and trouble, what we love and honour and what we hate and fear. The philosopher is fascinated and threatened, seduced and mocked: woman is the vanishing point for which he lacks any true perspective, since the perspective *he* has guarantees he cannot know *her*, while the impossibility of knowing her is itself *his* perspective, women produced as 'the woman', *das ewig Weibliche*, the function of this discourse of mask and behind, that mask behind which man suspects some hidden danger.

Listen to physicians who have hypnotized women. Listen to analysts the history of whose psychoanalysis starts with hypnosis, women, hysteria. And hysteria is what? *Failed* masquerade. The hysteric will not play the game, misses her identity as woman: 'Speaking as a whole', writes Freud, 'hysterical attacks, like hysteria in general, revive a piece of sexual activity in women which existed during their childhood and at that time revealed an essentially masculine character.'[21] Playing the game is how a Lacanian analyst, Moustapha Safouan, puts it with reference to the patient described in Riviere's paper: 'When Joan Riviere's patient falls into the masquerade, it is out of rivalry. What I call playing the game, is abandoning the masquerade inasmuch as it covers such a rivalry.'[22] The game to be played is that of being the phallus. With the mother as initial object, the child seeks to be the phallus she wants, lacks-desires (the phallic phase); with the father as law, the child is forbidden that fantasy and pushed into division, sexual difference (the castration complex). No one has the phallus, it is a signifier, the initial signifier of 'the lack-in-being that determines the subject's relation to the signifier'.[23] The phallus inscribes the subject in a relation of desire as division, the subject's lack-in-being, and assigns the subject to sexual difference, boy or girl as having or not having the phallus. No one has the phallus but the order of the phallus as initial signifier identifies as having or not having: the subject is constituted in lack *and* the woman represents lack. In the Oedipal moment of the articulation of sexual difference as identity, male and female, the woman concedes to phallic *jouissance* (Riviere's attainment of full heterosexuality coincident with genitality): 'she invests the man as having the phallus. But she cannot thus invest him without the wish to be, herself, for him, the phallus . . . in the end she finds her being not as woman but as phallus (this is the sense of the fundamental alienation of her being).'[24] In other words, she becomes the woman men want, the term of phallic identity, phallic exchange.

So Lacan credits Riviere with pin-pointing in the masquerade 'the feminine sexual attitude': the woman's 'on-the-off-chance of preparing herself so that the fantasy of The man in her finds its moment of truth.'[25] The masquerade serves to show what she does not have, a penis, by showing – the adornment, the putting-on – something else, the phallus she becomes, as woman to man, sustaining his identity and an order of exchange of which she is the object – 'the fantasy of The man in her finds its moment of truth': 'Such is the woman behind her veil: it is the absence of the penis that makes her phallus, object of desire.'[26] Adornment *is* the woman, she exists veiled; only thus can she represent lack, be what is wanted: lack 'is never presented other than as a reflection on a veil'.[27] Disguising herself as a castrated woman, the woman represents man's desire and finds her identity as, precisely, woman – genuine womanliness and the masquerade are the same thing, as Riviere insists, or, in the words of the Lacanian analyst Eugénie Lemoine-Luccioni, 'the veil is constitutive of the feminine libidinal structure'.[28]

It is the question of the *constitutive* – and with it the status of the feminine, the identity of the woman – that is crucial here. Its psychoanalytic context (Lacanian-Freudian) includes the following emphases: (1) The subject is given divided in the symbolic; the drama of the subject in language is the experience of its lack in being and that experience is a movement of desire: 'desire is a relation of being to lack . . . not lack of this or that but lack in being by which the being exists'.[29] Thus nothing can make up division, no object can satisfy desire – what is *wanting* is always wanting, division is the condition of subjectivity. (2) Sexual division is the crucial articulation of symbolic division, it enacts the fundamental splitting of subjectivity itself. The phallus is the term – the signifier – of this articulation-enactment; it comes to figure lack and so to order desire. In Juliet Mitchell's words: 'The phallus – with its status as potentially absent – comes to stand in for the necessarily *missing* object of desire at the level of sexual division.'[30] (3) That no one has the phallus is an expression of its reality as signifier of lack: if division cannot be made up, desire satisfied, then the phallus is not an end, not some final truth, but, paradoxically, the supreme signifier of an impossible identity. (4) Insisting on sexual identity as constructed from division, from the castration complex which gives the phallic mark of sexual distinction, and not ordained in nature, psychoanalysis stresses that identity as precarious, uncertain. (5) Nevertheless, precisely, psychoanalysis describes that construction in terms of an assignment of identity, male and female, the attainment – or not – of heterosexuality round the phallus and castration. (6) For Freud both sexes repudiate femininity; this is the bedrock that analysis strikes: 'the repudiation of femininity can be nothing else than a biological fact, a part of the great riddle of sex.'[31] Pre-Oedipally, both sexes have a masculine relation to the mother, seeking to be the phallus she wants; the prohibition of the mother under the law of the father – the recognition of castration – inaugurates the Oedipus complex for the girl, she now shifting her object love to the father who seems to have the phallus and identifying with the mother who, to her fury, does not: henceforth the girl will desire to have the phallus, which is the bedrock repudiation for her, the point in analytic work more than any other at which the analyst's efforts are felt to have been in vain, 'trying to persuade a woman to abandon her wish for a penis on the ground of its being unrealizable.'[32]

With these emphases in mind as the psychoanalytic context, we can return to the masquerade. The masquerade is a representation of femininity but then femininity is representation, the representation of the woman: 'images and symbols of the woman's cannot be isolated from images and symbols of the woman.'[33] Representation gives not essential but constructed identity, which is uncertain and, as the perspectives slide, precisely masquerade, mask, disguise, threat, danger. Michèle Montrelay notes that 'man has always called the feminine defenses and masquerade *evil*'[34] and we can remember Riviere's comment on man's suspicion of some 'hidden danger' behind the mask, as well as Nietzsche's demonstration of that very suspicion, the woman's always '"giving herself"'. The woman is situated as subject *vis-à-vis* the symbolic, lack in being, the phallus as mark of sexual division, but she lacks nothing in the real, has a problematic relation (to say the least) to castration and the Oedipus complex. Somewhere women do not *fit*, and for Freud and Lacan returning late in their careers to the *Was will das Weib?* Just as the scandal of women that torments Nietzsche is what can the phallus signify to them, what can it say of them? They 'give themselves' even when they give themselves, they are never who they, phallically, are, never *really* the woman.

The masquerade says that the woman exists at the same time that, as masquerade, it says she does not. This tourniquet of reassurance and disturbance can be considered both from the side of the man and from that of the woman. He has the woman, who is, however, fantasy (whence her confirmation in show, spectacle, cinema). She becomes the woman that she is not, assumes a feminity in a movement that Safouan calls 'playing the game' but also 'the fundamental alienation of her being'.

'Alienation' is a social and political term which is here used in the psychoanalytic abstract:

> Let us limit ourselves to the psychoanalytic side of the question. If symbolic castration results in a benefit for the man as regards having, since it conditions 'the attribution of the penis to his person', all is not loss for the woman. But it is as regards being that the benefit is situated for her, since it is her very lack that confers on her her 'price' – a price without equal as there is nothing to pay for it![35]

Alienation quickly becomes a *structural* condition of being a woman (overlying the alienation which for Lacan is a structural condition of subjectivity in general, the subject's division in the symbolic) and can be transposed into playing the game (and in which the woman is said to benefit, said to profit). Alienation is playing the game which is the act of womanliness and the act is her identity (remember Nietzsche on the genius of women), she *sticks* to it. The problem for Riviere's patient is her *distance* from womanliness, the gap between her and femininity – *she*, the case-history says, is disturbed.

At a meeting of the Lacan School a woman analyst comments: 'The nature of femininity is to be cause of man's desire and, as corollary, not to be able to be recognized other than by a man is the nature of femininity. I know that the MLF [Women's Liberation Movement] will be super-angry but I'll carry on . . .'[36] It is not clear why the MLF should be 'super-angry' (my rendering of the here trivializing *furax*, a kid's slang version of *furieux*, furious) at what can be taken at once as a statement of the male economy of femininity within which women are held, forced to masquerade – *at the cost* of their desire (Luce Irigaray: 'the masquerade . . . is what women do . . . in order to participate in man's desire, but at the cost of giving up theirs'[37]). Women as subjects are subjected, men too, but the masquerade-femininity is the representation of this subjection to men, a male order, and so must be broken: 'Women always experience at certain moments of their lives that "femininity" is a masquerade,' writes Monique Plaza in the first issue of the journal *Questions féministes*,[38] and we can reread Riviere's patient as experiencing just that, just that alienation.

For the psychoanalyst, however, the social-political analysis of the masquerade towards which the idea of an alienation can pull must be problematic. The analyst who thinks the MLF will be super-angry does so because she is announcing exactly a nature of femininity, what being a woman is in the human articulation of identity round the phallus. Riviere herself runs the masquerade back into 'genuine womanliness' and in Oedipal terms makes the latter an attainment, not an alienation but a fulfilment (there is a moment too when she seems almost to posit a given 'capacity for womanliness', the property of every woman, p.38). In other words, the masquerade comes out as a basic fact of female identity, which can then only doubt and question any social-political analysis of it. If the masquerade goes, taking femininity with it, what is left? Thus another woman analyst: 'When women give up the masquerade, what do they find in bed? Women analysts, how do they cause erections? This difficulty is the price they pay when they leave the masquerade.'[39]

This is crude enough (though its particular concern with phallic identity and exchange can be turned round and read back into the world of Riviere's patient, as into the world of the writing of her paper, the reality of the Freud–Jones–Riviere triangle, their problem with her, the woman analyst, as erotic type) but the question is insistent and important: what is left behind the mask of womanliness? The Oedipal story replies with masculinity; in Freud's words, 'the development of femininity remains exposed to disturbance by the residual phenomena of the early masculine period.'[40] The display of femininity, the masquerade, hides an unconscious masculinity; which is Riviere's account of womanliness as the defence against masculinity that the normal woman achieves, just as it is Nietzsche's worry precisely at that womanliness as defence, the fear of it as mask and so of what may lie behind (the intellectual woman, the feminist, the hysteric, a different sexuality). On the other side, over and against the Oedipal story, resisting the masculine answer, are replies that look to something lost, really the woman's. Both answers come together, have a certain oneness, the one truth they envisage, phallus or anti-phallus, the man/the woman (Irigaray again: 'She does not constitute herself as *one*, does not oppose the masculine truth with a feminine truth; which would be tantamount once more to playing the game of castration'[41].)

No one has the phallus but the phallus is the male sign, the man's assignment; so Safouan talks about his benefit in having 'the attribution of the penis to his person'. The man's masculinity, his male world, is the assertion of the phallus to support his having it. To the woman's masquerade there thus corresponds male display (*parade* is Lacan's term), that display so powerfully described by Virginia Woolf in *Three Guineas*: 'Your clothes in the first place make us gape with astonishment . . . every button, rosette and stripe seems to have some symbolical meaning.'[42] All the trappings of authority, hierarchy, order, position make the man, his phallic identity: 'if the penis was the phallus, men would have no need of feathers or ties or medals . . . Display [*parade*], just like the masquerade, thus betrays a flaw: no one has the phallus.'[43] Which can be read ironically in the reactions of the university lecturer to whom Riviere briefly refers:

> When lecturing, not to students but to colleagues, she chooses particularly feminine clothes. Her behaviour on these occasions is also marked by an inappropriate feature: she becomes flippant and joking, so much so that it has caused comment and rebuke. She has to treat the situation of displaying her masculinity to men as a 'game', as something *not real*, as a 'joke'. (p.39)

Riviere reads clothes and behaviour as inappropriate, though at the same time appropriate to women as women, but we can turn things round to this woman displaying *their* masculinity to men as a game, as a joke, much as Woolf does in *Three Guineas* (a strong social-political, feminist joke): she cannot, indeed, contemplate herself on equal terms with men – she isn't, and why should she? For her colleagues, for that *rank* of men (*not* for her students, there she simply does her job), she puts on a show of the femininity they demand, but inappropriately, keeping her distance, and returns masculinity to them as equally unreal, another act, a charade of power. But then masculinity is real in its effects, femininity too, the charade is *in* power (Woolf's theme again in *Three Guineas*); this woman's life is marked by power and effects, is caught up in the definitions of masculinity/femininity, the identifications of the man and the woman. Her behaviour and dress are about that; Oedipally reading one way only, Riviere misreads, and protest becomes merely sadism – sexual politics gives way to a psychology of sex.

In the end we come back to a now familiar problem. Psychoanalysis gives us sexual identity as construction and an understanding of that construction that makes good sense; reading 'Womanliness as a masquerade' is surely evidence enough of this. At the same time, the terms of that understanding give us a pattern of development – for instance, the little girl's passage 'from her masculine phase to the feminine one to which she is biologically destined'[44] – which seems to fix things for ever in the given, and oppressive, identities, with no connections through to the *social-historical* realities that it also seems accurately to be describing; 'Womanliness as a masquerade' surely provides evidence of this too. The argument crystallizes again today round femininity and woman's identity, for obvious reasons. Psychoanalysis tells us that identity is precarious and that women will bear the traces of its difficult achievement; but it *is* an identity and it is, normally, achieved, and individual women can be understood – analysed – in relation to it. Riviere does just this with the patient in her paper and the paper gives us the psychical and the social together and simultaneously keeps them apart, returning to the former over the latter. No doubt it is an articulation of the psychical and the social in the construction of sexuality and sexual identity that we need to break the deadlock, the articulation that psychoanalysis lays a basis for and continually suggests but never makes. Easier said than done.

And cinema? The masquerade is obviously at once a whole cinema, the given image of femininity. So it is no surprise that cinema itself can be seen as a prime statement of the masquerade, nor then that the masquerade as a concept should have a presence today in film analysis, thinking about film. The collective analysis by the *Cahiers du cinéma* editorial group of Sternberg's *Morocco* in 1970 is one moment of its introduction; Claire Johnston's account of Tourneur's *Anne of the Indies* in 1975 is another.[45]

A whole cinema . . . Cinema has played to the maximum the masquerade, the signs of the exchange femininity, has ceaselessly reproduced its – their – social currency: from genre to genre, film to film, the same spectacle of the woman, her body highlighted into the unity of its image, this cinema image, set out with all the signs of its femininity (all the 'dress and behaviour'). Which is not to say that women in those films are only those signs, that image, but simply that cinema works with the masquerade, the inscription of the fantasy of femininity, the identity of the woman. 'Works with' in the sense of runs on, and in the sense that the masquerade is a work of film and cinema, something to be made up again, *re*inscribed.

The films of the classic Hollywood cinema – more or less contemporary with Riviere's paper and her main analytic contributions – know the difficulties of the masquerade and genuine womanliness, the problematic of who *she* is. The *Cahiers du cinéma* analysis takes *Morocco*, Marlene Dietrich directed by Sternberg who had made her image in *The Blue Angel* only months before and who is fascinated by the very cinema of cinema, the extremes of elaboration. Dietrich wears all the accoutrements of femininity *as* accoutrements, does the poses as poses, gives the act as an act (as in so many films, she is a cabaret performer); writing of a much later performance by her, Sylvia Bovenschen talks of watching 'a woman demonstrate the representation of a woman's body.'[46] We are at an extreme: Dietrich gives the masquerade in excess and so *proffers* the masquerade, take it or leave it, holding and flaunting the male gaze; not a defence against but a derision of masculinity (remember the bric-à-brac of male attire that Dietrich affects in her most famous poses – top hat, dress jacket, cane).

Max Ophuls again develops the masquerade as pure cinema, the hyper-spectacle of fantasy. *Madame de . . .* sets out the woman, no name, just Madame de . . . , the object–possession–identity, the luxurious feminine of jewellery, furs, mirrors, and the man, the men, all their display of uniforms, military rituals, codes of honour. Everything turns on a pair of earrings: 'I've a right to do what I like with them', she says at the beginning of the film, but no, she hasn't; she doesn't *have*, she *is*. The circulation of the earrings produces the spectacle of the film, all the show of femininity, and the catastrophe to which its narrative leads, closing on her death; the masquerade again in excess – but then it *always* is: *was will das Weib?*, the trouble of her identity.

Hitchcock does it differently. In *Suspicion* and again in *Rebecca* Joan Fontaine is offered us as genuine, which means a certain submissive insignificance, the absence of the masquerade that the film will nevertheless quote in order to fill its spectacle contract (in *Suspicion*, for example, the close-ups of Joan Fontaine as she calms her horse) at the same time that it will explicitly reject it (in *Rebecca*, for example, the ball-dress scene where she fails to be the spectacle of the woman, is different from the dangerous Rebecca). Spectacle and narrative, image and movement, cinema in its films exasperates the masquerade and also tries to get women right, know her identity as reassurance – which rightness itself, however, can only be masquerade, fetishization, a whole cinema: the genuineness of the Joan Fontaine character is just another image, womanliness *is* masquerade.

The fetishization of the masquerade that cinema captures is the male distance: having, possession, the woman as phallus as the term of the fantasy of the man, her identity for him. Mary Ann Doane has recently been emphasizing women's lack of distance here or, to put it another way, the claustrophobia of this cinema:

> Above and beyond a simple adoption of the masculine position in relation to the cinematic sign, the female spectator is given two options: the masochism of overidentification or the narcissism entailed in becoming one's own object of desire, in assuming the image in the most radical way. The effectivity of masquerade lies precisely in its potential to manufacture a distance for the image, to generate a problematic within which the image is manipulable, producible, and readable by the woman.[47]

The problem is thus the refusal of the masquerade, making films outside of cinema, its images (so Anne Friedberg will see Lizzie Borden's *Born in Flames* in this way: 'you never fetishize the body through masquerade . . .

the film seems consciously deaestheticized'[48]), or perhaps its use, breaking the closeness of femininity for women (Doane's suggestion, taking the masquerade as artifice, destabilizing the image – remember Riviere's lecturer again). The former is a question of representation – what is an alternative image and an alternative to the image? – while the latter is a question in representation – what are the breaks, the contradictions, the possible skewings in the system? The former is the utopian actuality of a new spectatorship, the latter the current disturbance of the old positions (in fact, Doane stresses the difficulties here, of seeing through the masquerade in a different way – Riviere's lecturer disturbs but is also caught up in the given identities in the very form of her disturbance).

I know nothing of Riviere's experience of the cinema. Her life remains to be written and, unlike Woolf or Richardson or H.D. or Bryher (all of them contemporaries of her paper, literary figures with an awareness of psychoanalysis), she seems to have written nothing herself directly concerning film. Of course, we can wonder: the year of the 'Masquerade' paper saw the release in Berlin of Pabst's *Pandora's Box*, a study in feminine identity and the masquerade in the male system of the woman; the previous year had seen the publication in *Close Up* (the London film journal with which Bryher, H.D. and Richardson were involved) of its first article by Freud's close collaborator Hanns Sachs, 'Film psychology'. Perhaps, probably, Riviere knew of these things, and many others, but that is all we can say. So we are left with her paper and the possibilities of the idea of the masquerade, the various ways it can go, in thinking about cinema as in thinking generally about the construction and representation of sexual identity. We are left with that and with her other writings and her translations; and then with the world of the paper, her world – the seashell path, the scarlet parasol, the conversation that should have been on theatres but might have been on Freud, this woman 'of all things' . . .[49]

## Notes

References to Riviere's paper 'Womanliness as a masquerade' are given in brackets in the body of the text and are to its reprinting in the present volume.

1. J. Strachey, obituary notice for Joan Riviere, *The International Journal of Psychoanalysis*, (*IJPA*) vol.44 (1963), p.228.
2. J. Riviere, letter to Ernest Jones, 25 October 1918, cit. V. Brome, *Ernest Jones: Freud's Alter Ego*, London, Caliban Books, 1982, p.113; Jones, letter to Freud, 21 January 1921, cit. Brome, op.cit., p.131.
3. E. Jones, letter to Freud, 21 January 1921, p.131.
4. ibid.
5. See A. Carotenuto, *A Secret Symmetry: Sabina Spielrein Between Jung and Freud*, New York, Pantheon Books, 1982.
6. E. Jones, letter to Freud, 1 April 1922, cit. Brome, op.cit., p.135.
7. E. Jones, *Sigmund Freud: Life and Work*, London, Hogarth Press, 1955, vol.II, p.469.

8. J. Riviere, 'An intimate impression', *The Lancet*, 20 September 1939, p.765; in E. Jones, *Sigmund Freud: Life and Work*, vol.II, pp.450–3.

9. See J. Strachey, op.cit., p.228 and P. Heimann, obituary notice for Joan Riviere, *IJPA*, vol.44 (1963), pp.232, 233.

10. K. West, *Inner and Outer Circles*, London, Cohen & West, 1958, p.26.

11. E. Jones, 'The phallic phase' [1933], in E. Jones, *Papers on Psychoanalysis* (fifth edition), London, Baillière, Tindall & Cox, 1948, pp.452–84; reference to Riviere's paper, p.480.

12. See S. Freud, *Jokes and their Relation to the Unconscious* [1905], *The Standard Edition of the Complete Psychological Works of Sigmund Freud*, ed. J. Strachey, London, Hogarth Press, 1953–74, (*SE*), vol.VIII, p.179; 'A seventeenth-century demonological neurosis' [1922], *SE*, vol.XIX, p.104.

13. J. Lacan, 'La signification du phallus' [1958], *Écrits*, Paris, Seuil, 1966, pp. 685–95; reference to the masquerade, p.694; trans. *Écrits: A Selection*, London, Tavistock, 1977, pp.281–91, reference p.290, and J. Mitchell and J. Rose (eds.), *Feminine Sexuality: Jacques Lacan and the École Freudienne*, London, Macmillan, 1982, pp.74–85, reference p.84.

14. J. Lampl-de Groot, 'The evolution of the Oedipus complex in women', *The International Journal of Psychoanalysis*, vol.9, 1928, pp.332–45. See also K. Horney, 'On the genesis of the castration complex in women', *IJPA*, vol.5 (1924), pp. 50–65; 'The flight from womanhood', *IJPA*, vol.7 (1926), pp.324–39; M. Klein, 'Early stages of the Oedipus complex', *IJPA*, vol.9 (1928), pp.167–80.

15. E. Jones, letter to Freud, 21 January 1921, p.132.

16. F. Nietzsche, *Beyond Good and Evil* [1886], Harmondsworth, Penguin, 1973, p.84.

17. ibid., p.145.

18. ibid., p.144.

19. ibid., p.145.

20. F. Nietzsche, *The Gay Science* [1882], New York, Vintage Books, 1974, p.317.

21. S. Freud, 'Some general remarks on hysterical attacks' [1909], *SE*, vol.IX, p.234.

22. I. Diamantis and M. Safouan, 'Entrevue avec Moustapha Safouan', *Ornicar?*, no.9 (1977), p.104.

23. J. Lacan, *Écrits*, p.710.

24. M. Safouan, *La Sexualité féminine dans la doctrine freudienne*, Paris, Seuil, 1976, pp.136–7.

25. J. Lacan, *Le Séminaire, livre XI, Les quatre concepts fondamentaux de la psychanalyse*, Paris, Seuil, 1973, p.176; trans. *The Four Fundamental Concepts of Psychoanalysis*, Harmondsworth, Penguin, 1979, p.193; *Télévision*, Paris, Seuil, 1974, p.64.

26. J. Lacan, *Écrits*, p.825; *Écrits: A Selection*, p.322.

27. J. Lacan, *Le Séminaire, livre II, Le moi dans la théorie de Freud et dans la technique de la psychanalyse*, Paris, Seuil, 1978, p.261.

28. E. Lemoine-Luccioni, *La Robe*, Paris, Seuil, 1983, p.124.

29. J. Lacan, *Le Séminaire, livre II*, p.261.

30. J. Mitchell, *Feminine Sexuality*, p.24 (I draw generally here on the introductions by Mitchell and Rose to *Feminine Sexuality*).

31. S. Freud, 'Analysis terminable and interminable' [1937], *SE*, vol.XXIII, p.252.

32. ibid.

33. J. Lacan, *Écrits*, p.728; *Feminine Sexuality*, p.90.

34. M. Montrelay, *L'Ombre et le nom*, Paris, Minuit, 1977, p.71; trans. 'Inquiry into femininity', *m/f*, no.1, 1978, p.93.

35. M. Safouan, 'Entrevue avec Moustapha Safouan', p.104.

36. I. Roublef, intervention, Journées des Cartels de l'École Freudienne de Paris [1975], *Lettres de l'École Freudienne*, no.18, 1976, p.211.

37. L. Irigaray, *Ce Sexe qui n'en est pas un*, Paris, Minuit, 1977, p.131.

38. M. Plaza, 'Pouvoir "phallomorphique" et psychologie de "la Femme"', *Questions féministes* no.1, 1977, p.112; trans. '"Phallomorphic power" and the psychology of "Woman"', *Ideology and Consciousness*, no.4, 1978, p.27.

39. 'Entrevue avec Moustapha Safouan', p.104.

40. S. Freud, *New Introductory Lectures on Psychoanalysis* [1933], *SE*, vol. XXIII, p.131.

41. L. Irigaray, *Amante marine*, Paris, Minuit, 1980, p.92.

42. V. Woolf, *Three Guineas* [1938], Harmondsworth, Penguin, 1977, p.23.
43. E. Lemoine-Luccioni, op.cit., p.34.
44. S. Freud, *New Introductory Lectures*, p.119.
45. '*Morocco* de Josef von Sternberg', *Cahiers du cinéma*, no.225, (1970), pp.5–13; C. Johnston, 'Femininity and the masquerade: *Anne of the Indies*', in C. Johnston and P. Willemen (eds.), *Jaques Tourneur*, Edinburgh, Edinburgh Film Festival, 1975, pp.36–44.
46. S. Bovenschen, 'Is there a feminine aesthetic?', *New German Critique*, no.10, (1977), p.129.
47. M.A. Doane, 'Film and the masquerade: theorising the female spectator', *Screen*, vol.23, no.3–4 (1982), p.87.
48. A. Friedberg, 'An interview with filmmaker Lizzie Borden', *Women and Performance*, vol.1, no.2 (1984), p.44. Cf. T. de Lauretis, 'Aesthetic and feminist theory: rethinking women's cinema', *New German Critique*, no.34 (1985), pp.154–75.
49. For an initial bibliography of Riviere's writings, see *IJPA*, vol.44 (1963), p.235.

Francette Pacteau

# THE IMPOSSIBLE REFERENT:
## representations of the androgyne

*For it was impossible to think of him as a woman . . . and yet whenever I thought of him as a man I felt a sense of falseness.*
                                    Ursula K. Le Guin, The Left Hand of Darkness

Discussions of androgyny invariably seem to come up against a resistance – not so much, or not only, from the speaking subject, but from language itself. Any attempt to *define* androgyny reveals an ever evasive concept which takes us to the limits of language. Not that definitions are impossible – for example, we might characterize androgyny as a mixing of secondary masculine and feminine sexual characteristics – but, confronted with the ubiquitous representations of the figure of the androgyne disseminated across visual and literary texts, such definitions ask for their own *dépassement*. The physiological discourse, in terms of which the above definition is offered, speaks of physical features but does not account for the mental processes at work in the *fascination* exercised by sexual ambiguity. Androgyny cannot be circumscribed as belonging to some being; it is more a question of a relation between a look and an appearance, in other words *psyche* and *image*. I do not encounter an 'androgyne' in the street; rather I encounter a figure whom I 'see as' androgynous. That is to say, the androgyne does not exist in the real – and this presents us with a major stumbling block in trying to organize a meaning for androgyny, for the impression is always that androgyny *does* so exist. To even approach the inherent difficulties of the subject, I must posit androgyny not as entity, but as symptom – in the psychoanalytic sense of indicative of a repressed desire.

In *Beatrix*, Balzac describes his androgynous-looking heroine, Camille de Maupin, as 'an amphibious being who is neither man nor woman' – a swift slide here from 'appearing', to 'being', to 'not being'; from an ambiguous sexual appearance to a non-sexual identity. When I see somebody as androgynous, I still *know* that the person I am looking at is either a man or a woman. However, somewhere behind the rationalization of the sexually ambiguous figure looms the vertiginous possibility of a dual sexual identity – vertiginous in that from dual sexual identity to non-sexual identity, in effect non-identity, there might be only one step.

As I have already observed, I know that the person I am looking at is either a man or a woman, but *nevertheless*, s/he is neither man nor woman. In psychoanalytic terms, a process of 'disavowal' is operative here (I shall return to this concept later) – two levels, the real (or rather, 'reality'), and the fantasized, between which I constantly oscillate in search of an impossible resolution.

In the impulse which propels me into fantasy I locate a wish. Androgyny can be said to belong to the domain of the imaginary, where desire is unobstructed; gender identity to that of the symbolic, the Law; it is at the nodal point where symbolic and imaginary meet that resistance occurs. The androgynous-looking figure presents me with an impossibility, that of the erasure of difference, that very difference which constructs *me* as a subject. From the instant my biological sex is determined, my identity is defined in difference – I am either a boy or a girl. I shall consequently take up my position in society on one side of the sexual divide, behave according to the genderized codes, reaffirm the difference. The androgynous 'position' represents a denial, or a transgression, of the rigid gender divide, and as such implies a threat to our given identity and to the system of social roles which define us. How can I reconcile the observation of *threat* with that of desire? Desire here has to be understood in a particular psychoanalytic acceptance of the term: an unconscious wish, indissolubly attached to memory traces, evoked through certain stimuli and associations; desire born out of the first loss of the mother's breast – and whose subsequent demands may require the hallucinatory reproduction of the traces of those earliest perceptions which have become the signifiers of lost primal satisfactions. In this context the wish correlative to the androgynous fantasy would be attached to archaic memories of early childhood; the disavowal of sexual difference therefore represents the fantasized re-enactment of an early pleasurable perception – another topic to which I must return later.

I mentioned earlier the resistance inherent in the language used in discussing androgyny. Having linked the androgyne fantasy to early infantile perceptions, it will be easier to understand the cause of this difficulty. Androgyny belongs to the realm of the primary processes: psychic energy happily shifting from one representation to the other through displacement and/or condensation, accommodating the unconscious wish in the most direct way. In relating androgyny to 'infantile sexuality', we are however using a 'secondary process' language of differences to refer to a domain of experience – the pre-Oedipal – in which difference is not acknowledged. Just as language does not cater for the 'neither . . . nor' of androgyny, neither does the term 'bisexuality', with its inherent assumption of *two* sexes, adequately express the nature of infantile sexuality. In popular culture the notion of bisexuality is invoked often and loosely in connection with androgyny (as in the media coverage of Bowie and Boy George). However, in the psychoanalytic view, 'bisexuality' is not the outrageous behavioural attribute of the few, but the psychic condition of us all. The psychoanalytic concept of bisexuality has been too widely discussed in recent theory to require representation here.[1] The important point is that, in opposition to the notion of a fixed sexual identity, determined by the subject's biological sex, Freudian theory disengages psychic masculinity and femininity from physiological male-ness and femaleness. It is necessary to distinguish between the *biological* concept of femininity/masculinity, dealing with primary and secondary physiological sexual characteristics; the *sociological*, referring to actual 'male' and 'female' subjects, their semiotic functions and 'gender roles' in a given society; and the *psychosexual*: 'anatomy can point out the characteristics of maleness and femaleness, psychology cannot. For psychology, the contrast between the sexes fades away into one between *activity* and *passivity*'[2] (activity, we must add, having too readily been associated with the man, passivity with the woman). Pre-Oedipal sexuality is undifferentiated – a common ground in the history of the libido in which passive and active instinctual aims alternate in both male and female subjects; the dissolution of the Oedipus complex marks the passage from a disseminated sexuality to a heterosexual organization under the primacy of the genitals. However, the positions adopted by the male and female subjects through identification are precarious. As Juliet Mitchell points out, 'it is always only an adoption'.[3] (Dora's identification was with her father, and her love object one belonging to her own sex.[4])

## Splitting

In 1768, Jean Baptiste Robinet, a philosopher, proposed his own theory of human evolution, which went as follows: Before attempting the creation of man, Nature tried her hand out on stones, as shown by the existence of fossil feet, hands, ears . . . etc. From those fragments Nature was to work towards achieving a complete, autonomous being. Although Robinet could quote the fact of 'un moine qui s'engrossa lui-même' (a monk who impregnated himself), Nature was striving for the realization of a far more aesthetic project, removed from the monastic reality:

> 'When Nature will have accomplished the unification in one and the same individual, of the perfect organs of the two sexes, these new beings will combine, to advantage, the beauty of Venus with that of Apollo: which is perhaps the highest degree of human beauty.[5]

Aristophanes' myth has us as two-faced spherical beings, endowed with four legs and four arms, happily rolling around. Some of us were half

Alexandre Séon, frontispiece of *L'Androgyne* by Joséphin Péladan. Part VIII of *L'Ethopée ou La Décadence Latine*, 1891. (Illustration from the Catalogue of the Salon de la Rose Croix, Paris, 1892)

woman and half man, others half woman and half woman and a third category, half man and half man. But, as a punishment for having angered the gods, each little round thing was split into two, and thus condemned to wander divided, each part endlessly looking for its lost half. Apollo proceeded to twist each head around, to the side of the wound, so that man and woman would be incessantly reminded of the chastisement. He then closed the gaping wound by bringing the skin to the centre of the abdomen and tying it at this point that we came to call navel. Zeus had achieved his objective: those earthly beings were now greater in number, and weaker in strength, a potentially exploitable workforce. However, efficiency and obsessive desire are incompatible; the once happy things would now wander, night and day, in an unharmonious motion, pining for their other half, clinging to each other, thus dying of starvation and inertia. This sight greatly afflicted the gods. Zeus conceded each man and woman a sexual organ.

> And after the transposition the male generated in the female in order that by the mutual embraces of man and woman they might breed, and the race might continue; or if man came to man they might be satisfied, and rest, and go their ways to the business of life.[6]

From fragments to whole or from whole to fragments the desire is respectively for union and re-union. The psychic development of the child fits perfectly the temporal sequence of Aristophanes' myth, from a being who extends beyond the boundaries of its own body, incorporating its environment, as full and replete as Plato's little spherical things, to an ever 'starving' subject: somewhere in between, when the smooth rolling motion is broken, the split and consequent loss. Psychoanalytic theory provides us with a picture of the constitution of the subject in a history punctuated by losses and separations – separation from the breast, 'mirror-phase', division of the subject in language and so on – engendering a split desiring subject who incessantly threatens our conscious subjective organization. It is important to remember that to be assigned one or the other sex entails a loss: that of the sexual position the subject has to surrender. Little Hans wanted to have children; he had to come up against the realization that as a little boy he would never be able to do so. 'Because I should so like to have children; but I don't ever want it, I shouldn't like to have them.'[7]

Meanwhile the post-Oedipal subject carves statues in the shape of sleeping hermaphrodites, writes about a world called Winter, situated in a distant corner of the galaxy, whose inhabitants are all of one sex, paints curvaceous, hairless Endymions, watches movies about Victorias who pose as Victors and enormously enjoys the confusion s/he creates by dressing up in the codes of the opposite sex.

Bartolo de Fredi, *The Creation of Eve*, Italy, fourteenth century. (Collegiato di San Gemignano (Siena), Italy)

Hermaphroditus, the offspring of Hermes and Aphrodite, once bathed in a lake where Salmacis, one of Diana's nymphs, dwelt. She fell in love with him at first sight.

> She longed to embrace him then and with difficulty restrained her frenzy. Hermaphroditus, clapping his hollow palms against his body, dived quickly into the stream. As he raised first one arm and then the other, his body gleamed in the clear water as if someone had encased an ivory statue or white lilies in transparent glass. 'I have won, he is mine', cried the nymph, and flinging aside her garments, plunged into the heart of the pool. The boy fought against her, but she held him, and snatched kisses as he struggled, placing her hand beneath him, stroking his unwilling breast, and clinging to him, now on this side, now on that. . . . 'You may fight, you rogue, but you will not escape. May the gods grant me this, may no time to come ever separate him from me, or me from him.' Her prayers found favour with the gods: for as they lay together, their bodies were united, and

from being two persons they became one. As when a gardener grafts a branch on to a tree, and sees the two unite as they grow . . . so when their limbs met in that clinging embrace the nymph and the boy were no longer two, but a single form, possessed of a dual nature, which could not be called male or female, but seemed to be at once both and neither.[8]

Caenis, the daughter of Elatus was famous for her beauty; she refused to marry anyone, but the story spread that:

As she was wandering on a lonely part of the shore, she was forcibly subjected to the embraces of the god of the sea. The same report went on to tell how Neptune, when he had enjoyed the pleasures of his new love, said to the girl: 'You may pray for anything without fear of being refused. Choose what you want.' 'The wrong I have suffered,' replied Caenis, 'evokes the fervent wish that I may never be able to undergo such an injury again. Grant that I be not a woman, and you will have given me all.' The last words were uttered in deeper tones: that voice could be taken for the voice of a man, as indeed it was. For already the god of the deep sea had granted Caenis' prayer, bestowing this further boon, that the man Caeneus should be proof against any wound, and should never be slain by the sword.[9]

## Reunion

What is at stake in the representation of the concept of the androgyne is a narcissistic as well as a fetishistic impulse. I would argue that whether or not I find somebody androgynous has to do with whether or not I can identify with the ambiguous figure. The process at work would be one where through identification with this 'ideal', because complete, other, I can shift positions, oscillating between the feminine and the masculine. Our identity is constructed – in similarities and differences – in identification with whomever we grow up with. Subsequently the everyday encounter with the other reminds us incessantly of this identity. When the other is not identifiable, my own position wavers. The consequent psychic oscillation would allow me, so to speak, to regain my other half, to reform the ideal image lost and found in the mirror.

The wish for reunion implies a state of self-sufficiency which recalls the auto-eroticism of early infancy, or perhaps more accurately the earlier *objectless* stage at the dawn of consciousness, and further back the plenitude of intra-uterine life. To regain this state of self-sufficiency would imply the abolition of the other who constantly evokes the difference, the loss. Initially it is the mother's breast which is 'lost' as not belonging to the infant's body, as other. Saint Agatha carries her severed

Auguste Rodin, *Paola and Francesca in Clouds*, marble, 1894. (Musée Rodin, Paris)

breast. Difference here annihilated in the violent gesture of which the saint's body bears no mark, a body which 'would appear to trace the image of a "feminineman" ("homme féminin")'.[10] The breast as first object is here denied and with it the very identity of the subject. The breast offered to us on a plate as of food – the breast the infant incorporates in a state of complete undifferentiation. In Slava Tsukerman's film *Liquid Sky*, the sexually ambiguous-looking heroine literally does away with the other(s) – whoever fucks her disintegrates in a whirl of colours. Narcissistic identification is one such process of annihilation of difference. In explaining why she finds Boy George androgynous, a friend spoke of his non-threatening sexuality. In the myths of Caenis and Caeneus and Hermaphroditus, it is the rape, respectively of the woman and the man's body, which provokes the metamorphoses. The injury made to a body that wants itself whole is repaired through abolition of the other. Hermaphroditus and Salmacis become one; Caenis becomes the other. The threatening distance is abolished. 'Tout corps étranger est menace, tout désir déjà corps étranger'.[11]

From the self-sufficient androgyne derives a non-desiring, asexual being. Catherine Clément speaks of the androgynous Virgin Mary, a woman who conceives by herself, an autonomous asexual being.[12] Desire born from the split between subject and object is located outside the subject's body, in a distance – between the infant and the breast, between the child and its image in the mirror. Fantasy does away with distance; the androgyne figure is situated at the locus of desire, but never itself desires.

The fantasized abolition of sexual difference as the resolution of the narcissistic desire for completeness and self-sufficiency is correlative to fetishism. Inherent in the androgyne fantasy is a process of disavowal that allows me to see somebody as a man *and* as a woman: 'I know . . . but nevertheless.' The narcissistic interest of the little boy in his penis promotes anxiety at the real or imagined threat to his sexual integrity and identity. In order to keep the threat at bay, the boy disavows what he now perceives as its actualization – the woman's 'lack' of the penis. Pontalis stresses the desire to abolish sexual difference as a desire to protect oneself from its *effects*. The process at work, in his account, is one of defence against what comes to stand as the signifier of all losses, castration. To be assigned to one sex deprives one of the powers of the other and conjures up castration. The androgyne would represent the possession of both 'maternal and paternal phallus'; in disavowing the difference, both sexes regain their 'lost half' and the power that comes with it. Pontalis seems to propose a parallel route to the androgynous resolution for woman and man until he comes to the conclusion that 'The positive androgyne cannot exist outside myth. Incarnated, seen, it is effectively and simultaneously castrated man and woman'.[13] Pontalis speaks of the man. In referring to the maternal phallus, one could hope for the man's desire to regain the power lost when separated from its feminine half; there may be some grounds for such optimism, as I shall discuss further. However, in a symbolic order in which the woman's body stands for signifier of lack, the androgyne figure invariably evokes castration: 'I see somebody as a woman' – its affirmation – 'and as a man' – its negation. Following a quote on the paramount male principle in our Western society, Catherine Clément speaks of the 'monstrous' figure of the Virgin Mary. For Clément the androgynous holy virgin is 'the occultation of the feminine principle beneath the masculine ideal',[14] a man-made fantasy, the virilization of the woman, a means of oppression and alienation because emanating from a culture where the male principle dominates.

In Proust's *Le temps retrouvé*, the creator feels himself grown big with 'this work which I bore within me . . . anxiously embraced with the fragile protection of its own pulpy and quivering substance'. He is writing a book. In a 'supremely important appointment with myself',[15] he will combine the powers of man, woman, and God, in order to carry his project through. Hermaphrodite, in casting a spell on the waters that made him half-man, half-woman, engenders a whole line of little Hermaphrodites. President Schreber wanted to conceive; when penetrated by the sun's rays he perceives his entire body as an erogenous zone, as a woman's body.[16] Pontalis' account of psychic bisexuality offers a negative androgyny and a positive androgyny: the impotency of the asexual being and the plenitude of the pre-Oedipal. At the unconscious level, where the androgyne belongs, conciliation of the positive and the negative is possible; the fantasy oscillates between desire and its correlative threat. Androgyny, as a fetishistic resolution of castration anxiety – providing the woman with the penis she lacks – could also evoke the possibility of the pregnant man: a more cheering proposition for the woman in that her body does not only signify a lack in relation to the man's castration anxiety, but also a plenitude in relation to the man's incapacity for conception. For the man, therefore, the woman's body could come to signify a *double* castration. By this token, the woman is *twice* repudiated in the androgynous figure. Catherine Clément shudders at the prospect of 'an ideal world without women, where men can live amongst themselves, an asexual world of warriors'.[17] Robinson Crusoe, by making love to the earth, engenders a new species of white flowers. An imperfect androgynous gesture; he still had to resort to the other. (Friday's botanical offspring bear black stripes.)[18]

The fantasy of the androgyne is also reminiscent of a more primitive imago of early childhood located prior to the recognition of sexual difference – the 'phallic' mother whom the child perceives as complete and autonomous. The belief in the mother who is all and everything is held by both the male and the female child. Genetically constructing the mother in his own image, the little boy attributes the penis to her. This image will be retained in spite of subsequent knowledge of sexual difference – an aspect of disavowal, a form of defence against castration anxiety.

## The clothed androgyne and the naked hermaphrodite

'The dreamer, in a state of nocturnal sexual excitation, will throw a woman down, strip her and prepare for intercourse – and then, in place of the female genitals, he beholds a well-developed penis and breaks off the dream and the excitation'.[19] In relation to the idea of the phallic mother, its correlative 'woman with a penis' may be linked to the composite figure of the hermaphrodite. Although I assume a similar desire at the roots of

Hermaphrodite statue, Greece. (Nationalmuseum, Stockholm)

*Satyr Uncovering a Sleeping Hermaphrodite*, Roman cameo (Reproduced by courtesy of the Trustees, The British Museum).

representations of both the androgyne and the hermaphrodite, the psychical processes at work have to be distinguished.

> The distinction established from time to time between the terms 'androgyne' and 'hermaphrodite' have always been purely arbitrary and consequently often contradictory. . . . Rather than attempt to choose from or add to the already excessively long list of extremely doubtful distinctions it is preferable to consider the two terms exactly synonymous, by accepting their broadest possible meaning: a person who unites certain of the essential characteristics of both sexes, and who consequently, may be considered as both a man and a woman, or as neither a man nor a woman, or bisexual or asexual.[20]

Busst's broad definition seems to be saying that by ignoring distinctions, we can get over the problems arising from drawing such distinctions. As a piece of logical thinking, his collapsing of androgyny, and hermaphroditism into one definition bears some weight; both exhibit mixed sexual characteristics, therefore they are one and the same thing. However, what Katharine Hepburn's boyish look in *Sylvia Scarlett* means, what impact it has on the psyche, will undeniably differ from the meaning we invest in the full frontal display of a being endowed with both male and female genitals, which itself has to be distinguished from the Greek hermaphrodite exhibiting both breast and penis.

What sets the androgyne and the hermaphrodite apart dwells in one gesture: the uncovering of the body. In his dream, Freud's patient unveils the woman's body; Herculine Barbin's body is cut open for medical investigation.[21] A gesture that positions the hermaphrodite on the side of the visible – reminiscent of the child's disposition to curiosity. Representations of the hermaphrodite in Greek antiquity or in Beardsley's drawings are closer to the dreamer's creation than to its somatic equivalent in one fundamental aspect: the dreamer sees a woman with a penis; the distinguished doctor from la Rochelle finds, in an atrophied state, both male and female genitals. The common representation of the hermaphrodite is that of a figure endowed with breasts and a penis; the female genitialia do not figure. The male infant does not acknowledge a sex other than his own. Seen in this light, the hermaphrodite appears less as a woman with a penis and more as a man with breasts – the reiteration in the post-Oedipal of a primitive creation of early childhood which passed into the unconscious through repression; the flaunting of visible, 'significant' signifiers in the hermaphrodite, resembles childhood perception, when the child who does not yet speak occupies a space which is essentially visual. The belief in the phallic mother has to be surrendered with the acknowledgement of sexual difference, in the case of the little boy marked by the castration threat. The figure which survives in the unconscious is a *compromise-formation*[22] – the woman with a penis/man with breasts accommodates both belief in the phallic mother and processes of defence. In its function it is a protection against castration. Although the absence of an 'absence', the non-representation of the female genitals, points to a denial of the woman's sexuality, the structure is not that of fetishism. Confronted with the representation of the hermaphrodite, there is no disavowal. What one sees is a woman with a penis. There is no fetishistic substitute, no 'stand-in' for it. There simply *is* a penis in place of a vagina. And yet the hermaphroditic figure, in its *visibility*, stands *on the side of* the fetish: a tangible substitute in the real for something that does not exist. The hermaphrodite as 'Fétiche de l'objet total',[23] a shapely substitute for the lost state of wholeness.

The hermaphroditic figure, in its generous display of breasts, emphasizes the maternal. About the symbolism of the breast, James Hall writes:

*Harlequin Breastfeeds his Son*, engraving, Holland, eighteenth century.
(Illustration from *La Comédie Italienne* by P.L. Ducharte, Paris, 1927)

> As a source of life and nourishment, the breast came to have several shades of meaning. The milk from Juno's breast ensured immortality for Hercules. A woman pressing milk from her breast personifies Mercy, and the kindred virtue of Benignity who tempers Justice. . . . The milk of creative inspiration may fall from the breast of a Muse on to the page of a book or a musical instrument, etc.[24]

The breast as privileged signifier of abundance and nurturance is the child's first object. It recalls a phase of plenitude when the mother, who is all and everything, can give all and everything. It is also that which the little boy, as he comes to realize, will never have.

> Little by little, I resigned myself to the fact that other men and boys had a bigger penis than mine, that they could urinate higher and further. But I shall never forget a memory which torments me to this very day, linked to the following incident: the wet-nurse had taken my brother, who was roughly eight years younger than I, on her knees to breastfeed him. . . . She took one of her breasts in her hand and squeezed it; a thin and powerful jet of milk squirted from the breast, into my face. This unexpected process provoked in me admiration and dread. The sensation which inscribed itself in me was: You will never be able to do that, it is an advantage that women have.[25]

For the male subject, not having the breast implies the impossibility to take part, again, as mother, in the pleasurable experience he once had sucking at his mother's breast; he is denied the powerful status he himself attributed to his mother. In this light, the hermaphrodite becomes a figure of excessive power, endowed with both female and male signifiers of fertility – breast and penis.

The androgyne and the hermaphrodite as manifestations of a similar repressed desire; the hermaphrodite, a childhood construction that reaches adult fantasy life in its primitive guise – one might assume because of its capacity to avoid the defence erected by the ego; the androgyne, furtive, a post-Oedipal creation from the tensions between desire and threat. In a short novel entitled *A Scandal at the Convent*, Oscar Panizza reinterprets the story of the nineteenth-century hermaphrodite, Herculine Barbin. Michel Foucault remarks on the 'area of shadow' that surrounds the main protagonist. The story revolves around her and yet she is described only in terms of the others' perception of her, in terms of their own fantasies unleashed by her ambiguous figure. The 'uncovering of the body' takes place in the doctor's surgery. Narrator and reader sit outside imagining the scene behind the closed doors. Only the medical discourse of the practitioner's report fully endorses the reality of Alexina's sexuality. We are never confronted with it; Alexina leaves the narrative leaving no traces – the area of shadow remains. Panizza's Alexina belongs to the androgyne fantasy in the very fact that she is perceived but not seen. Foucault writes: 'Panizza did not even choose to fix her with a suicide, whereby she would become a corpse like Abel Barbin to which curious doctors in the end assigned the reality of an inadequate sex.'[26] The *fixing* of the look is contrary to the androgyne who can only ever be the object of a *searching* look. The hermaphrodite would be the resolution of the search, following the dreamer's unveiling gesture, when light is shed on the case.

## The visible androgyne

In order to bring to light the ubiquitousness of the androgyne, I have happily leapt across centuries and between forms of representation. The insistency with which the desire for re-union emerges in representation, from Plato's little spherical things to the sexually ambiguous figure of Boy George, justifies such leaps. I would argue for the universality of this 'desire for re-union', rooted in the fundamental and inevitable fact that at some stage of its history the subject must recognize *difference*. A contextualized analysis of the androgyne would enlighten us as to how specific social and historical conjunctures and formations favour or impede access of the fantasy to various representational forms; this is not my purpose here. As for the leap across differing representational forms, Barthes writes: 'There will still be representation for as long as a subject (author, reader, spectator or voyeur) casts his gaze towards a horizon on which he cuts out the base of a triangle, his eye (or his mind) forming the apex.'[27] Barthes' definition is useful here in its various implications – of a relation between a look and an object; of a *distance* between a subject and an object; of a 'sovereign' gesture of selection, 'découpage', appropriation; of a *unified* subject who firmly stands at the apex of its visual pyramid; and so on. The little boy *watches* the wet nurse breast-feeding his baby brother; what he *sees* is his own tiny body, his flat breast, his incapacity to produce such a powerful milky jet. He appropriates the scene in terms of his own fears and desires; he re-presents the scene. In the distance between the eye and the object of the look, psychic processes are operative. From the founding position where the little boy stands, everything as it were is taking place 'for him' – it is the same distance that allows the subject to take up a 'sovereign' position, unchallenged by the other, who is close enough, but not so close as to become a threat. In moving across different forms of representation, I wish to stress the fantasizing processes at work in *all* forms of representation, regardless of their formal and material outcome. Fantasy, rooted in the absence of an object, is contingent upon a distance; that between viewer and viewed,

*First a Girl*, 1935. (Gaumont British Films)

where the unconscious comes to rest, along which look and psyche travel.

The androgyne dwells in a distance. The androgynous figure has to do with *seduction*, that which comes before undressing, seeing and touching. It can only exist in the shadow area of the image; once unveiled, once we throw a light on it, it becomes a woman or man, and I (myself) resume my position on the side of the female. The perfect symmetry of the figure of the androgyne positions the viewer at the convergence of the

*First a Girl*, 1935. (Gaumont British Films)

feminine and the masculine where 's/he' oscillates. The androgyne is excessive in its transgression of the boundaries of gender identity; however, this threat of superabundance, of overflowing, is safely contained within the frame of the feminine and the masculine. The figure of the androgyne represents the gathering into one image of those various instances when the certainty in our identity wavers under the 'constant pressure of something hidden but not forgotten',[28] instances that we may

Fernand Khnopff, *Silence*, 1890. (Musées Royaux des Beaux Arts de Belgique, Brussels)

assume to be numerous. In this light, the figure of the androgyne appears at once formally impoverished and semantically overdetermined. The visible androgyne is 'degraded' to an amalgam of signifiers of femininity and masculinity. Katharine Hepburn rests on the set of *Sylvia Scarlett*.

The 'visible' androgyne presents me with a problem. The desire behind the ambiguous figure is one of non-sexual identity, an impossibility. The oscillatory motion can never stop at a position of equilibrium where one is neither man nor woman. The 'visible' androgyne, as an attempt to objectify desire, to reduce into one *still* image a process, is in itself contrary to the dynamics of the fantasy that produces it. Furthermore, the image does not exist outside the symbolic; it is irremediably caught up between the feminine and the masculine. Representation of the androgynous 'in between' is an impossibility. Perhaps it is because of the image's overwhelming concern with the 'body' as the site of all truth. The 'body' as an entity, as an end in itself, cannot contain the excess of the androgynous fantasy.

## Orlando

'The sounds of the trumpets died away and Orlando stood stark naked. No human being since the world began has ever looked more ravishing.' Has Robinet's Nature achieved its lofty aim? 'His form combined in one the strength of a man and a woman's grace.'[29]

Orlando inhabits a world where it is possible to change gender by changing costume. After Orlando has become a woman, the Archduchess Harriet becomes Archduke Harry: s/he and Orlando 'acted the parts of man and woman for ten minutes with great vigour and then fell into natural discourse'. Orlando's transformations are not aleatory acts, but the outcome of some 'deeper' impulse – 'it was a change in Orlando herself that dictated her choice of a woman's dress, because different though the sexes are, they intermix'.[30] Woolf's cheerful tale of transcendence of the body displaces identity from the body to the costume. We are what we wear/were.

As Orlando changes costume, the transvestite *dresses up* – the transvestite's feminine disguise enhances the masculinity it conceals, but at the cost of a doubly inferior social status: as woman and as deviant. To gain all at the imaginary level is to lose all in the symbolic.

Speaking for the man, Pontalis remarks that representation of the 'positive' androgyne is an impossibility because it would evoke a double castration. When the little girl becomes acquainted with sexual difference she has to change love object from her mother to her father – a difficult process, but, unlike that for the little boy, not marked by the castration threat. One might assume that the female child's entry into heterosexuality lacks the *conviction* which comes with the threat. The little boy's passage from polymorphous sexuality to an adult sexual organization is doubly determined. Were he to turn back he would lose his penis; but if he goes ahead he will gain the power which his organ has come to signify. Such deterrent and incentive are absent from the little girl's sexual development. She has to be convinced because no promise lies before her, but unconvinced she remains. Her continuing fantasy life is characterized by a wandering attempt to gather the fragments. The little boy's unconscious mobility is impeded by the memory of the castration threat. Furthermore, both the male and female child have to surrender the belief in the 'phallic' mother. For the little boy this entails the shattering of both belief *and* image. For the little girl, the *image* of the phallic mother remains intact since, we can assume, she has made the mother in her own image. The little boy has the added problem of having to erase a tenacious mental image which nevertheless does not fit reality. However, this difficulty should subsequently prove to be of some advantage: he possesses two incompatible (visual/mental) images, whereas the little girl is confronted with two incompatible *concepts*. Here again one might assume that the little girl is even less convinced in surrendering the belief in the mother who is all and everything. A process of disavowal is operative, which has nothing to do with fetishism. In disavowing the lack of the mother, the little girl disavows her own lack.

In describing these transitional scenarios, I am proposing for the woman a fantasy life which, in its fluidity and lack of focus, resembles infantile sexuality – a fantasy which is not fixed in an image by the trauma of the castration threat. Just as Orlando's journeys into the feminine and the masculine are lightheartedly undertaken, women would have a greater ability, literally and metaphorically, to change costumes. (Condemned to masquerade, men's sexual ambivalence would perhaps express itself more freely displaced on to the image of a not-yet-fully-sexual, a boyish, never manly, Katharine Hepburn and Jessie Matthews.) Clément says of the androgyne, 'She is a man'.[31]

The sunny scene is delineated by shadow, absence. In the primal wish for union, difference, and therefore identity, is abolished. From its contradictory position – both 'this' and not 'this', a position therefore logically outside systems of signification, the androgyne demands not to be talked about, not to be represented (hence the difficulty, the impossibility of pinning it down, of arresting it in an image).

The androgynous fantasy is a narcissistic 'caress' in which the subject annihilates itself. In this double movement of pleasure and destruction, the fantasy allies itself with the 'death drive', the regressive tendency towards the restoration of a less differentiated, less organized, ultimately inorganic state. The androgyne at once immortal and annihilating, the perpetually youthful Orlando lives on. 'How to reach what transgresses, not the internal order of the sexual paradigm (a transvestite would have inverted this order but not destroyed it . . .), but the very existence of difference which generates life and meaning; the ultimate horror is not death but that the classification of death and life should be broken off.'[32]

# Notes

1. For an account of the concept of 'bisexuality' see J. Laplanche and J.B. Pontalis, *The Language of Psychoanalysis*, London, Hogarth Press, 1973.
2. S. Freud, 'Civilisation and its discontents', [1930] *The Standard Edition of the Complete Psychological Works*, ed. J. Strachey, London, Hogarth Press, 1953–74 (*SE*), vol.XXI, p.106.
3. J. Mitchell and J. Rose, *Feminine Sexuality: Jacques Lacan and the École Freudienne*, London, Macmillan, 1982, p.22.
4. S. Freud, 'Fragments of an analysis of a case of hysteria', [1905] *SE*, vol.VII.
5. J.B. Robinet, quoted by A.J.L. Busst in 'The image of the androgyne in the nineteenth century', *Romantic Mythologies*, London, Routledge & Kegan Paul, 1967, pp.2–3.
6. Plato, 'The Symposium', in *The Portable Plato*, Harmondsworth, Penguin, 1982, pp.145–6.
7. S. Freud, 'Analysis of a phobia in a five-year-old boy', [1907] vol.X, p.93.
8. Ovid, *Metamorphoses*, book IV, Harmondsworth, Penguin, 1980, pp.102–4.
9. Ovid, ibid., book XII, pp.272–3.
10. M. Gagnebin, 'Les Seins coupés d'Agathe', in D. Anzieu *et al.*, *Art et Fantasme*, Seysell, Champ Vallon, 1984, p.142.
11. J.B. Pontalis, 'L'insaisissable entre-deux', in 'Bisexualité et différence des sexes', *Nouvelle Revue de Psychanalyse* (printemps 1973), p.16.
12. C. Clément, *Vies et Légendes de Jacques Lacan*, Paris, Grasset, 1981, pp.99–100.
13. J.B. Pontalis, op. cit., p.17.
14. C. Clément, op. cit., p.99.
15. M. Proust, *Le Temps Retrouvé*, quoted by J.E. Rivers in 'The myth and science of homosexuality', in *À la Recherche du Temps Perdu, Homosexualities and French Literature*, Ithaca, NY, Cornell University Press, 1979.
16. S. Freud, 'Psychoanalytic notes on an autobiographical account of a case of paranoia (*dementia paranoides*)', [1911] *SE*, vol.XII.
17. C. Clément, op. cit., p.100.
18. M. Tournier, *Vendredi ou les Limbes du Pacifique*, Paris, Gallimard, 1967.
19. S. Freud, 'The sexual theories of children', *SE*, vol.IX, p.216.
20. A.J.L. Busst, op. cit., p.1.
21. H. Barbin, *Memoirs of a Nineteenth-Century French Hermaphrodite*, introduced by M. Foucault, Brighton, Harvester Press, 1980. 'Brought up as a poor and deserving girl in a milieu that was exclusively feminine and strongly religious, Herculine Barbin, who was called Alexina by her familiars, was finally recognised as being "truly" a young man. Obliged to make a legal change of sex after judicial proceedings and a modification of his civil status, he was incapable of adapting himself to a new identity and ultimately committed suicide' (M. Foucault).
22. *Compromise–formation*: 'Form taken by the repressed memory so as to be admitted to consciousness when it returns in symptoms, in dreams, and more generally, in all products of the unconscious: in the process the repressed ideas are distorted by defence to the point of being unrecognisable. Thus both the unconscious wish and the demands of defence may be satisfied by the same formation – in a single compromise.' Laplanche and Pontalis, in *The Language of Psychoanalysis*, p.76.
23. Fetishism attests in Freud's view to the possibility of the sexual instinct's fixation to a part-object – part-objects being part of the body, real or fantasised (breast, faeces, penis). Freud defines the fetish as a substitute for the mother's penis. Pontalis' use of the term 'objet total' has to be understood in relation to the term 'part-objet'. Fetishism in this case takes as its support the *complete* body.
24. J. Hall, *Dictionary of Subjects and Symbols in Art*, London, John Murray, 1979, p.52.
25. F. Boehm, 'Le complexe de féminité chez l'homme', in 'Bisexualité et différence des sexes', *Nouvelle Revue de Psychanalyse*, 1979, p.289.
26. H. Barbin, op. cit.
27. R. Barthes, 'Diderot, Brecht, Eisenstein' in *Image, Music, Text*, London, Fontana, 1977, p.69.

28. J. Rose, 'Sexuality in the field of vision', in *Difference*, New York, New Museum of Contemporary Art, 1984.
29. V. Woolf, *Orlando*, London, Panther, 1977, p.86.
30. ibid, pp.117–18.
31. C. Clément, op. cit., p.100.
32. R. Barthes, *S/Z*, Paris, Seuil, 1970, p.202.

Victor Burgin

# DIDEROT, BARTHES, *VERTIGO*

The title of this essay[1] came by way of 'Diderot, Brecht, Eisenstein', an essay by Roland Barthes to which I shall refer later. Recent theory has been very interested in the facts of which my extemporaneous substitution of one phrase for another is an instance: meaning is only ever produced in difference, and the final closure of meaning is only ever deferred – the combination of observations which Derrida enshrined in his neologism, *différance*, but to which C.S. Peirce had already referred in his notion of 'unlimited semiosis'. Meaning is never simply 'there' for our consumption, it is only ever *produced* in a process of substitution of one term for another in a potentially limitless series. In the *social* world, however, meaning must come to rest somewhere; what is it that sets limits on the meanings of images?

The meaning of the photograph in my passport derives ultimately from the authority of the state, which may in the last resort assert its truths by physical force. However, most images we encounter in daily life derive their meanings from more complexly mediated interdependent systems: concrete institutions, discursive formations, scripto-visual codes, and so on. All of these determinations have been, and are being, discussed in theories of representations – they demand a sociology, a social history, a political economy and a semiotics of the image, and they are concerned with what 'common sense' tells us about an image. However, it has been objected that such theories are unable to account for those meanings which are 'subjective', irreducibly individual, inviolably private; moreover, it has been maintained that, at least in respect of art, it is *these* meanings which are the most important.

It is partly in response to this lacuna of theory that, in recent years, a psychoanalytically informed semiotics has been evolved. There has been considerable criticism of this development of theory, not least from a 'left' which disparages psychoanalysis as being concerned with the 'merely subjective'. It seems to me that a 'progressive' politics indifferent to subjective experience, in *all* of its aspects, is itself a mere parody of the political impulse, but apart from this the charge against psychoanalysis is simply false. Psychoanalytic theory does not construct a realm of the 'subjective' *apart* from social life. It is a theory of the internalization of the social *as* 'subjective' and, as such, has profound implications for any theory of ideology.[2] What follows is intended as a sketch account of one aspect of the workings of a putative 'transindividual unconscious',[3] characteristically manifested in the form of fleetingly inconsequential subjective affects, but which nevertheless underpins the meanings of images. My point of departure is from some observations by Barthes, observations he leaves untheorized, but which I suggest should be seen as indicating a necessity for a 'psychopathology of everyday representations'. Most particularly, my discussion concerns a type of relation between 'movie' and still images.

*

At the beginning of his 1970 essay, 'The third meaning',[4] Roland Barthes speaks of his being fascinated by film stills, but while he is watching the film, he says, he forgets the stills. Reading this, I was reminded of a recurrent experience of my own: often, having seen a film, all that remains of it in my memory is an image, or a short sequence of images. The film still, a material entity; the mnemic image, a psychic entity: what they have in common is that they are both *fragments* abstracted from a whole, but fragments which have nevertheless achieved a sort of representative autonomy. In his 1973 paper, 'Diderot, Brecht, Eisenstein',[5] Barthes again touches on the 'representative fragment', this time in discussing a concept in the work of Diderot – *tableau*.

The concept of the tableau has a history prior to Diderot: humanist scholars of the mid-sixteenth century elaborated a theory of painting which they based on isolated remarks in the writings of classical authors. From Aristotle's *Poetics* they took the doctrine that the highest calling of any art is to depict human action in its most exemplary forms; the human body, they held, was the privileged vehicle for the depiction of such 'histories'. The consequent programme of so-called 'history painting', which dominated painting in the West from the mid-sixteenth to the mid-eighteenth centuries, was elaborated in great detail in the body of humanist art theory now known by the emblematic slogan '*ut pictura poesis*' – 'as is painting, so is poetry' – a device abstracted from the *Ars Poetica* of Horace, which the Renaissance reversed in emphasis to establish the dependency of the visual image on the written text.[6] As the painter of 'histories' had to show in a single instant that which took time to unfold, then that instant had to have a singularly privileged position within the total action. It was therefore recommended that the moment selected by the painter for visualization should be the *peripateia*, that instant in the course of an action when all hangs in the balance. Thus, for example, Rubens paints Paris in the act of extending the golden apple towards the group of three goddesses who await his judgement and

Peter-Paul Rubens, *The Judgment of Paris*. (Reproduced by courtesy of the Trustees, The National Gallery, London)

arrests Paris at that precise moment when alternative futures open before him. In the very next instant, however, *Venus* will receive the golden apple, and the fate of Paris, and that of his nation, will be irrevocably sealed, committed to war, with Paris himself to be among the dead.

By the beginning of the eighteenth century the ideal of discursive clarity, embodied in human gesture, had become lost or subsumed within the increasingly decorative practices we know as Rococo. The work of Diderot's contemporary Boucher exemplifies this transition from the semantic to the decorative body. Where 'history painting' – painting rooted in a discursive programme – survived, it tended to take the form of allegory of an ever increasing complexity and obscurity. Allegory in the Renaissance had begun with conventional symbols whose range of references was legislated by such 'dictionaries' as Andrea Alciati's *Emblematum liber* of 1531 (the first) and Cesare Ripa's *Iconologia* of 1593 and 1603 (the definitive);[7] by the eighteenth century, however, symbolism had become increasingly esoteric and/or a matter of purely individual invention, to the point where it often was felt necessary to produce extensive explanatory pamphlets along with the painting.[8]

It was against the Rococo tendency towards formal decorativeness and semantic obscurity that the concept of the *tableau* emerged: first, at the beginning of the eighteenth century, in the writings of Lord Shaftsbury, and later, with more elaboration, in the work of Diderot and some of his

François Boucher, *The Toilet of Venus*, 1751. (The Metropolitan Museum of Art, New York. Bequest of William K. Vanderbilt, 1920)

contemporaries. The concept of the tableau represented, at least initially, a reaffirmation of the values of *ut pictura poesis*; it represented the ideal of a formally unified, centred, *concentrated*, composition whose meaning would be communicated 'at a glance', intelligible, in Diderot's words, to 'a man of simple common-sense'. (We should note that Diderot's recom-

Jean-Baptiste Greuze, *The Broken Mirror*, 1763. (Reproduced by permission of the Trustees, The Wallace Collection, London)

mendations for painting here are practically indistinguishable from his ambitions for the theatre, where his intervention was primarily on behalf of the *mise-en-scène*: 'Gesture', he writes, 'should frequently inscribe itself (*s'écrire*) in the place of discourse'; and he speaks of some scenes in his *Père de Famille* as being 'more difficult to paint', than others[9]). The concept of peripateia once again became central (although the paintings of Greuze, much approved of by Diderot, seem most often concerned with *post-*peripateian triste). Although Barthes does not use the term 'peripateia' in

'Diderot, Brecht, Eisenstein', he does speak of this moment. He remarks that it is the moment Lessing calls the 'pregnant moment' (we might add that still photography inherits this concept under the title of 'decisive moment') and he further remarks that Brecht's theatre and Eisenstein's cinema are composed of series of such 'pregnant moments'. The word Barthes takes from Diderot to name *this* moment is 'hieroglyph'.

Western interest in the hieroglyph goes back at least as far as 31 BC when Egypt became part of the Roman Empire. Part of the humanist project of reconciling the texts and artefacts of antiquity with Christian doctrine involved a theory of the hieroglyph. The theory was derived, via the Neo-Platonists, from the Platonic doctrine of two worlds, and the mode of communication operative within each: in the murky and imperfect world in which we mortals are condemned to live, verbal discourse is the appropriately confused medium through which we are condemned, impossibly, to attempt to communicate; in the luminous and perfect 'upper world' however, all meaning is communicated instantaneously and unambiguously through the medium of *vision*. Thus the humanist Ficino translates this passage from Plotinus: 'The Egyptian sages ... drew pictures and carved one picture for each thing ... each picture was a kind of understanding and wisdom and substance given all at once, and not discursive reasoning and deliberation.'[10] The hieroglyph then, by definition, communicates instantaneously and stands *outside* discourse; this, certainly, is the way in which Diderot understood the term. For Diderot, the syntactically ordered linear progression of speech and writing is alien to the actual experience of *thought*: 'Our mind does not move in stages, as does our expression.' Such alienating linguistic structures may, however, be partially overcome as language approaches the condition of poetry, where words succeed in effacing themselves as words by giving rise to *images*. It is this state of language that Diderot refers to as 'hieroglyphic'. Here 'discourse is no longer simply a suite of energetic terms which expose thought nobly and forcefully, but a tissue of hieroglyphs gathered one upon the other which paint what is to be represented.'[11] We should note that in Diderot, as in the Barthes of 'Diderot, Brecht, Eisenstein', the ideal of a radically *extra*-discursive, 'hieroglyphic' mode of communication tends always to be attracted into the gravitational field of discourse, convention, morality. Nevertheless, in 'The third meaning' (an essay which complements 'Diderot, Brecht, Eisenstein') Barthes does speak of a meaning which will not be pinned down by words. In his 1970 paper Barthes calls it the 'obtuse' meaning; ten years later, in *Camera Lucida*, he calls it the *punctum*.

Fragments of certain photographs, Barthes says, move him in a way which is strictly incommunicable, purely personal. Certainly there are photographs which many people, in common, may find moving, but here,

James Van der Zee, *Portrait of a Family*, 1926

he says: 'emotion requires the rational intermediary of an ethical and political culture'. The *punctum*, on the contrary, is unpredictable and private, it is that in the image, says Barthes, which is 'purely image' (which is, he says, 'very little'); the meaning of the *punctum* is perfectly clear, but yet it cannot be made public. The privileged example of the *punctum* offered by Barthes in *Camera Lucida* occurs in his discussion of a photograph of a New York family by James Van der Zee[12] – 'privileged' for my purposes here because, in a book which is not a text of theory, it nevertheless indicates the path a theorization of the *punctum* must take. The detail which 'touches' him in this image, he says, is the strapped shoes of one of the women: 'This particular *punctum* arouses great sympathy in me, almost a kind of tenderness.' Barthes makes no further comment until, ten pages later, he 'remembers' the photograph ('I may know better a photograph I remember than a photograph I am looking at'). He now realizes it was not the shoes which moved him, it was the necklace the woman wore: 'for (no doubt) it was this same necklace (a slender ribbon of braided gold) which I had seen worn by someone in my own family.' The relative he has now been reminded of is a deceased maiden aunt who had spent most of her adult life looking after her mother: 'I had always been saddened when I thought of her dreary life'; after the aunt died her necklace was 'shut up in a family box of old jewelry'. What Barthes does in this brief account is to retrace, as it were 'in reverse', part of the path taken in the original investment of the image-fragment (the strap) by a feeling ('a kind of tenderness'). The terminal point of the cathexis is the ankle-strap. In 'stepping stone' fashion the next displacement is from the circle around the neck. From here, the movement is from the neck of the woman in the photograph (material image) to the neck of the aunt (mental image): the aunt whose necklace was 'shut up in a box', whose body in death was 'shut up in a box', and whose sexuality in life had remained 'shut up in a box'. We arrive here at a preliminary account of the sources of the emotion in memories circulating around the themes of death and sexuality, played out within the space of the family, which are the substance of psychoanalysis.

In the example of Barthes' commentary on the Van der Zee photograph we might say that a highly cathected image-fragment 'takes the place of', 'stands in for', a narrative: it is the *representative* of a narrative. Barthes' expansion of the narrative, the written 'transcription', is itself laconic in the extreme; it is only *vaguely* a narrative: 'her necklace was shut up in a box.' What stands out, as if 'in focus' against an incomplete background of indistinct detail, is 'a situation in an image'. We are here in the presence of *fantasy*. What for the moment I can only call an 'ambivalence in respect of movement' is implicit in psychoanalytic accounts of fantasy, something of which I must now resume.

*

Unlike most other animals, the human infant is born into a state of nurseling dependency in which it is incapable of actively seeking its food; nourishment must be brought to *it*, as when the mother provides the breast. When hunger reasserts itself, therefore, the suckling initially has no recourse but to attempt to resurrect the original experience of satisfaction in hallucinatory form. Thus Freud writes, 'The first wishing seems to have been a hallucinatory cathecting of the memory of satisfaction.' We may see in this scenario the Lacanian schema according to which 'desire' insinuates itself between 'need' and 'demand': the infant's *need* for nourishment is satisfied when the milk is provided; the infant's *demand* that its mother care for it is also met in that same instant. *Desire*, however, is directed neither to an object (here the substance, 'milk') nor to a person, but to a *fantasy* – the mnemic traces of the lost satisfaction. It should be noted that the origins of fantasy here are inseparable from the origins of *sexuality*. In the 1905 *Three essays on the theory of sexuality*, Freud posits a 'libido' present, quantitatively, 'in full' from birth but nevertheless having, as it were, no 'address' until it progessively colonizes, 'props' against, zones of the body associated with important physiological functions. Thus, in the above example, the act of sucking, initially functionally associated with the ingestion of food, becomes enjoyed as 'sensual sucking', an activity in its own, erotic, right. In this earliest emergence of sexuality, in which it is supported by a life-preserving function, the functional and libidinal are but two faces of the same experiential coin: on the one side the ingestion of milk, on the other the accompanying excitations. It is at this stage that the infant must construct out of the primal flux of its earliest perceptions that primitive hierarchy in which the breast can emerge as 'object'. Hardly has this been achieved, however, than the object is 'lost' with the realization that the breast, in real terms, belongs to the mother. The first fantasy then is most fundamentally motivated by the desire to fill the gap thus opened between the infant and the maternal body, but a body itself already fantasmatically displaced in relation to the real:

> . . . the real object, milk, was the object of the function, which is virtually preordained to the world of satisfaction. Such is the real object which has been lost, but the breast – become the fantasmatic breast – is, for its part, the object of the sexual drive. Thus the sexual object is not identical to the object of the function, but is displaced in relation to it; they are in a relation of essential *contiguity* which leads us to slide almost indifferently from one to the other, from the milk to the breast as its symbol.[13]

An important qualification must now be made. From the above schematic account it might seem we could posit a simple parallelism: on the one hand *need*, directed towards an object; on the other hand *desire*, directed towards a fantasy object. Fantasy, however, 'is not the object of desire but its setting . . . the subject does not pursue the object or its sign: he [*sic*] appears caught up himself in the sequence of images.'[14] In this perspective, then, the fact that the infant may be observed making sucking motions even after its hunger has been satiated is not to be construed as the outward manifestation of the intentional aim of a desiring subject towards a fantasy object. Rather, what we are witnessing is the display of auto-erotic pleasure in the *movement* itself, to which we must assume an accompanying fantasy not of *ingestion* (functional), but of *incorporation* (libidinal). The fantasy-precipitating sequence *having/losing* the object, then, also institutes *auto-eroticism*, (it is a mistake to consider auto-eroticism a 'stage of development' *prior* to object choice): 'The "origin" of auto-eroticism would therefore be the moment when sexuality, disengaged from any natural object, moves into the field of fantasy and by that very fact becomes sexuality.'[15] Even at the most primal moment, 'satisfaction' (the lost object) is not a unitary experience. In so far as it survives, it does so as a constellation of visual, tactile, kinaesthetic, auditory, olfactory, etc., mnemic traces; it is such a fantasy *configuration* which is indelibly inscribed as an ever present principle of organization in the psychic life of the subject.

> The signs accompanying satisfaction (the breast accompanying the offering of nursing milk) will henceforth take on the value of a fixed arrangement, and it is that arrangement, a *fantasy* as yet limited to several barely elaborated elements, that will be repeated on the occasion of a subsequent appearance of need, . . . with the appearance of an internal excitation, the fantastic arrangement – of *several representative elements linked together in a short scene*, an extremely rudimentary scene, ultimately composed of partial (or 'component') objects and not whole objects: for example, a breast, a mouth, a movement of a mouth seizing a breast – will be revived.[16] (my emphasis)

'Incorporation' rather than 'ingestion' – the psychoanalytic concept of 'incorporation' implies a range of objects vastly more extensive than food as, for example, in Melanie Klein's description of the fantasy world of the infant, in which the parental imagos fragment into relatively autonomous 'part objects', body parts which the child may destroy, repair, identify with, combine and, of course, incorporate. Moreover, the mouth is not the only organ of fantasy incorporation – for example, it would be particularly pertinent here to recall Lacan's discussions of the eye as an incorporative organ.[17] The fantasy then, in our 'original' example, albeit metonymically linked to the ingestion of milk and the image of the breast, is not to be *reduced* to such terms, for they will themselves be subject to further substitutions of a metaphorical, as well as metonymical, order.

In the above scenario of emergent sexuality, with its emphasis on the fixation of 'signifier' to 'satisfaction' we may see exemplified the Lacanian maxim, 'Desire is the alienation of the instinct in a signifier'. It is this *privileged* signifier which stops 'the otherwise endless sliding of the signification'; it is that which Laplanche and Leclaire call the 'elementary signifier' of the unconscious,[18] and which in Freud would be one of the senses we may give to 'ideational representative' of the instinct. As I have observed, although the position of 'representative of the instinct' is a permanent one, more than one signifier may be elected to the same post, and these signifiers in turn may elect delegates from amongst their derivatives and semblances – a process which will continue throughout the life of the subject as a process of *elaboration*. For example, in Laplanche and Leclaire's paper, 'The unconscious: a psychoanalytic study', we read of a child, during the time he is beginning to speak, experiencing thirst on a beach and addressing a demand to the woman who is caring for him. Become adult, and now in analysis, amongst the elementary particles of one of his dreams are 'the memory of a gesture engraved like an image' (cupped hands) and 'the formula, "I'm thirsty"'. The gesture here ('enactive') belongs to the kinaesthetic and visual. Moreover, the 'verbal' expression is not verbal in the linguistic (lexical, syntactical) sense – the child in question here is French, and at a stage of linguistic development when the use of 'shifters' is not yet fully mastered. The initial sound of '*J'ai soif*' ('I'm thirsty'), the terminal sound of '*moi-je*' (me-I), and the ultimate syllable of *plage* (beach) become condensed, collapsed together, to result in a dense phonic image, '*zhe*' inseparable from a meaning purely personal to the child.

We may reasonably suppose that it is this type of process that is at work behind the production of the phenomenon Barthes names *punctum*. Just as the phonic fragment '*zhe*' belongs both to, in Saussure's expression, 'the common storehouse of language' and at the same time to a universe of meaning which is purely private to the patient Philippe, so the *punctum* appears at one and the same time in a public and a private context. In some remarks on Freud's insistence on 'the independence and the cohesion' of the conscious and unconscious systems, Laplanche and Leclaire remark:

> It is important to note at what level the passage from one system to another operates: it cannot be the global passage of the same structure from one mode of organisation to another, similar to the oscillatory effect at work in the perception of an equivocal image. What passes from one *Gestalt* to another is always *an isolated equivocal element*.[19] (my emphasis)

He finds a more appropriate analogy in 'those puzzle drawings in which a certain perceptual attitude suddenly makes Napoleon's hat appear in the branches of the tree that shades a family picnic', observing that 'if this hat is able to appear, it is because it can be related to an entirely different "anecdote", which is not at all present in the rest of the drawing: the "Napoleonic legend".' It is precisely such an 'intertextual' mutual imbrication of 'anecdotes', pinned together by a fragment, which allows Barthes to see his own family history in that group portrait from another time and another culture, and which makes '*je*' more than simply a 'shifter' for Philippe. I say 'allows' Barthes, but he himself insists he has no choice but to feel that *affect* which 'pierces' him. Two things must be stressed here; not only the *involuntary* nature of the unconscious irruption, but the fact that, like the hat in Laplanche's example, it may also derive from an inscription which may be *trans-individual*, rather than, like the *punctum*, exclusively personal – assertions which require some elaboration.

*

In the story which 'begins' (in the arbitrary *découpage* of narrative convention) with Philippe on the beach, we may see historically later stages in the vicissitudes of the oral drive, 'alienated in a signifier', for a particular individual. The fantasy *complex* to which the ramifications of this alienation have given rise has left its traces in all aspects of the unconscious organization of the subject. The unconscious, however, knows no time; psychoanalytic accounts of fantasy present us with a *simultaneous* continuum of degrees of elaboration. 'Topographically', the fantasy may be conscious, preconscious, or unconscious. Thus the fantasy, says Freud, is encountered 'at both extremities' of the dream – both in the secondary elaboration of the waking report, and in the most primitive layers of the latent content, where it is linked to the ultimate unconscious desire, the 'capitalist' of the dream. Freud finds the fantasy present in the form of the hysterical symptom, in the delusional fears of paranoiacs, in 'acting out', and, as is well known, he believed such cultural manifestations as 'art' to represent the highly elaborated, disguised, expressions of unconscious fantasies. In a sense therefore 'the' fantasy is only ever encountered in the *wake* of continual exchanges, transformations and transcriptions, of and between signifiers. In its most primitive form the fantasy complex will consist of *thing-presentations*, the register of the imaginary – thus, with Philippe, 'a gesture engraved like an image'. Later may be found fragments attracted into the 'gravitational field' of the primitive fantasy at the moment of acquisition of language; for example, the compound sound, '*zhe*'. Later still, the adult Philippe will produce the dream of a unicorn, whose image is the transformation (according to 'considerations of representability') of derivatives of a complex of *words*: that aspect of the fantasy which is ensnared within the *symbolic*.

    In bringing Philippe's story to my consideration of the anecdote told by Barthes, however, I face a difficulty – Barthes' book is *not* a case-history. I shall therefore take the liberty of incorporating the anecdote of the 'ankle-strap' *punctum* into a convenient fiction to illustrate a point I wish to make here. Suppose that a very small child is inquisitively playing with a ring on its mother's finger; in a playful demonstration the mother takes off the ring and slips it on to one of the child's fingers; then she takes it back. Other circumstances being favourable, the mnemic trace of this event could become structurally reinforced and re-cathected by the previously established trace of the mouth circling the nipple, and the nipple's subsequent withdrawal. Later in the history of the subject, knowledge of the significance of the giving of the ring in marriage could, by 'deferred action',[20] further reinforce and intensify the cathexis of this image of the 'encircling of a body-part', producing the sort of affective and semantic consequences Barthes describes. By juxtaposing this diagrammatically simple myth of origin with Philippe's story I wish simply to make the point that, although the oral drive will have an effect on the unconscious organization of all subjects alike, the particular *form* of the effect will vary according to individual history. Nevertheless, such individual elaborations of representatives of the drives coexist alongside, and may become imbricated within, fantasy scenarios whose *common* outlines may be detected across differences between individual 'versions'.

Freud was so impressed by the ubiquitous *transindividuality* of a certain small number of fantasies – which 'emerge' in the history of the subject, and yet which seem always already to have been in place – that he suggested they might be transmitted by hereditary factors. These are the 'primal fantasies', as he first called them – 'primal scene', 'seduction', 'castration' – all of which devolve upon major enigmas in the life of a child, enigmas concerning origins: origin of the subject, of sexuality, and of sexual difference. As Laplanche and Pontalis have pointed out, however, we do not need to invoke the idea of phylogenetic inheritance to explain the ubiquitousness of the primal fantasies. These fantasies are the precipitate of the early familial complex in which each child finds itself, at once irreducibly unique in its historical, cultural, and biographical detail, and universally shared, in that every newcomer to the world is lodged under the same sign of interdiction of incest. (At the risk of stating the obvious, to acknowledge the Oedipal nucleus of the primal fantasies is not thereby to place *all* fantasy scenarios on the Oedipal stage. To acknowledge *this*, though, is not necessarily to embrace the anarchistic voluntarism exemplified by the Deleuze and Guattari of *Anti-Oedipus*, for so long as it makes sense to say we are living in a 'patriarchal society' we may be sure that we remain, at the most fundamental level, locked in the Oedipal matrix.)

It is the privileged 'families' of related signifiers of the desire of the subject which serve as the *points de capiton* (Lacan), 'buttoning down' the otherwise endless dispersions of Derrida's *différance*, Pierce's 'endless semiosis'. In the history of the subject it is precisely this overall structural *stability* of the fantasy, albeit constantly subject to transformations, which serves to regulate and organize the otherwise formless displacements of desire. As Jean-Michel Ribettes has put it: 'To such potentially anarchic and polymorphous movements of desire, fantasy opposes the constancy of its forms; to the erratic, fantasy opposes the hieratic.'[21] It is because of the *mise-en-scène* of desire, which is fantasy, that dissemination does not 'centrifugally' dissipate itself but rather 'circles back' on itself to repeat – but *differently*. That is to say, to extend my metaphor, that the movement describes not so much a circle, closed, but a *spiral*, perpetually renewing itself by conquering new territory while nevertheless tracing the same *figure* (no grammar of the unconscious, but a rhetoric). Thus, for example, Freud speaks of the day-dream as having a 'date-stamp' on it. In the field of public human affairs, we may think of the popular newspaper, endlessly repeating itself in the form of 'news'; or, scandalous to add, in the realm of politics, those 'real struggles' – conflicts which renew and repeat themselves precisely to the extent that the fantasmatic which informs them remains untouched by them. (My slide here from the 'internal' to the 'external' world is deliberate – I shall return to this later.)

I have spoken of the quality of 'arrest' in fantasy. By my own argument this very attribution is itself a form of arrest, the abstraction of a notional 'elementary' form of fantasy from the multifarious ways in which 'it' is actually encountered. In speaking of 'arrest', however, I wish to emphasize just this insistence in psychoanalytic theory on the structural constancy of fantasy across a 'spectrum' of forms of elaboration. Moreover, although the fantasy is an imaginary *sequence* in which the subject plays a part, or parts (the precise mode of integration of the subject, as Freud has demonstrated, being variable – the subject may be represented as observer, as actor, even in the very *form* of an utterance), the 'sequence' is characteristically of such brevity that it may be summarized in a short phrase – 'her necklace was shut up in a box'; or again, a classic example, the title of one of Freud's essays, 'A child is being beaten'. It is in this that I allow myself to identify the sequence which paradoxically takes on the characteristic of the *still*; for there is no doubt that in this band of the 'spectrum' of elaborations (the band, moreover, of greatest affective density) the fantasy may be represented in an image, and what better word for *this* image, this *mise-en-scène*, than *tableau*?

May we not say then that the fantasy is a tableau which stands to the otherwise formless indeterminacies, dispersions, displacements of desire of the individual subject, precisely as the tableau of Diderot stands to the endless dispersions and indeterminacies of the meanings of material events, of 'history'? Two contrasting kinds of claim are frequently made in respect of certain images: 'this image captures, in a single visual statement, the essence of an event which would otherwise take many words to describe'; and, 'this image has a significance which transcends its literal content, and which may not be expressed in words'. The first type of claim defines the tableau, the second defines the hieroglyph. The terms 'tableau' and 'hieroglyph', used by Diderot in his discussion of painting and theatre, and by Barthes in respect of theatre and cinema, label concepts which were already long established in art theory by the time Diderot came to use them in the eighteenth century. They are still with us today, albeit they are now less formally described. If we are to account for the longevity of these concepts in the history of theories of representation in the West, we might usefully consider the possibility that they are the *projection*, into the field of material representational practices, of fundamental psychological processes described in psychoanalysis.

*

The question now arises of how, in terms of the analogy I am proposing between certain art-historical and psychoanalytical categories, the relations of the various key terms I have mentioned are to be conceived. In 'Diderot, Brecht, Eisenstein' Barthes effectively *conflates* the concepts 'hieroglyph', 'pregnant moment' (peripateia), and 'tableau'; my argument here must separate them. First, peripateia and tableau must be placed in a logical hierarchy. The relation of peripateia to tableau is a relation of *text* to *staging*: the peripateia is an instant arrested within, abstracted from, a narrative flow; the tableau is a particular *realization* of that as yet purely notional instant (the doctrines of *ut pictura poesis* were concerned precisely with detailing recommended 'correct' procedures for such *mise-en-scène*). Further, in belonging to a *common* ground of meaning, rooted in, in Barthes' words, 'an ethical and political culture', the tableau is clearly situated in the field of what Barthes first calls the 'obvious meaning' and then, ten years later, the '*studium*'. The *punctum*, we will remember, is, on the contrary, unpredictable and private; it is that 'very little' in the image which is 'purely image'. As the meaning of the *punctum* takes the form of an affect which cannot be translated into discourse then, equally clearly, the 'hieroglyph' is on the side of the *punctum*.

The separation between tableau and hieroglyph which we may see in the history of the concepts, and the oscillation between them in Barthes' paper, map the distinction we have inherited from Lacan between the registers of the 'symbolic' and the 'imaginary'; to complete the picture we need to take into account that necessary third Lacanian category, the 'real'. As Barthes' account of the *punctum* is, for my purposes here, incomplete, I have juxtaposed it with the case history of Philippe – a history of 'stages' of transformation of the alienation of the oral drive in a 'succession' of signifiers (with the understanding that 'stage' and 'succession' here in no way imply 'supercession'). Resumed most briefly, and as the story of

Philippe illustrates, the fantasy may be considered as 'standing in for' that which is radically unrepresentable: the absence *in* the real, and the absence *of* the real in discourse. The real then, as Ribettes remarks, is one of the 'three dimensions' of fantasy; the imaginary is that dimension which is outside discourse, attached to (but not assimilable to) the pre-Oedipal; the symbolic is the 'later' dimension of combination, syntax, transcription. In a schematically descriptive 'triangle' of fantasy, therefore, the real would be located at one point, and at the other two could be grouped, respectively, the terms: 'imaginary'/'elementary signifier'/'*punctum*'/ 'hieroglyph' and 'symbolic'/'fantasy scenario'/'*studium*'/'tableau'.

This is indeed sketchy, and is no doubt in the spirit of a structuralism of which we have grown suspicious, but I believe there is enough accuracy in it at least to serve my purpose here. A major limitation of this schema is its implication of segregation; in fact, the more highly cathected, most primitive, elements will have the capacity to 'unfold' upon the very scenarios in which they figure, either directly or in a displaced manner. Thus the 'piercing' image of the 'ankle-strap' gives way to the short scene, 'her necklace was locked in a box', which in turn figures . . . , we know not.

Some clarification of what I have in mind here may be gained by reference to Herman Rapaport's essay, 'Staging: Mont Blanc'.[22] Rapaport begins his essay with a reference to Plato's allegory of the cave, the purpose of which is to communicate the doctrine of pure forms. But, Rapaport remarks:

> what is most interesting is the way a prop such as the cave image can suddenly turn into a stage, how an image, itself framed, can suddenly stage itself as stage and in that way absent itself or disappear from the viewer's consciousness as image, object, or prop.

Rapaport then moves to the example of the Wolf Man case-history, in which Freud, in Rapaport's words:

> documents what happens to a small child who has been exposed on repeated occasions to a picture of a wolf, an image that can be seen with or through like a kind of optic glass and thus can frame what will become a traumatic fantasy, a nightmare about six or seven wolves in a tree.

Having quoted Freud's transcription of his patient's account of the nightmare, Rapaport comments:

> Here the image of the wolf has been phantomized, has faded out, and frames or stages this dream. *Although the wolf image has disappeared in its original form, its effect or impression energizes the dream*, and it is

repeated six or seven times within the image's little 'production'. (my emphasis)

With the word 'production' I am returned again to thoughts about the cinema, and particularly to the relation of film to still with which I began.

*

When I first read a short essay by Freud called, 'A special type of choice of object made by men',[23] I was struck by the similarities between the syndrome of male desire Freud describes and the pattern of behaviour 'Scottie' (James Stewart) exhibits in Hitchcock's film *Vertigo* (1958). The first condition determining the choice of love-object by the type of man discussed in Freud's essay is that the woman should be already attached to some other man – husband, fiancé, or friend: in the film, Scottie falls in love with the woman he is hired to investigate, the wife of an old college friend. The second precondition is that the woman should be seen to be of bad repute sexually: 'Madeleine' (Kim Novak), the college friend's wife, suffers from a fixated identification with a forebear whose illicit love-affair and illegitimate child brought her to tragic ruin. The type of man described by Freud is 'invariably moved to rescue the object of his love', and prominent amongst the rescue fantasies of such men is the fantasy of rescue from water: Scottie rescues Madeleine from San Francisco Bay. Finally Freud observes, 'The lives of men of this type are characterized by a repetition of passionate attachments of this sort: . . . each is an exact replica of the other', and he remarks that it is always the same physical type which is chosen: following Madeleine's death, Scottie becomes obsessed by 'Judy' (Kim Novak), a woman who physically resembles Madeleine and whom he sets about 'remaking' into an exact replica of Madeleine. Behind the pattern of repetitious behaviour he describes, Freud identifies a primary scenario of male Oedipal desire for the mother – already attached to the father, her sexual relations with whom bring her into ill repute in the eyes of the little rival for her love. The ubiquitous fantasy of rescue from water represents a conflation of 'rescue' with 'birth'. Just as he was, at birth, 'fished from the waters' and given life, so will he now return this gift to his mother in a reciprocal act of recovery from water. Finally, the adult man's love-attachments form an endless series of similar types for the simple reason that, as mother surrogates, they can never match the irreducibly unique qualities of the original.

When I fish Hitchcock's film from the depths of my memory it surfaces in the form of two images superimposed as one: Madeleine's face above the shadow of her lifeless body below the waters of the bay; Judy's face floating through the green-tinged gloom of the hotel room where she has just emerged from her final transformation, in the bathroom, into the

John Everett Millais, *Ophelia*, 1851. (The Tate Gallery, London)

image of the dead Madeleine.[24] I can, of course, recall many other images, actions, snatches of dialogue, and so on, but the first, composite, image comes as if unbidden, spreading itself as if to form the very screen upon which my memory of the *reel*-film (the object of 'criticism' and most film theory) is projected. Paraphrasing Rapaport, I might say: 'although the film has disappeared in its original form, its effect or impression energizes the image'; or beyond, more fundamentally, 'although the fantasy has been repressed in its original form, the displacement of its cathexis energizes the film'. Away from the cinema now, away from the insistence of the film's unreeling, this privileged image opens on to that skeletal narrative I find both in *Vertigo* and in Freud's paper on men's desire; but a narrative whose substance is undecidedly (n)either text (n)or tableau; and this in turn immediately dissolves into a myriad other delegates from a history of Western representations flooded with watery images of women – from the *Birth of Venus* to the *Death of Ophelia*. For example, in pursuit of these last two, I am returned to *Vertigo* by way of the bridge over the bay, in whose shadow Madeleine casts flowers on the water as she prepares to jump, leaping the gap between Hitchcock's and Botticelli/Millais' images of woman/water/flowers. As I now recall that Botticelli's *Birth of Venus* depicts the goddess at the moment of her *landfall* at Paphos, eliding the circumstances of her birth out at sea from the bloody foam produced when Saturn casts the genitals of the newly castrated Uranus into the ocean, I

*Vertigo* 1958. (Copyright © by Universal Pictures, a Division of Universal City Studios, Inc. All rights reserved. Courtesy of MCA Publishing Rights, a Division of MCA Inc.)

find that my re-entry into the text of the film is by a different route – one destined to take me through a different sequence of images, until I have traversed the text again, to regain another exit into the intertext, from which I shall be returned again . . . and again, until the *possible* passages have been exhausted, or until I find that the trajectory of associations has become attracted into the orbit of some other semantically/affectively dense textual item, some other fantasy.

    In a certain (phenomenological) sense, the cinema is the 'negative' of the gallery (the museums which now house the paintings Diderot wrote about; our galleries of contemporary art). In the cinema we are in darkness; the gallery is light. In the cinema we are immobile before moving images; in the gallery it is we who must move. In the cinema we may interrupt the sequence of images only by leaving; in the gallery we may order the duration of our attention in whatever sequence we wish. The much remarked 'hypnosis' of cinema suppresses our critical attention; in the gallery the critical faculty is less easily beguiled. I could continue this list of 'oppositions' but the point is that, as in all positive/negative processes, the one situation implies the other. It is precisely their mutual reliance which concerns me here. Just as Malraux, in assessing the fortunes of the work of art in the age of mechanical reproduction, found it necessary to speak of a 'museum without walls', so there is a 'cinema without walls' in the form of the countless stills and synopses to which we are exposed. These in their turn dissolve into the broader flood of images (from 'news' to 'advertising') issuing from our 'society of the spectacle' – mutually affective *tableaux* which stage not only the legitimizing narratives of human existence but also, in the process, each other.

I was once in Padua and took the opportunity to visit the Scrovegni Chapel to see its famous frescoes by Giotto. In form the chapel is a simple box, whose interior faces display the 'grand narrative' of human existence in the fourteenth century – the redemption of man, guaranteed by the exemplary lives of the Virgin and Christ. In addition to the narration of the ideal mother and her ideal son we are shown personifications of the vices and the virtues. Although the father does not make a personal appearance his will is conspicuously seen to be done throughout, and most vividly in the large final scene of the Last Judgement, which (Giotto being no Bosch) appears appropriately as quite a *domestic* affair. Only a couple of hundred yards from the Scrovegni Chapel is the Church of the Eremitani which in 1944 took a direct hit from allied bombs (thereby losing some works by Mantegna). In my fantasy, however, it is the Scrovegni Chapel which explodes, raining its fragments upon the city of Padua like the scattered contents of a huge Giotto jigsaw puzzle. The grand narrative of human existence – the meaning of life, the source of inspiration and legitimation of all social institutions and individual actions – is not destroyed, but it is now encountered in a very different way, as representative fragments whose connections and ultimate meanings must be implied. The narrative/ideological coherence of this material heterogeneity depends upon a psychological investment, largely unconscious, and therefore radically inaccessible to the discourses of an 'ethical and political culture', except in so far as these discourses themselves issue from an unconscious matrix as the heavily elaborated transcriptions of common fantasy scenarios. In Padua today, as in all our Western cities, this is precisely the way in which we encounter the grand legitimating narratives of our existence: on billboards, in magazines, in family albums, in newspapers, on picture postcards and, of course, outside the cinema – from the metaphorical and metonymical webs of this most general environment of (mainly photographic) images which *prefigure* the film, to the particular film poster and film still. It is all this which 'conducts the subject, from street to street, poster to poster, to finally plunge one into a dark, anonymous, and indifferent cube'.[25] As I have remarked elsewhere:

> The darkness of the cinema has been evinced as a condition for an artificial 'regression' of the spectator; film has been compared with

hypnosis. It is likely, however, that the apparatus which desire has constructed for itself incorporates *all* those aspects of contemporary Western society for which the Situationists chose the name *spectacle* . . . desire needs no material darkness in which to stage its imaginary satisfactions; day-dreams, too, can have the potency of hypnotic suggestion.[26]

Discussions of fantasy and cinema have concentrated on structures 'near the surface' of the film, predominantly the obviously Oedipal scenarios of 'family dramas'. I have suggested how an elaborate film narrative (here *Vertigo*) may figure an Oedipal scene in a more displaced form (Scottie's behaviour). I have further suggested that, just as the 'manifest narrative' of the film in my example opens upon ('stages', 'frames') an Oedipal scenario, so *this* narrative in its turn unfolds upon an *image*, of hieroglyphic affect (both the *mise-en-scène* of a moment of narrative crisis, and the cryptic inscription of a moment of narrative truth) which is nothing but a point of condensation of the laconic tales which *it* figures ('a woman is in the water', 'I am rescuing the woman', etc.). These, in *their* turn, open on to all those representations which are (male?) fantasies of birth. In all this perpetual motion, through which the subject exists, there is no rest, no arrival at a point of origin. Nor, clearly, is there any point at which we may be sure we have left the domain of the 'political' (Oedipal structures as structures of *authority*) for some other.

In a sense, psychoanalysis comes into existence with the recognition that what we call 'material reality', the 'real world', is not all that is real for us. Unconscious wishes, and the unconscious fantasies they engender, are as immutable a force in our lives as any material circumstance. Freud's observation that unconscious fantasy structures exert as actual a force on the life of the subject as do, for example, socio-economic structures, is signified in his use of the expression *psychical-reality*. Psychical reality is not to be equated with the contingent and ephemeral phenomena of 'mental life' in general. On the contrary, what marks it is its stability, its coherence, the constancy of its *effects* upon perceptions and actions of the subject. Severe cases of 'mental disturbance' are only the most dramatic-ally obvious manifestations of the *fact* of psychical reality. Although, almost a century after the birth of psychoanalysis, it still suits many to draw a line of absolute division and exclusion between such 'abnormal' behaviour and their own 'normality', psychoanalysis recognizes no such possible state of unambiguous and self-possessed lucidity in which the external world is seen for, and known as, simply what it *is*.

Common fantasy structures contribute to the construction of 'reality' in the realm of representations. I say 'construction' rather than 'mediation' to emphasize that no reality is known to us *outside* representations. There is no question of 'freeing' representations ('reality') from the determinations of fantasy. There is, however, a considerable benefit to be achieved from an *awareness* of the agency of unconscious fantasy in representations: the representations of women by men; the representations of blacks by whites; the representations of 'homosexuals' by 'heterosexuals'; and so on. The purpose of my remarks has been to argue that the systematic development of such an awareness in the field of theories of representations has been impeded by too restricted a framing of notions of the 'specificity' of objects of study ('painting', 'photography', 'film').

In approaching the phenomenologically given field of representations theoretically, we have tended to divide it empirically, and according to an implicit sociologism. Beyond a certain limit, however, attention to the 'specificity' of a representational practice – grounded most usually in its material substrate and material mode of production – becomes unhelpful, as, for example, when 'specificity' is fetishized for professional convenience, to conserve the putative sanctity of the 'discipline', or to respect the reality of academic institutions and markets. Certainly we need a social history of the news photograph, a semiotics of the cinema, a political economy of advertising, and so on, but we should avoid the risk of 'failing to see the wood for the trees' – we need to take account of the *total* environment of the 'society of the spectacle', at least if it is a theory of ideology which is at issue. In order to achieve this we must deconstruct not only the supposed absolute difference between 'fine art' and 'mass media' – with its implication of what Benjamin so accurately, and so long ago, identified as, 'this fetishistic, fundamentally anti-technical notion of *Art*' – but also the differences between such equally hallowed and uninterrogated academic categories as 'art history' and 'film studies'. I recommend this not in the interests of some spurious argument that the objects of these categories – paintings, photographs, films – are somehow 'the same', but rather in order that we may begin to construe their differences *differently*.

# Notes

1. In an abbreviated form, this paper was first given at the symposium, 'Film and Photography', at the University of California, Santa Barbara, May, 1984.

2. I am careful to specify psychoanalytic *theory* here, as the history of the *institution* of psychoanalysis, as a professional practice, has tended to elide the socially radical nature of Freud's legacy. See, for example, R. Jacoby, *The Repression of Psychoanalysis, Otto Fenichel and the Political Freudians*, New York, Basic Books, 1983.

3. To avoid possible misunderstanding at the start, I would stress that *no* implication of a Jungian 'collective unconscious' is intended here. I do, however, assume a collective *preconscious* (in the sense in which the notion is encountered in both Freud and Lacan). I further assume that the 'mechanisms' of the unconscious (primary processes) are held in common (much as all speakers of English hold English syntax in common, albeit syntax belongs to the preconscious); moreover, I assume that certain unconscious contents (e.g., fantasy 'scenarios') will be held in common by all individuals in a given society, in a given historical period – albeit the particular forms of representation of these contents will vary according to biographical circumstances (see section III).

4. R. Barthes, 'The third meaning', in *Image–Music–Text*, London, Fontana, 1977, p.52.

5. ibid., p.69.

6. See R.W. Lee, *Ut Pictura Poesis: the Humanistic Theory of Painting*, Norton, 1967.

7. For a succinct account of allegory in Renaissance painting, see J. Hall, *A History of Ideas and Images in Italian Art*, London, John Murray, 1983.

8. See, for example, Thornhill's commentary on his *Allegory of the Protestant Succession*, quoted in R. Paulson, *Emblem and Expression: Meaning in English Art of the Eighteenth Century*. By way of correcting my perhaps over-schematic characterization of the evolution of allegory as 'simple to complex', see also Rubens' late (1638) letter of description of his *The Horrors of War*, quoted in W. Stechow, *Rubens and the Classical Tradition*, Harvard, 1968, pp.87–9.

9. D. Diderot, *Discours sur la poésie dramatique* [1785], quoted in J.C. Bonnet, *Diderot*, Livre de Poche, 1984, pp.182–3.

10. Quoted in R. Wittkower, 'Hieroglyphics in the early Renaissance', in *Allegory and the Migration of Symbols*, Westview Press, 1977, p.116.

11. D. Diderot, *Oeuvres Complètes* (22 vols.), ed. J. Assézat and M. Tourneaux, vol.III, p.190; quoted in N. Bryson, *Word and Image: French Painting of the Ancien Régime*, Cambridge, Cambridge University Press, 1981, p.179.

12. R. Barthes, *Camera Lucida*, Hill & Wang, 1981, pp.43 and 53.

13. J. Laplanche, 'The order of life and the genesis of human sexuality', in *Life and Death in Psychoanalysis* (trans. and intro. by J. Mehlman), Baltimore, Johns Hopkins University Press, 1976, pp.19–20.

14. J. Laplanche and J.-B. Pontalis, 'Fantasy and the origins of sexuality', *The International Journal of Psychoanalysis*, vol.49 (1968), part 1, p.17. Reprinted in this volume, p.25.

15. ibid., p.16. Reprinted in this volume, p.26. (It is this perspective which allows Derrida to locate the error in Rousseau's condemnation of masturbation as a deplorable ancilliary to sexuality; it is in this 'supplement', the grubby margin to the bright page of human affective relations, that sexuality reveals itself most essentially.)

16. J. Laplanche, 'The ego and the vital order', in *Life and Death in Psychoanalysis*. op.cit.

17. J. Lacan, 'Of the gaze as *Objet Petit a*', in *The Four Fundamental Concepts of Psycho-Analysis*, London, Hogarth Press, 1977, pp.67–105.

18. J. Laplanche and S. Leclaire, 'The unconscious: a psychoanalytic study', *Yale French Studies*, no.48 (1972), p.118.

19. ibid., p.135.

20. For an account of this concept, see J. Laplanche and J.-B. Pontalis, *The Language of Psychoanalysis*, London, Hogarth Press, 1973, pp.111–14.

21. J.-M. Ribettes, 'La troisième dimension du fantasme', in D. Anzieu *et al.*, *Art et Fantasme*, Seyssel, Champ Vallon, 1984, p.188.

22. H. Rapaport, 'Staging: Mont Blanc', in M. Krupnick (ed.), *Displacement: Derrida and After*,

Bloomington, Indiana University Press, 1983, p.59.

23. S. Freud, *The Standard Edition of the Complete Psychological Works of Sigmund Freud*, ed. J. Strachey, Hogarth Press, 1953–74, vol.XI, p.165.

24. For Hitchcock's own fascinating comments on this scene, '. . . the scene which moved me most', see *Hitchcock/Truffaut, Edition Definitive*, Ramsay, 1983, pp.208–9.

25. R. Barthes, 'En sortant du cinéma', in *Communications*, no.23, Seuil, 1975.

26. 'Looking at photographs', in V. Burgin (ed.), *Thinking Photography*, London, Macmillan, 1982, p.153.

John Fletcher

# POETRY, GENDER AND PRIMAL FANTASY

This essay is an attempt at reading three poems, Blake's 'I saw a chapel all of gold', Elizabeth Barrett Browning's 'A Musical Instrument' and Emily Dickinson's 'I started early took my dog', in order to disclose the way they work and rework fantasies that bear on sexual difference and desire. My readings are in some sense then 'sexual political' readings, taking the sexual field constructed by the poems as organized around relations of domination, submission and resistance. The moments and movements of desire in each poem, I shall argue, are bound up with and against these relations of power.

For any account of the relations between desire and power, of a *politics* of sexuality, a theory of fantasy as a production of meanings and identities is essential. Psychoanalysis will figure in the account as that discourse which addresses itself most sustainedly to sexuality as both difference and identity; to sexuality, not as a fixed biological given, but in its emergence and organization, its precariousness and mobility in relation to language and the symbolic. In their essay 'Fantasy and the origins of sexuality',[1] which continues Lacan's structuralist rereading of Freud, Laplanche and Pontalis attempt a critical reintegration of the semiotic and the sexual in Freud's thought around the concept of fantasy, which they claim is the fundamental object of psychoanalysis.

Psychoanalysis in its Lacanian form and derivatives challenges a privileged theme in the literary tradition – the primacy of the intending, expressive individual as origin of meaning. Much orthodox Freudian interpretation, however, seems to operate with what might be called a biological theory of symbolism, involving a privileged repertoire of sexual contents and bodily parts: breasts, penis, mouth, womb, etc. We seem to be forever in the presence of an importunate natural body insinuating its multiple urges into every product and utterance. This clamorous organism and its instincts emerges, not just as the theme or object of unconscious fantasy, but as its expressive origin or source. The bypaths and indirect crooked ways of fantasy and symbolism seem to have a trick of converging back on the same set of stubborn itches, behind and beyond the beleaguered ego and its vengeful superintendent. The creative genius of literary tradition is simply replaced by the biological subject with its preset trajectory through the zones and stages of libidinal maturation.

## The psychical order and its effects

Psychoanalysis begins, however, with the postulation of a level of psychical reality distinct from the body, and exceeding both consciousness and the ego. The initial objects of psychoanalytic attention, as it emerges from medico-psychiatric practice in the 1890s, are the symptoms of mental illness, especially hysteria. These are understood as the meaningful but distorted expressions of wishes, ideas, fantasies of which the subject is not conscious. The symptom is read as a distorted signifying act, a twisted signifier, such that with the conscious working through of its repressed significations, the hysterical paralysis, amnesia, obsessional behaviour or phobia disappears. Central to psychoanalysis then is the Unconscious as a system of repressed psychical contents, ideas, memories, wishes, which are split off and denied access to consciousness and expression in a sort of internal quarantine. This splitting is bound up with the organization of sexuality and the acquisition of gender.

The status of these unconscious mental contents remains permanently problematic in Freud's writing. Initially they are understood within a trauma theory, as the memories of disturbing actual events, split off in a process of defence, with their accompanying emotions undischarged and pathogenic. Neurotics were suffering from reminiscences. Freud moves, by his own account, from a trauma theory of neurosis based on real incidents to a fantasy theory of neurotic symptoms as the expression of unconscious wishes. Famously the common stories of paternal seduction told by his female hysterics are re-identified, with considerable relief, as the expression of repressed infantile wishes directed towards the father. Together with the determining force of unconscious fantasy is the postulation of infantile sexuality as an active set of wishes and masturbatory activities. The literalist seduction theory, we are told, gives way to the discovery of the Oedipus complex, of which the stories of paternal seduction are the typical feminine expression in fantasy. Potentially psychoanalysis might be said to lay the groundwork, not for a biological theory of symbolism but for a symbolic, even a narrative theory of sexuality.

Laplanche and Pontalis challenge the simple account of a transition from the seduction theory to the Oedipus complex. They discern various tendencies or currents in Freud's thought productive of rival or contradictory emphases, all of which persist to some degree throughout his work. One of these is a biological conception of a spontaneous infantile sexuality, endogenously determined by a sexual constitution, unfolding through a set of natural and regular stages, oral, anal, phallic towards a naturally given norm of heterosexual genitality involving masculine (active and phallic) and feminine (receptive and vaginal) positions, serving the functions of reproduction. The effect of this still dominant conception, Laplanche and Pontalis argue, was to marginalize for twenty years the early recognition of the Oedipus complex and its structure of fantasies even in the Three Essays on Sexuality (1905). As late as 1924 in the paper on 'The dissolution of the Oedipus complex', we find Freud still supporting the view that the Oedipus complex passes 'just as the milk-teeth fall out . . . bound to pass away according to programme when the next pre-ordained phase of development sets in'.[2] As a result, fantasy in this perspective is no more than a secondary expression, a purely imaginary efflorescence of an innate biological programme. What is obscured at the very moment fantasy is discovered, Laplanche and Pontalis argue, is its structural status in the determining of sexuality, what they call Freud's intuition of a pre-subjective structure that transcends either the punctual event, its protagonists or its internal imagery.

## The reality of fantasy

Freud never finally abandons, however, the regressive, detective search for the originating event or actual scene behind the neurosis and its unconscious fantasies. He is never content to accept such scenes and memories as entirely imaginary products. Both features of the old seduction theory reappear in the case-study of the Wolf Man (1918):[3] a concern to derive the smallest details of the subject's symptoms and fantasies by reconstruction from the actual observation of parental coitus at the age of 18 months: a hot summer's day towards five o'clock in the afternoon; the parents half undressed, in white underclothes; the sexual act taking place three times, from behind, with the mother kneeling on all fours and the father upright; the infant witness interrupting the primal scene by passing a motion and crying out. The memory remaining dormant, as an encysted foreign body, is then activated at the age of 4 in a belatedly sexualized form after a series of enabling events (seduction by his sister, the threat of castration by his nurse), producing the famous dream of the white wolves and the beginnings of his phobias and delusions. There is the persistent attempt to ground the production of fantasies, both in their details and in their structure, on the bedrock of an originating event (albeit the first of a complemental series). At the high point of this concern with the biographical actuality of the primal scene, however, an alternative conceptualization emerges: the primal scene is primal fantasy, constructed from the perception of copulating animals and projected backwards on to the parents in the form of an earlier infantile memory. The text of the Wolf Man case history oscillates between an insistence on the reality of the scene as memory and its equivalent reality as fantasy.

The latter conception of the compelling psychical reality of primal fantasies is elaborated by Freud, both in the case study of 1918 and the earlier 1916 lecture,[4] as an inherited endowment, a phylogenetic heritage, that supplements the gaps in individual experience with pre-historic experience. This store of unconscious primal fantasies, possessed not just by neurotics but by all human beings, underlies the whole spectrum of psychical productions from dreams, to conscious day-dreams, to all forms of neurotic and psychotic symptoms. The reality of what Freud calls 'these phylogenetically inherited schemata',[5] postulated beneath the individual elaborations of fantasy, has 'an autonomous and structural status with regard to the subject who is totally dependent on it' (p.17). Freud draws an analogy with the Kantian transcendental categories of time, space, causality, etc. which organize the influx of sense data:

> like the categories of philosophy, [they] are concerned with the business of 'placing' the impressions derived from actual experience. I am inclined to take the view that they are precipitates from the history of human civilization. . . . Wherever experience fails to fit in with the hereditary schema, they become remodelled in the imagination.[6]

The example of the Wolf Man is given by Freud as an instance of the hereditary schema triumphing over individual experience, for the boy's father becomes in fantasy the castrating figure and threat to his sexuality, despite the boy's *inverted* Oedipus complex (desire for the father, identification with the mother), and a literal castration threat actually made by his female nurse.

Even where Freud's insistence on the 'transcendental' and structuring function of primal fantasies is clearest, its formulation within the dubious framework of phylogenesis, binds it still to the foundation of an originating primal event. The bedrock of the event is now displaced from the fortuitous experiences of personal biography to the prehistory of the race. The originating event in question is now the mythic murder of the primal father, despot of the primal horde and possessor of its women, by the rebellious sons, as elaborated in *Totem and Taboo* (1913). The primal fantasies are then the inherited, unconscious memory-traces, finding expression in myth and legend, of the originating primal crime and its 'scene'. In Freud's search for the bedrock of the originating event an imaginary biography gives way to an imaginary anthropology.

Laplanche and Pontalis suggest a way of reading this encapsulation of the structuring role of primal fantasies within the framework of phylogenesis, 'as a prefiguration of the "symbolic order" defined by Lévi-Strauss and Lacan in the ethnological and psychoanalytic fields respectively'. Its function is 'to assign limits to the "imaginary" which cannot contain its own principle of organization' (p.17). Prehistory and its phylogenetic heritage becomes an alibi for a missing concept of structure, a premature structuralism *avant la lettre*.

## Primal fantasy as the drama of difference

One of Freud's earliest extended discussions of what comes to be called primal fantasies occurs in his essay on 'The sexual theories of children' (1908).[7] These speculations, in defiance of adult mystification, rework fantasies based on the component drives and erotogenic zones to produce oral, anal and phallic explanations to the questions, 'Where do babies come from?' and 'What is the difference between the sexes?' The latter question, of sexual difference and its meaning, comes gradually to the fore as the primary one for Freud. In his later discussions of primal fantasy the bizarre variety of infantile speculations is pared down to three scenes: seduction, castration and parental intercourse. In their classic formulation these fantasies form a triptych in which the earliest recognized fantasy of the daughter's seduction by the father is joined by the fantasy of the son's threatened castration by the father. These form attendant pieces on either side, so to speak, of the central piece which alone comes to be designated in the singular as *the* primal scene: a fantasy of sadistic coupling, a primal rape or wounding of the mother by the father.

Laplanche and Pontalis make the connection with infantile speculation central to their discussion of the primal fantasies, which they describe as subjective myths of origins:

> Like myths, they claim to provide a representation of, and a solution to, the major enigmas that confront the child. Whatever appears to the subject as something needing an explanation or theory, is dramatized as a moment of emergence, the beginning of a history.
>
> Fantasies of origins: the primal scene pictures the origin of the individual; fantasies of seduction, the origin and upsurge of sexuality; fantasies of castration, the origin of the difference between the sexes (p.19).

There is a certain elegance in this handling of the three fantasies as Freud's two questions become three and receive each their particular 'mythic' solution. Behind each scene a separate question and answer. It is not at all clear, however, that each scene can be quite so cleanly distinguished from the others as the staging of a separate enigma. In Freud's handling of them in different texts they blend into each other, overlap and repeat the same or similar preoccupations from different positions. Neither is it at all clear that the Wolf Man's dream of wolves, his phobias and delusions, represent the origins of babies as the leading question behind the primal scene. The primal scene stages castration as the hidden 'truth' of difference as much as any other scene, and the seduction scene presupposes and compensates for it (the father's gift to the daughter). What enables the neatness of Laplanche and Pontalis's explication is the reduction of scene to theme, with the consequent obscuring of the subject positions involved. The primal fantasies entail not just the theme of castration or seduction in general, but typically the *father's* castration of the son, the *father's* seduction of the daughter. All three scenes are haunted by the fantasy of castration-as-difference just as they are dominated by the figure of the castrating, phallic father. Seduction as 'the origin and upsurge of sexuality' is located in the pre-Oedipal relations between mother and infant (as Laplanche and Pontalis have themselves outlined it),[8] and as such is radically different from seduction in the Oedipal register where it is the typical relation in fantasy between father and daughter. It is precisely their abstraction from the Oedipal structure that enables the separation of the three enigmas and the three solutions. The 'themes' of castration and seduction as primal fantasies are not explicable apart from the primal scene and the overall scenario of the Oedipus complex in which they figure.

From both Freud's particular work of analysis of the Wolf Man's dream, and his subsequent generalization of the psychical operations by which the masculine Oedipus complex is dissolved, it is clear that the primal scene is inseparable from the staging of sexual difference as castration, with a different address to the masculine and feminine subjects whose positions it constructs. In 'The dissolution of the Oedipus complex' (1924), Freud formulates its operations for the bisexual male infant for whom the threat of castration is the organizing term in the relations constructed in fantasy with the phallic father (whether of desire or of rivalry). Castration is the price to be paid, whether as punishment or precondition, for what Freud calls 'the satisfaction of love in the field of the Oedipus complex'.[9] The primal fantasies operate so as to reorganize the pre-Oedipal sexual field through the alignment of a set of identifications and object attachments which are dramatized for the subject as alternatives. This assigns a meaning, as Freud notes, to the gender positions it constructs: masculine/active, feminine/passive. It also secures particular identifications as modes of access to particular objects. Access to the father as libidinal object is now through a feminine identification with the mother, with a consequent loss of phallic activity.

What the primal fantasies leave out is therefore as important as what they include. They inscribe a set of relations to the father for son (threat of castration) and daughter (seduction) which turn on a prior relation of the father to the mother, hence its 'primal' status, as always already there. They do not include direct relations between mother and child which constitute the pre-Oedipal sexual field they exclude precisely so as to transform. Access to the mother is now regulated by the function or place of the father. The premise of bisexuality in the infant and the either/or structure of the Oedipal field means that there is no simple determinism that consigns the biological individual to a given gender position. Gender positions are given in relations (active/passive) to each other but not to the anatomy of the subject who must negotiate certain identifications at the price of certain object choices. Indeed Freud enunciates a general principle that identifications are formed out of abandoned object-cathexes, and that 'identification is the sole condition under which the id can give up its objects'. The ego structured through identifications is 'a precipitate of such abandoned object choices'.[10] This suggests that the object of desire that the threat of castration is designed to forbid to the bisexual male subject is not the mother, with whom a sublimated object-relation must be retained, but the phallic father himself. Homosexual desire for the phallic father is at once the necessary condition and the potential obstacle to the required masculine identification with the phallic father. Correlatively it is the identification with the formerly phallic mother, now repositioned as castrated in the primal scene, that also lays the subject under the same threat. This is certainly the logic of Freud's analysis of the Wolf Man. The Wolf Man lives out the traumatic fantasy of castration, with its phobias and delusions, not for any rivalry with his father for the mother, but, according to Freud, for his repressed but stubborn homosexual desire for satisfaction from the father.

Freud's analysis of the Wolf Man might suggest that the primal fantasies and the Oedipal structure turn, not on the incest taboo in Lévi-Strauss's sense, but on the imperatives of heterosexual genitality. However, it also suggests the lack of any *given* alignment between anatomy and gender position. What is in question is not the abstracted biological function of reproduction, but a set of psycho-social relations and positions bearing on a particular form of the genital order of sexed reproduction, and the movements of desire within and against those relations and positions, to which it is held and in which it constantly fails. The negotiations of the subject in relation to the proscriptions and injunctions of the primal fantasies reveal sexuality precisely as a field of vicissitudes and discontents.

The register of the 'primal', for Freud, is bound to the symbolic father and his law; it is a secondary revision of an earlier organization, that of the drives bound to the maternal imago, a revision that stages itself as an origin. This restructuring of identifications and desires is the effect of the primal fantasies and their narratives. While these narratives turn on the rigid symbolic opposition phallic–castrated, the negotiation of subject positions in and through fantasy is a revisionary work (involving repressions, displacements, substitutions, losses and remedies), a work of narrative as such. Fantasy, Laplanche and Pontalis insist, is 'the stage-setting of desire', 'not the object of desire but its setting' (p.26). The primal fantasies, those repetitive scenarios limited in thematic scope, yet prolific in their range of productions, are characterized by both a fixity of terms yet a mobility in their narrative combination and staging. Not the 'expression' of a pre-given subject, the primal fantasies Laplanche and Pontalis argue, 'are characterized by the absence of subjectivization . . . the subject is present in the scene . . .' Subject positioning is the effect of a desiring movement in and through the terms and images of the narrative.

> In fantasy the subject does not pursue the object or its sign: he appears caught up himself in the sequence of images . . . in the very syntax of the sequence in question (p.26).

The emphasis on syntax and sequence, on the work of narrative as a desiring movement that stages and restages the subject, precludes any simple determining of externally opposed positions and identities. What we have is a constant reshuffling of the court cards, 'those *dramatis personae* . . . [who] receive their notation from a family legend which is mutilated, disordered and misunderstood' (p.22). The most striking and bizarre example of this is Laplanche and Pontalis's commentary on the primal fantasy of seduction, which can be summarized as 'a father seduces a daughter'.

> The indication here of the primary process . . . is a scenario with multiple entries, in which nothing shows whether the subject will be immediately located as *daughter*; it can as well be fixed as *father*, or even in the term *seduces* (p.22–3).

This dispersal of the subject through the sequence, even the syntax of the text, characterizes the three poems I shall be concerned with. All show signs of a *troubling* of syntax, sequence, and enunciation. Similarly, in being read in relation to the triptych of primal fantasies and the issues of identity, difference and desire they stage, the compounding of scenes and positions in each poem precludes any clearcut separation of the scenes into the three separate enigmas and solutions as envisaged by Laplanche and Pontalis.

## Fantasy and literature

The reformulation of sexual identity and desire as symbolic productions, the effects of a narrative positioning and revision within the scenarios of primal fantasy, will alter radically any general account of the relations between the psychical order, object of psychoanalysis, and the institution of Literature. Traditional accounts have often tended to posit a specialized sexual content (oral, anal, genital impulses), seeking expressive detours around the censorship by social taboos. Even a more semiotically oriented account such as Francesco Orlando's model of the literary text, based on Freud's essay on negation, repeats this traditional opposition. Beginning with his initial proposition that 'literature or poetry is the seat of a socially institutionalized return of the repressed',[11] a typology of five formal possibilities is deduced, each possibility defined by a different relation between the repressed content and the addressee of the text. The repressed content returns but remains unconscious, becomes conscious but is not accepted, is accepted but not supported, is supported but not authorized, is authorized but not by all codes of the culture. Despite some concern with the literary question of address, with the addressee as textual position rather than as empirical reader, the basic opposition between repression and repressed remains an external one. The five formal distinctions register the degree to which some natural or given content is refused or conceded a space of expression in the field of the social. The role of fantasy and a symbolic order in the constitution of identity and desire precludes any such functionalist model of the literary text as licensed safety-valve for non-social forbidden contents. For all Orlando's emphasis on the text as compromise formation, repression is being thought within a naturalist dualism, a pre-given exteriority of the natural or individual to the social as a power to negate or refuse expression. The extrapolation of Freud's account of negation makes the model of repression/return of the repressed peculiarly vulnerable to Foucault's critique of the negative conception of power as a simple refusal or exclusion.

The problems with Orlando's position are exemplary. If I were to risk an alternative general proposition, it would be to Laplanche's critical return to the seduction theory, and his more recent concern with the underdeveloped theory of sublimation, that I would turn. Laplanche's concern with the recruitment/seduction of the infant to parental fantasy in the very formation of the sexual drives has always been in effect a concern with the positive and productive effects of power in the field of the psychical. Rather than a simple dualism of repression and repressed, Laplanche has described a double and reverse formation of the ego and sexuality, through a dialectic of inscription and repression, seduction and threat. Seduction is understood not as an event but as a situation or structure of seduction, in which 'the fantasy of implantation represents the implantation of fantasy'.[12] The propping of the sexual on the non-sexual at the bodily site of maternal care and unconscious seduction is reversed in sublimation. He postulates a genesis of 'higher', culturally valued activities (aesthetic representation, intellectual investigation and analysis) and their objects (myths, religious and cultural representations) which are propped in turn on the sexual. Propping is Laplanche's reworking of Freud's term *Anlehnung* (translated by Strachey as *anaclisis*). It is a structural relation of derivation, divergence and analogy, in which the sexual drives emerge, through a metaphorization of aims and a metonymic displacement of objects, from the biological instincts.[13]

All *general* models of the literary/psychical relation are necessarily speculative and provisional, but if sublimation, its activities and objects are propped on seduction and its effects, then a useful starting point would be the proposition that Literature is the site of a socially institutionalized seduction. The literary text is precisely a situation or structure of seduction, in which the implantation of fantasy through a sublimatory reverse solicits and sustains a set of readerly identifications as textual effects.[14] (For Freud the mechanisms of identification and sublimation have an identical recourse to the ego and its incorporations as aspects of the same process.) In Laplanche's dialectic of seduction and sublimation one might recognize a psychoanalytic parallel with the old Horatian prescriptions from the *Ars Poetica* that the function of literature is both to delight and to instruct, or in Sir Philip Sidney's version, to instruct by delighting.

Between them, a 'seduction theory' of literature and a narrative/symbolic theory of sexuality might open the possibility of a non-reductive articulation of the literary and the psychical. However, the question of the historical specificity of literary texts and genres, indeed of the literary institution itself, raises unresolved difficulties for the appropriation of psychoanalytic thought for literary theory. Freud and his structuralist successors appear to propose a transhistorical symbolic order and set of fantasies which in principle could claim explanatory pertinence for the reading of literature in any genre or period. The incidence of the primal fantasies would not be restricted to any particular period. This would *not* be to claim that they were a necessary or universal constituent of all fantasy or all literary production. While one would expect to be able to read their effects in texts and genres that are explicitly concerned with love, sexuality and gender, it would not be possible to specify, in advance of particular analyses, a necessary general connection between a given thematic material at a manifest textual level and a latent nucleus of structuring fantasies, that would obtain in all cases.[15]

What the literary theorist confronts at this point is the failure of any systematic attempt to ground the psycho-symbolic order described by psychoanalysis, not in an originary event, but in historically determinate sets of social relations. Lacan invokes Lévi-Strauss's structuralist theory of kinship and the symbolic function organized around exogamy and the incest taboo. Laplanche and Pontalis distance themselves in a long footnote (p.31, n. 34) from the reductive effects of structuralist abstraction on the specificity of the primal fantasies and the Oedipus complex (hesitating between *parole* and *langue*). Contemporary feminist theories of patriarchy have attempted with only partial success to provide an historical grounding in an account of the social relations of reproduction.[16]

In a recent essay Catherine Belsey has attempted to read certain late-eighteenth- and early-nineteenth-century texts, the early Gothic novel and the poetry of Wordsworth and Coleridge, as sites of what she calls 'the Romantic construction of the Unconscious' where 'the Unconscious is *for the first time* produced in discourse'. She argues that 'it makes no sense to talk of a mediaeval unconscious'[17] because the medieval subject, as in the morality plays, is openly presented as the locus of contending forces, dispersed, vacillating, in process, with no recourse to the fixity and unity of the *cogito*. Echoing Foucault's accusation of a psychoanalytic essentializing of sexuality as the 'truth' of the subject, she seeks to give psychoanalysis an historically specific object, bourgeois subjectivity, and to locate its radical potential in a critique of the imaginary pretensions of the bourgeois subject. The Unconscious is produced by Romantic literature as the site of meanings that disrupt the bourgeois subject's claim to sovereignty and autonomy.

A number of problems are raised by Belsey's attempt to historicize psychoanalysis and the Unconscious in relation to literature. It privileges the literary to the extent that the Unconscious appears as virtually a literary, as distinct from a discursive, construction. Historically, of course, Romanticism does not exhaust the epoch of the bourgeois subject, and many seventeenth-century texts (Shakespearean drama, Milton, etc.) make as productive a response to psychoanalytic interrogation, even if one grants Belsey's correlation of psychoanalysis with the epoch of bourgeois social relations. Accepting *tout court* Foucault's charges of essentializing sexuality, relocating its radical potential as a critical theory of the subject as unified ego, Belsey effectively desexualizes psychoanalysis, producing a radicalized mirror-opposite of American ego psychology. The Unconscious is not just the site of *any* disruptive meaning, but specifically of the primal fantasies, the Oedipal order, and the unstable fictions of sexual identity. Laplanche and Pontalis describe how the narratives of sexual difference function as myths of origin in the emergence of the subject. The subject and the Unconscious are inextricably bound up with sexual difference, for better or for worse. Between the patriarchal family and market relations, between Renaissance man and the Romantic individual, psychoanalysis continues to slip undecidably away from our best materialist attempts to give its airy nothings a local habitation and a name.

While tentatively aligned with the attempt to locate the Oedipal order within the *longue durée* of the patriarchal family in its various forms, I have nevertheless chosen for analysis three poems that merit the conventional designation of Romantic. All three construct a privileged literary space for the exploration of the psychical and its productions. As Cora Kaplan has observed of certain kinds of Romantic poetry,[18] they focus states of feeling in abstraction from any social context of causation, or from any realist representation of a public world. In the poems by Blake and Barrett Browning, however, the fantasy situations are the results of a poetic reworking of public mythologies, classical or Christian. Only Dickinson's poem answers to anything like a conventional account of first-person Romantic lyric, yet even its personalised whimsy shares with the greater impersonality of Blake's vision-form and Barrett Browning's ballad-form, a clearly marked narrative sequence. Whether the romance worlds of Spenser, the celestial and infernal worlds of Milton or the mock-heroic worlds of Pope, mythological traditions (like the Gothic worlds of later periods) offer to literature a sanctioned symbolic domain for the fabrication of 'another scene' of extremity, exorbitance and excess.

## Blake and the Oedipal impasse

The first poem I am concerned with is Blake's visionary poem from the Rossetti Manuscript, 'I saw a chapel all of gold'. Its central image of the chapel is a reworking of material from a simpler poem from the *Songs of Experience*, 'The Garden of Love', which serves as a useful approach to it. Both poems stage a fantasy of confrontation between a desiring subject (implicitly, then explicitly, male) and the institutions of patriarchal law with its exclusions and repressions.

In the earlier poem an allegory of sexual repression is represented by the building of a chapel surrounded by graves in the midst of the childhood Garden of Love 'where I used to play on the green'. The chapel is signalled as the representative of organized religion through its bearing the standard formula of prohibition from the Ten Commandments: '"Thou shalt not" writ over the door'. The theme of repression, the binding of energy and desire, is part of Blake's critique of reason and traditional moral codes in *The Marriage of Heaven and Hell*. Repression is identified clearly with the Church and its agents in the poem's paralysed conclusion:

> And priests in black gowns were walking their rounds,
> And binding with briars my joys and desires.[19]

The passivity of the speaker/seer before this vision is not without a certain implication of him in the scene. Explicitly it is '*my* joys and desires' that are being bound by the priests. Implicitly his apparently passive process of turning and viewing is caught up in the deathly transformation of the garden. The effect might be summed up by a line from *The Mental Traveller* as 'the eye viewing alters all', for the garden scene turns from flowers to graves even as he turns to view it. It is a momentary effect that hints at some unspecified complicity between the visionary and his vision. It disturbs the relatively clearcut allegory of institutionalized repression seen as over there and at a distance.

A further counter-suggestion concerns the characterization of the chapel – 'and the gates of this Chapel were shut'. The shut gates seem at first to enforce the prohibition 'Thou shalt not' and the binding of joys and desires. However the chapel itself, along with the joys and desires, seems to be under prohibition. This might imply that another state of the chapel – its doors open – could be compatible with the unbinding of joys and desires.

Both the hinted implication of the visionary in the destructive transformations of his vision, and an alternative significance of the chapel, its opening to joys and desires, are important for Blake's poetic reworking of the scenario of repression. The later poem begins by making the chapel explicitly the object of prohibition:

> I saw a Chapel all of gold
> That none did dare to enter in,
> And many weeping stood without,
> Weeping, mourning, worshipping.
>
> I saw a Serpent rise between
> The white pillars of the door,
> And he forc'd and forc'd and forc'd;
> Down the golden hinges tore,
>
> And along the pavement sweet,
> Set with pearls and rubies bright,
> All his shining length he drew,
> Till upon the altar white
>
> Vomiting his poison out
> On the Bread and on the Wine.
> So I turn'd into a sty,
> And laid me down among the swine.[20]

The poem's initial situation is one of exclusion: the 'Chapel all of gold' is precious but under some unspecified taboo – 'none did *dare* to enter in'.

The result is a group, presumably a potential congregation, who would, if they dared to, enter in, but who are excluded and grieving. Their attitude is reverential, 'mourning, worshipping', from afar or without, rather than aggressive or rebellious.

Aggression or rebellion is figured by the serpent who rises up as if in response to the situation of the first stanza. The serpent brings with it conventional echoes of Genesis and the myth of the Fall, but these are displaced, or at least disputed, by its unserpentlike energy of attack – 'forc'd and forc'd and forc'd' – and the object of attack, 'the golden hinges' and so by metonymic extension the doors that shut out and exclude the weeping multitude of the first stanza. In line with Blake's rewriting of the myth of the Fall and his valorization of Satan as an incandescent figure of energy and desire, 'none other than he who dwells in flaming fire',[21] the serpent might be read as a liberating force, opening out the chapel to the excluded. This is reinforced in the third stanza where the serpent's entry into the chapel is dwelt on in a stage by stage progress – 'and along the pavement . . . till upon the altar' – with a lyrical, celebratory note: 'all his shining length he drew . . .' This is the central action and object of the stanza's attention. The word 'shining' associates the serpent with the chapel 'all of gold' and the pavement 'set with pearls and rubies bright'. It is placed midpoint in the extended sentence that constitutes the main portion of the poem, overspilling the stanza boundaries. The tight grammatical closure characteristic of the sharply delineated stanza form of Blake's songs is opened out. An unusually long, accumulating syntactical movement, snakes its way, so to speak, from stanza to stanza, as if designed to exhibit and draw out for the reader's regard 'all his shining length.'

The rhythmic impetus of the serpent's forward movement is carried over across the stanza break, transgressing the poem's formal divisions, to be released violently in the first word of the final stanza:

> Vomiting his poison out
> On the Bread and on the Wine.
> So I turn'd into a sty,
> And laid me down among the swine.

There is a sudden reversal of the serpent's apparent significance, as what seemed to be a liberating force, as radiant as the chapel it opens up, climaxes in an act of violation. The altar with its bread and wine might remind us of the excluded worshippers whose entry in the shining serpent seemed to make possible. Instead of an act of communal eating and drinking, a sacred, sacramental meal, there is vomiting and poison. The final act of the serpent produces an effect of shock, even of trauma, as the hitherto minimally present speaker/seer of the vision responds with an act of self-loathing and self-disgust. The complicity of visionary and vision is here more strongly marked. The serpent's action produces self-disgust in the speaker, a placing of himself in the sty and among swine. The emblematic status of swine in the gospels, contrasting the bestial and the precious – not casting one's pearls before swine – suggesting demonic possession – the Gadarene swine – are all potentially in play. The connection between the serpent's act and the speaker's act is marked syntactically, 'so I turn'd into a sty', as if there were an unstated even unconscious identification between serpent and speaker. This is borne out by the syntactical oddity of the final stanza. Normal sentence construction requires something like:

> Till upon the altar white
> *He vomited* his poison out

Blake's preference for present participial verbs – 'vomiting' – defers grammatical closure once again, keeps the sequence mobile and open, requiring a further main verb to complete it. The effect of closure and conclusion comes in the final two lines with '*So* I turn'd . . .'. There is a hiatus, however, caused by the change of person in the main verb, from 'he' to 'I', when it does come. The sentence structure when picked out goes: 'all his shining length he drew/till . . . Vomiting . . . I turn'd into a sty . . .'. Out of the sequence of images and actions enacted by the serpent, and in the wake of its sudden reversal of value, a subject position is crystallized and assumed by the anonymous speaker. 'I' is precipitated and held to a state and a judgement. The work of fantasy bears the mark of the primary processes that characterize Freud's account of the dream-work, where single unconscious elements find multiple representatives in the manifest content, and the dreamer's identity is dispersed through agents and delegates, in the acting out of unacknowledged and prohibited impulses.

The poem seems to begin as an allegory of repression and liberation along the lines of 'The Garden of Love', transforming that poem's paralysed passivity into energetic rebellion. Something goes unaccountably wrong and the act of liberation capsizes into an act of violation. Part of the problem lies in the cultural coding of rebellious desire as phallic, aggressive, penetrating. The very configuration that seems to indicate the rebellious, phallic nature of the serpent, rising up between the white pillars of the door, also makes the serpent's attack – 'and he forc'd and forc'd and forc'd' – look uncomfortably like a rape. Alternative versions of certain lines record a struggle to establish the image of the shining serpent as positive and liberating by directing its violence away from the chapel as object of desire:

> And he forc'd and forc'd and forc'd
> Till he broke the pearly door.[22]

The change from 'pearly door' to 'golden hinges' can be read as an attempt to exclude connotations of beauty, delicacy, purity, even fleshliness, virginity under attack, and to refocus the aggression on the decidedly unfleshly 'golden hinges', with their connotations of mechanism, barriers, prohibition. However, ambivalence centres on more than the chapel as representation both of repression and the object of desire. The nature of the serpent and its energies is also at stake. An alternative version of another line reads: 'all his slimy length he drew'.[23] In such a sequence – breaking down the pearly door, slimy length – the climactic act of violation, 'vomiting his poison out', comes as no surprise. What we have is a text which stages a symbolic scene whose possible meanings are deeply contradictory.

The serpent as figure of rebellious desire is positioned within an Oedipal dynamic of repression, exclusion and answering violence. This Oedipal positioning of the serpent as phallic rebel is a reworking of the primal fantasy of father and son rivalry, the term of whose relation is castration. Its effect, however, is to reproduce within the poem the primal scene or rape itself as a relation to the object of desire. One primal fantasy entails another, as if the very constitution of the Oedipal rebel as phallic through rivalry with the law and its prohibitions, installs him in the place of the phallic father *vis-à-vis* the mother. Such a blighting recognition closes the longer version of 'Infant Sorrow', also from the Rossetti Manuscript:

vii

> I beheld the Priest by night;
> He embraced my Myrtle bright:
> I beheld the Priest by day,
> Where beneath my vines he lay.

viii

> Like a serpent in the day
> Underneath my vines he lay:
> Like a serpent in the night
> He embraced my Myrtle bright.

ix

> So I smote him, and his gore
> Stain'd the roots my Myrtle bore;
> But the time of youth is fled,
> And grey hairs are on my head.[24]

The jealous infant smites the phallic, serpentine priest/father and, ageing instantaneously, seems in effect to become the very figure he strikes down. Caught up in such a dynamic, Oedipal rebels are no liberators.

Where 'Infant Sorrow' lucidly addresses the impasse of Oedipal rivalry and struggle, the present poem presses further the implications for the object of desire. Where the myrtle with its promises of 'delight', both proscribed and possessed by the priest/father, is stained with the gore of parricidal violence, here the chapel is itself the object of violation. Despite Blake's revisions, of 'pearly door' to 'golden hinges', the ambivalence of the chapel persists both as object of desired entry and as obstacle and barrier. The violence generated in one scenario (father/son/castration) appears to be discharged within another (father/mother/rape), and that violence is bound up with 'castration' and its effects.

Castration does not appear as such in the poem and Lacan's argument seems to be that its effects are only ever registered in displaced or condensed symbolic form. The poem's phallic violence, 'forc'd and forc'd and forc'd', and violation, 'vomiting his poison out', are instances of symbolic surplus or excess. Just as serpents don't smash their way through doors unless caught up in an Oedipal economy as representatives of the phallus, so also they spit their poison out rather than vomit it. The symbolic overdetermination that substitutes 'vomiting' for 'spitting' makes it an affair of the stomach. The intensification of appetite as desire and in a hostile relation to its object suggests the operation of vengeful oral fantasies: to *vomit* poison one must first have swallowed it. Vomiting here is an act of aggression against that precious and prohibited place which once entered offers the satisfaction of appetite, the bread and wine. The recasting of pre-Oedipal oral fantasies centring on the desired mother into the religious discourse of Christian myth, chapel/altar/bread and wine, reverses the desired object into poison.

Bread and wine in the Christian sacramental tradition are symbols of flesh and blood, flesh and blood that can be symbolically consumed only because it has first been sacrificed. The flesh and blood in question is that of the Son, and the sacramental meal with its *mise-en-scène* of altar and chapel is a symbolic repetition of the sacrifice of the Son on the cross to appease the anger of the Father ('Die he or Justice must', *Paradise Lost*, Book III, l.210).[25] The dominant Pauline interpretation of the crucifixion is precisely in terms of the discharge of the debt incurred by the primal crime against the Father. The sacrifice of the Son's flesh and blood is a theological/mythic equivalent to the figure of castration as submission to the law of the father.[26] At the heart of the oral fantasy and its desired object, through its transposition into the symbolic complex of altar/ sacrificial meal specific to Christianity, lurks the threat of castration, the son's submission in blood to the law of the father. No wonder the Oedipal serpent/rebel vomits, both poisoned and poisoning.

The violence of that climax, gagging on castration, generated within the father/son relation, is discharged as I have argued through a slide of meaning round the chapel symbol, against the maternal object of desire in a re-enactment of the primal scene of forcible entry and violation. After such a climactic defilement of the mother's image in the Oedipal struggle, the speaker's final desolating gesture places himself, like the Prodigal Son he has become, among swine.

This overtaking of the shining serpent's apparent promise of liberation in Blake's poem by that set of unconscious symbolic determinations, the primal fantasies, suggests that the relation to the symbolic father and his law, figured in the dramas of castration, cannot be simply repudiated or evaded. It lies in wait, built into the very terms chapel/altar/bread and wine, in which the poem stages desire.

## Barret Browning: castration and the music of *jouissance*

Elizabeth Barrett Browning's 'A Musical Instrument' figures directly a sadistic, phallic figure and again the staging of desire through narrative and symbolic setting brings in train reversals and surprises that overtake the poetic project.

The poem appears to elaborate more directly the features of the primal scene. Its interest is less in this playing out of a common sado-masochistic scenario, than in the ways it positions its speaker and solicits readerly identifications, and the oscillations and disavowals that mark them.

I

What was he doing, the great god Pan,
   Down in the reeds by the river?
Spreading ruin and scattering ban,
Splashing and paddling with hoofs of a goat,
And breaking the golden lilies afloat
   With the dragon-fly on the river.

II

He tore out a reed, the great god Pan,
   From the deep cool bed of the river:
The limpid water turbidly ran,
And the broken lilies a-dying lay,
And the dragon-fly had fled away,
   Ere he brought it out of the river.

III

High on the shore sate the great god Pan,
   While turbidly flowed the river;

And hacked and hewed as a great god can,
With his hard bleak steel at the patient reed,
Till there was not a sign of a leaf indeed
    To prove it fresh from the river.

### IV

He cut it short, did the great god Pan
    (How tall it stood in the river!),
Then drew the pith, like the heart of a man,
Steadily from the outside ring,
And notched the poor dry empty thing
    In holes, as he sate by the river.

### V

'This is the way,' laughed the great god Pan
    (Laughed while he sate by the river),
'The only way, since gods began
To make sweet music, they could succeed.'
Then, dropping his mouth to a hole in the reed,
    He blew in power by the river.

### VI

Sweet, sweet, sweet, O Pan!
    Piercing sweet by the river!
Blinding sweet, O great god Pan!
The sun on the hill forgot to die,
And the lilies revived, and the dragon-fly
    Came back to dream on the river.

### VII

Yet half a beast is the great god Pan,
    To laugh as he sits by the river,
Making a poet out of a man:
The true gods sigh for the cost and pain, –
For the reed which grows nevermore again
    As a reed with the reeds in the river.[27]

    The poem appears to offer itself as an allegory of making, of the cost and pain attendant on the uprooting and transformation of the natural into the man-made, the human artifact. The making over of the reed into the pipe is offered as a figure of the making of a poet – 'making a poet out of a man'. The intensely invested details of the narrative are explicitly thematized, given a retrospective meaning and point, one might almost say a moral, in the final stanza. However, its sudden appearance at the close, and certain problems with its reference to the poetic details it is meant to organize, might lead one to think of its function in the economy of the poem, along the lines of Freud's 'secondary revision'.[28]

Freud describes the process of secondary revision as one of filling in the gaps of the dream-structure with shreds and patches, a reworking of the distorted results of the dreamwork, which has displaced and disguised the repressed dream-thoughts, but a reworking from the viewpoint of waking intelligibility and coherence. He sees it as a continuation of the activity of the psychical censor that has imposed censorship and disguise on the dream-thoughts in the first place, a continuation that reorders and renders acceptable the disproportion and oddity of the dream products. The allegory of 'making a poet out of a man' is offered as a thematic key to the symbolic figures and actions of the poem which, like the last-minute tidying of secondary revision, appears to give a retrospective and familiar point to the intensities and excesses of the poem's fantasy. Initially there might seem a loose plausibility about the allegory, for the figure of Pan as maker of pipes and music readily lends itself to being read as a figure of the artist. For the allegory to work, however, it is the reed being turned into the musical instrument that must be taken as the figure for the man made over into the poet. Who or what, then, is Pan? What of the intensity of interest that makes Pan and Pan's activities so central to the poem?

Mythologically, Pan as satyr, half goat and half god, is associated with brutality, even cruelty, and with lust. His desire and pursuit of the nymph Syrinx led to her tranformation into a reed in her desperate attempt to escape him, just as Daphne turned into a laurel in her similar flight from Apollo's attentions. It is Marvell who comes to mind with his witty inversion of the logic of the event:

> Apollo hunted Daphne so,
> Only that She might Laurel grow.
> And Pan did after Syrinx speed,
> Not as a Nymph, but for a Reed.[29]

The nymph/reed equivalence as objects of Pan's erotic interest are established in the poetic tradition from at least Ovid onwards. Taken as an allegory of the making of the artist, one is left with the problem that all the vigorous and brutal activities of pipe and music-making belong to Pan, and the reed is reduced to being a passive and gutted instrument, the product of Pan's mastery and power. This would be a puzzling account of the artist, uncharacteristic both of Barrett Browning herself and of the literary ideology of Romanticism within which she worked. It leaves the figure of Pan unaccounted for (if the reed/pipe is the man/poet, who is Pan?), and especially the Pan/reed/nymph complex as established in poetic mythology.

The river scene is central to the structure of the poem, which begins with its devastation and returns to it, complete with its cluster of lilies and dragonfly, for the climax of power and pleasure in the penultimate stanza. Pan is established as the dominant figure at the beginning of each stanza by the same balladlike repetitions that allude throughout to the river:

> What was he doing, the great god Pan,
> Down in the reeds by the river ? . . .

> Yet half a beast is the great god Pan,
> To laugh as he sits by the river, . . .

Each stanza, opening and closing, takes the river as a point of reference, not just the first two where the river is the object and scene of Pan's violence. The river is the object of a pervasive lyrical nostalgia through bracketed asides – '(How tall it stood in the river!)' – and at the close where we are told that, the true gods sigh, for the reed's lost state of reedhood:

> For the reed which grows nevermore again
> As a reed with the reeds in the river.

The significance of the reed/river scene in the poem's unconscious fantasy can be partly indicated by previous poetic workings of the Pan myth with its reed/nymph equivalence. This can be further explored by considering a similar image complex in another poem of Barrett Browning's 'The Romance of the Swan's Nest'.[30] This takes the form of a young girl's day-dream. Sitting down by the riverside and dipping her feet into the water, little Ellie fantasizes a perfect lover in the form of an idealized knight, equipped with a lute that 'shall strike ladies into trouble,/As his sword strikes men to death'. She sets him a series of morally testing tasks which she imagines herself as viewing from a high mountain. The final reward she imagines for him, when he comes to claim her hand, sounds through the poem as a quasi-refrain: 'Unto *him* I will discover/That swan's nest among the reeds.' The implication of the swan's nest image is so pointed, given its context, yet so decently veiled, that it might seem a case of indirect rather than unconscious representation. This is confirmed by the poem's close where little Ellie goes home the long way round in order to visit the swan's nest, only to find that 'the wild swan had deserted,/And a rat had gnawed the reeds.' The poem closes knowingly with a claim not to know whether Ellie ever found her perfect lover, only that she could never show him 'that swan's nest among the reeds'. The poem's air of knowingness is enforced by the epigraph that tells us that dreams and phantoms must give way to sharp realities.

The swan/lover/knight equivalence and the swan's nest as erotic reward and object of desire are fairly explicit in 'The Romance'. In 'A Musical Instrument' Pan clearly has affinities as much with the rat and its 'sharp reality' of violation as with the idealized phallic knight/swan. The 'swan's nest among the reeds' with its suggestion of the female body reappears in the idyllic scene of riverside, reeds, golden lilies and 'the deep cool bed of the river'. The poem's opening lines put these two symbolic complexes together and in a rush of excited curiosity formulates the classic childish question:

> What was he doing, the great god Pan,
> Down in the reeds by the river?

The answer to this leading question, laden with violence and ambivalent identification, is so thoroughly repressed that it appears only in disguised and distorted form. The reed/nymph connection is banished entirely from the poem's manifest content, as is any indication that the poem's preoccupations, like 'The Romance of the Swan's Nest', might be with desire and the terms of its fulfilment or disappointment.

The first two stanzas lay considerable emphasis on Pan's disruption of the idyllic river scene and his gratuitous destruction is in excess of any effort required to extract a single reed. The violence goes with the note of lyrical regret and pathos:

> The limpid water turbidly ran,
> And the broken lilies a-dying lay, . . .

In the following stanzas, however, the same excessive violence and the lyrical pathos which suggests sympathetic identification with reed and river scene are countered by a different note.

The adulatory ballad formula – 'the great god Pan' – develops into a tone close to overt admiration for a figure presented as exalted and masterful:

> High on the shore sate the great god Pan, . . .
> And hacked and hewed as a great god can, . . .

It is a highly unstable tone and attitude that passes quickly back into lyrical empathy for 'the patient reed' and nostalgia for its watery origins:

> Till there was not a sign of a leaf indeed
> To prove it fresh from the river.

Like Blake's serpent whose entry into the chapel and vomiting of poison are moments of symbolic surplus, Pan's hacking and hewing 'with his hard bleak steel' is in overdetermined excess of the operations necessary for trimming and hollowing a reed.

The significance of this overkill can be seen when the hacking and hewing give way to the operation of gutting the reed and the human analogy latent in the phrase, 'the patient reed', becomes explicit:

> Then drew the pith, like the heart of a man,
> Steadily from the outside ring,
> And notched the poor dry empty thing
> In holes, as he sate by the river.

The cutting and gutting of the reed, like that of a human heart, with its image of sadistically inflicted loss and mutilation, bring us up against an unconscious fantasy of castration. It separates the reed irrevocably from its primal state or origin. What is notable is that while the poem maintains a notional sympathy for the reed, yet in its description of the reed's reduced state, 'the poor dry empty thing', it is hard to distinguish pity from contempt. The poem's revisionary allegory of the making of a poet seems at its most inappropriate and implausible at this point.

Where Romantic expressivism locates the heart as source of feeling and origin of poetry, the making of the pipe requires the cutting out of the reed's pith or 'heart'. Within such an allegory the figure of Pan remains unspecified, yet throughout the poem's middle stanzas the swinging insouciant rhythm and balladlike repetitions make it impossible to distinguish the sadistic glee of Pan laughing and boasting from the sadistic glee with which he is envisaged and his operations acted out. Despite its nominal sympathy with the reed, the poetically dominant identification, through tone, rhythm and phrasing, is with Pan. Pan's gloating explanation, 'This is the way . . ./The only way . . ./To make sweet music', seems to be insisting on the symbolic violence of the previous stanzas, and the submission to castration it figures, as the necessary condition for the climax it moves towards.

It is striking that the identification with Pan as a castrating, phallic figure is combined with the positioning of the reed not only as castrated but as the necessary instrument of Pan's music. As castrated the reed is the object of contempt and a fairly notional pity, as instrument of Pan's music the reed becomes through a rapid oscillation the object of intense identification:

> Then, dropping his mouth to the hole in the reed,
> He blew in power by the river.

> Sweet, sweet, sweet, O Pan!
> Piercing sweet by the river!
> Blinding sweet, O great god Pan!
> The sun on the hill forgot to die,
> And the lilies revived, and the dragon-fly
> Came back to dream on the river.

If psychoanalytically the reed figures the feminine position in relation to the phallic term, where then does the voice speak from that enunciates the moment of climax? In terms of the formal structure of discourse it is the voice of the anonymous speaker/seer of the poem's action, the overhearer of Pan's music. This evades, however, the question of the speaker's relation to what figures in the discourse, of where the speaker is speaking from. The speaker addresses rather than describes – 'O Pan' – and does so in ecstatic outcry from a *jouissance* that offers itself as testimony to Pan's power, the vindication of his brutal transformation, and the truth of his boast, 'This is the way . . ./The only way . . ./To make sweet music'. At no point in the poem has even a minimal self-reference marked out or held the speaker's position as a distinct place comparable to the 'I' of Blake's poem. Consequently the sudden shift, in Benveniste's terms, from *histoire* to *discours*, from impersonal narration to direct address, together with those telltale gerunds, '*Piercing* sweet . . . *Blinding* sweet . . .', elides the position of the speaker and the reed. Pierced and blinded alike by the power of Pan, the poem speaks the *jouissance* of the reed, for three brief lines.

The final three lines of the stanza move back into *histoire*, impersonal narration, with a note of detached, even comic hyperbole: 'The sun on the hill forgot to die'. This entranced or arrested moment, time stopped, the lilies revived, the return of the dragonfly and its *dream* on the river, recapitulates the original river scene from the first stanza. Within the moment of phallic *jouissance* is the revival of the earlier scene, of the infantile fantasy of the mother, the pre-Oedipal 'dream on the river'.

One could read the apparent rejection of Pan in the final stanza simply as part of the poem's process of disavowal and secondary revision which I began by discussing. The turn against and away from Pan, 'Yet half a beast is the great god Pan,/To laugh . . .', produces out of nowhere the covering theme in terms of which we are invited to make retrospective sense of the poem's fantasy. The reed is a man, the pipe a poet, the question of difference and desire effaced. One might be tempted to read the close as mere disavowal but it is part of a larger contrast, for Pan is a beast to laugh while 'The true gods sigh for the cost and pain'. The revival of the river scene is not a simple return. What it foregrounds finally in the poem is the sense of loss – 'the cost and pain' – and the unassuaged nostalgia of a fantasy of *in*differentiation:

> For the reed which grows nevermore again
> As a reed with the reeds in the river.

My argument has been that 'A Musical Instrument' reworks the primal fantasies of castration and seduction as they bear on the construction of the feminine position as conceived within psychoanalytic theory. If these fantasies mark out a violently polarized pair of symbolic positions, phallic/castrated, yet the identifications and desires inscribed by the poetic discourse play across those positions in an oscillating and unstable way. Identifications and desires appear as a movement across and against that symbolic construction of difference as mastery and submission. If the overt or dominant identifications, tonally and rhythmically, are slavish, i.e. with the master, it is a mastery whose climax of piercing and blinding is a sweetness located elsewhere, in another subject and another scene; a sweetness figured as a restored 'dream on the river', the revival of a scene even earlier than that classically nominated as 'primal'.

In his enigmatic meditation on feminine *jouissance* in *Encore* Lacan asserts the impossibility of The Woman as a universal, a claim to essence, because 'of her essence she is not all'. Writing this contradictory claim as ~~The~~ Woman, under erasure, Lacan designates it *as* a fantasy, the representation of a lack (castration), within the phallocentric economy of the symbolic order and its language. Both necessary and impossible, 'there is woman only as excluded by the nature of things which is the nature of words'. This necessary and negative relation to language thus becomes the basis for Lacan's further claim that 'it is precisely that in being not all, she has, in relation to what the phallic function has of *jouissance*, a supplementary *jouissance* . . . a *jouissance* beyond the phallus'.[31] This oscillation from a 'not all' to a 'beyond' (*en plus*, something more) in relation to the phallus characterizes the poem's movement towards its *nachträglich* 'dream on the river'. If the gutting of the reed signifies castration, its remaking as the pan-pipe signifies the construction of woman-as-phallus. In Lacan's dialectic of having and being, she cannot *have* the phallus but must *be* the-phallus-for-the-man. As phallus the pan-pipe becomes the site of a *jouissance* which in the movement from stanza V ('He blew in power by the river') to stanza VI (the 'dream on the river') breaks elsewhere, beyond the phallic function.

A number of unanswered questions remain after such a reading. What after all is the *place of the poet* in such a system of figures? What would be the making of a poet out of a woman, especially the woman who made the poem and who is elided in the figurative leap from 'reed' to 'man'? Is such an elision the condition of the poem's regressive undoing of the moment of mastery, the articulation of cost and pain, of an origin that refuses to be effaced? Does the poetic articulation of the fantasy of ~~The~~ Woman, *as* phallic construction but *from* the woman's position (its reverse), of woman as desiring subject *beyond* the phallic terrain of the primal fantasies, require the cancellation of woman as writing subject (making a poet out of the woman)? Perhaps the poem's most 'blinded' question is that of the relation of feminine *jouissance* to writing.

## Dickinson: the pearls and perils of seduction

Elizabeth Barrett Browning's poem is marked by repression and divided against itself, not incidentally but as the very condition of its utterance, like the music whose 'cost' is blinding. Emily Dickinson's poem also addresses itself to questions of desire and identity through the detour of symbolic representation. It reworks the primal fantasy of seduction in a way that might challenge the claim made by Lacanian theory of an intrinsic connection between metaphor, symbolic substitution, even representation as such, and repression.

> I started Early – Took my Dog –
> And visited the Sea –
> The Mermaids in the Basement
> Came out to look at me –
>
> And Frigates – in the Upper Floor
> Extended Hempen Hands –
> Presuming Me to be a Mouse –
> Aground – upon the Sands –
>
> But no Man moved Me – till the Tide
> Went past my simple Shoe –
> And past my Apron – and my Belt
> And past my Bodice – too –
>
> And made as He would eat me up –
> As wholly as a Dew
> Upon a Dandelion's Sleeve –
> and then – I started – too –
>
> And He – He followed – close behind –
> I felt His Silver Heel
> Upon my Ankle – Then my Shoes
> Would overflow with Pearl –
>
> Until We met the Solid Town –
> No One He seemed to know –
> And bowing – with a Mighty look –
> At me – The Sea withdrew –[32]

I don't wish to attribute a simple transparency to the poem's symbolic processes, a secure self-consciousness or self-presence in whose service those processes function. The structural cleavage between the subject of the utterance and the subject of enunciation is not bridged or mastered by any simple myth of Wordsworthian overflow or expressiveness. The brisk colloquial opening gesture, 'I started Early – Took my Dog –', might seem to lay claim to autobiographical veracity, a Huck Finn-ish equivalent of 'I wandered lonely as a cloud', but the poem's fantastical whimsical scene displaces and overtakes the speaker with a series of surprises. The poem is concerned with the determination of self, even self-determination, but not through the idealist fiction of an act of pure will. If the maidenly speaker in some sense chooses or makes herself, it is, in a famous formula, in circumstances and out of materials not of her own choosing. The figuring of self in the poem takes an unexpected turn in the first stanza when the businesslike seaside visitor becomes not the secure subject of the look, but the object of the gaze, initiative and presumption of others:

> I started Early – Took my Dog –
> And visited the Sea –
> The Mermaids in the Basement
> Came out to look at me –
>
> And Frigates – in the Upper Floor
> Extended Hempen Hands –
> Presuming Me to be a Mouse –
> Aground – upon the Sands –

This reversal, whereby 'I' as a visitor coming to look finds herself the spectacle, coincides with the superimposition of house on sea, one startling effect of which is to cross-section the sea, setting up frigates and mermaids, upper floor and basement, in an upstairs/downstairs opposition. This opposition involves a positioning of masculine and feminine. If the feminine is a combination of submarine mystery (mermaids) and domestic service (maids in basements), the second stanza presents a wittily condensed image of friendly male condescension and patronage: the hempen hands are masculine, both metonymically (sailors' hands) and metaphorically (coarse and brown). Extended in friendly, helpful persuasion, they offer the speaker an image of herself, 'a Mouse –/Aground – upon the Sands –', in need of rescue, timidly waiting to be taken on board, which in a wry, meticulous way the speaker registers as indeed 'presuming'. Impervious to the frigates, solicitous and soliciting from their superior position in the upper floor, the speaker is finally 'moved' by a rising tide of erotic encroachment. The poem profiles her from her 'simple Shoe' upwards even as the tide threatens to engulf her inch by inch.

> But no Man moved Me – till the Tide
> Went past my simple Shoe –
> And past my Apron – and my Belt
> And past my Bodice – too –

> And made as He would eat me up –
> As wholly as a Dew
> Upon a Dandelion's Sleeve –
> And then – I started – too –

It is possible to recognize the figure of gentlewomanly composure and self-containment from other Dickinson poems, where the emblems of maidenly propriety are deployed against forces that have the power to threaten or unmake identity:

> Because I could not stop for Death –
> He kindly stopped for me –
> The Carriage held but just Ourselves –
> And Immortality . . .
>
> Or rather – He passed Us –
> The Dews drew quivering and chill –
> For only Gossamer, my Gown –
> My Tippet – only Tulle –[33]

In both poems the subject's relation to death or sexuality is figured in two ways: as an encounter between the maidenly speaker and a mysteriously overbearing gentleman; and as the destructive operation of natural forces on the stylized emblems of femininity. The exposure of gown and tippet, of gossamer and tulle to the deathly chill dews is comparable to the threat of the engulfing tide in the fourth stanza, where the dew image is not the carrier of a threat but an exquisite accessory on the flower/lady's sleeve, itself in danger of being dissolved and swallowed up by the tide. The tide accumulates a number of connotations and as Cora Kaplan has argued 'it is nature, lover, rapist, gentleman'.[34] The moment of starting as from a trance is provoked by recoil from the threat of being devoured. A loss of self, of dew in the ocean, is the consequence of allowing oneself to become the object of the other's appetite or desire. Where the unavoidable effects of mortality are figured in an ironic fiction of 'Civility', 'Because I could not stop for Death –/He kindly stopped for me, –' here a measure of choice is possible, even if only strategic retreat, in negotiating sexual positioning.

> But no Man moved Me – till the Tide
> Went past my simple Shoe –

'Moved' might seem to have the implication of flight or retreat in the light of the final stanzas, where previously far from being 'aground' she has stood her ground. However, the tide isn't simply a figure of the other's desire, encroaching and devouring though it is. 'Moved' also suggests that, unlike the solicitations of the frigates that left her unmoved, this 'man' does move her own desire. The item-by-item encroachment has a repetitive, quasi-hypnotic excitement, 'And past my Apron – and my Belt/And past my Bodice – too –, even as it delineates her as a spectacle for herself, the spectacle of her own desirability, exquisite, deliquescent, edible.

> And He – He followed – close behind –
> I felt His Silver Heel
> Upon my Ankle – Then my Shoes
> Would overflow with Pearl –
>
> Until We met the Solid Town –
> No One He seemed to know –
> And bowing – with a Mighty look –
> At me – The Sea withdrew –

The startling, overtaken, quasi-fetishistic contact 'close behind' of silver heel on ankle and the exotic 'overflow' it produces establishes the sea as a seductive domain of submarine transformations. Like the 'full fathom five' of Ariel's Song in *The Tempest* it is a moment of 'sea change/Into something rich and strange'. The fear of loss in the previous stanza is succeeded by a magical transformation of those simple shoes, the emblems of the speaker's propriety and fixity. Those are pearls that were her shoes. Like the double value of the rising tide as a figure of the feelings of both self and other, the pearl is both the sea-foam breaking over the feet of the averted, departing speaker on the sea-shore and an aroused, erotic overflow in response to the touch of the silver heel.

The poem ends with the safety of 'the Solid Town' as opposed to the sea's dissolution and transformation. In contrast to the Death poem, the fiction of 'Civility' here, a courteous encounter, suggests a capitulation of the threatening forces and the speaker's escape.

> And bowing – with a Mighty look –
> At me – The Sea withdrew –

However the 'Mighty look' contains a continuing menace, not just of an outmanoeuvred but still powerful force, but of a 'look – /At me'. The speaker is still the object of that attention. Between 'the Solid Town' and the 'Mighty look' the poem gives the speaker no more precise or distinct a localization, on the margins. The poem appears to stage a moment of choice, of seduction and refusal, a disengagement from the networks of desire and desirability which are not simply excluded, disavowed or repudiated. The poem's symbolic processes do not function as the exclusion/return of the repressed. The rising tide and the overflow of pearl open up a field of experience where self and other are overlaid and inextricable. It is from a fascinated acknowledgement of the inextricability of loss and transformation that the speaker's fragile and precarious self-retrieval and self-conservation begins. She is neither outside the sexual domain of desire and its sea-change nor has she succumbed to it, securely positioned. Her identity is at once implicated, responsive to the pressure of its solicitations, but at one remove, marginal, negotiating between the devil and the deep blue sea.

## Poetry and the question of gender

All three poems rework fantasies of seduction, castration and rape and in doing so they restage the central scenarios of what psychoanalytic theory calls 'primal fantasy'. These are designated by Freud as philogenetic schemata, historical precipitates of the development of civilization, and by Laplanche and Pontalis as a pre-subjective structure of signifiers that constitute a symbolic order as conceptualized by Lévi-Strauss and Lacan. Certainly something like a combinatory of binary oppositions, phallic/castrated, domination/submission, appears to map relations of power on to gender positions. Yet Freud's account of primal fantasy and the Oedipus complex presents certain resistances to any smooth assimilation to classic structuralist notions of code or combinatory. Laplanche and Pontalis indicate this when they warn that 'it is less easy to assimilate it [the Oedipus complex] to a language system than to the complexities of a particular speech' (p.31, n. 34). With characteristics both of *parole* and of *langue* (see note 15), the primal fantasies institute one set of meanings and relationships and exclude others (pre-Oedipal, matrocentric and dyadic relations). Through them 'the subject is, admittedly, located in a structure of interrelationship, but the latter is transmitted by the parental unconscious' (p.31, n. 34). Certain combinations do repetitively occur that assimilate masculine/phallic/dominant in what Derrida calls a 'violent hierarchy'[35] over feminine/castrated/submissive. Within psychoanalytic theory, however, gender relations are not inscribed within power relations directly, but through a familial structure within which daughter, mother, son, are positioned in relation to the father through fantasies of seduction, rape and castration. Rather than three separate myths of origins, concerned with three separate enigmas, the primal fantasies all converge on relations to the father. All three are concerned with sexual difference as constructed within a patrocentric 'family legend' that organizes difference, identity and desire around the phallus, its possession, loss or reception.

Nevertheless, the three poems are not reducible to the scenarios they stage, whether singly or in combination; nor are they reducible to the normative gender positions that emerge from their incidence within the Oedipus complex as described by Freud. I have indicated that Laplanche and Pontalis themselves insist on the 'de-subjectivized', unpredictable subject-positioning in particular productions of the primal fantasies. In her discussion of psychoanalytic concepts of fantasy in relation to film criticism, Elizabeth Cowie has argued:

> What is interesting in the analysis of *Now Voyager* and *The Reckless Moment* is that, in different ways, in each film, the subject positions shift across the boundary of sexual difference, but do so in terms of sexual difference. Thus while subject positions are variable the terms of sexual difference are fixed. . . . While the terms of sexual difference are fixed, the places of characters and spectators in relation to these terms are not.[36]

Her arguments challenge the functionalist tendency of certain currents in recent film theory that have described the construction of the position of the spectator in normative gender terms that are relatively homogeneous and unproblematic. My reading of the three poems would bear out Cowie's account of subject mobility across a fixed terrain. For if Blake's 'shining serpent' reinscribes the phallocentric at the expense of a project of liberation, Barrett Browning's phallic Pan is displaced, his dominance momentarily breached by a *jouissance* that escapes beyond it. So also Dickinson's scenarios of looking and seduction close on a subject position of neither submission nor disavowal, but of strategic disengagement, provisional refusal. The trajectory of each poem passes through a series of often highly unstable investments, identifications, satisfactions and reversals, which cannot be unified as the 'expression' of a simple originary position (whether of the speaking/reading subject within the poem or the authorial biography that precedes it). Despite the fixed terms of sexual difference, the shifts and ruptures of enunciation and syntax, the symbolic densities of image and metaphor, are not reducible to the simple repetition of normative gender positions.

This raises the question as to whether gender is engaged, not by reduction to or coincidence with the fixed terms of difference, but by the *kinds* of mobility displayed. All three poems engage with imagined moments of phallic mastery or potency, yet close on positions of self-repudiation, disavowal or refusal. To what extent can these vicissitudes of poetic discourse be related to the fact that the first poem was written by a man and the other two by women? Certainly the readings I have given would seem to contradict or at least complicate the biographical 'myths' of revolutionary or rebellious emancipation in the case of Blake and Barrett Browning and of spinsterly self-repression in the case of Dickinson. To what extent can poetic mobility across the terms of gender be understood, not as an indeterminate 'free play', but as variously gendered strategies of complicity, resistance, fascination and elusion?

These questions cannot be answered by consideration of these three poems only, in the present context of analysis. It would require their reinsertion, to a greater extent than I have attempted here, into the authorial projects and oeuvres within which they were produced, and into the intertextual fields pertinent to each.

## Notes

1. J. Laplanche and J.-B. Pontalis, 'Fantasy and the origins of sexuality', *The International Journal of Psychoanalysis*, vol.49 (1968). References to this essay are given in brackets in the body of the text and are to its reprinting in the present volume.
2. S. Freud, 'The dissolution of the Oedipus complex' [1924], in *On Sexuality*, Pelican Freud Library (*PFL*), vol.7, (gen. ed. A. Richards, trans. A. and J. Strachey), Harmondsworth, Penguin, 1977–, p.315.
3. S. Freud, 'From the history of an infantile neurosis' [1918], in *Case Histories II*, *PFL*, vol.9.
4. S. Freud, 'The path to the formation of symptoms' [1916], Lecture 23, in *New Introductory Lectures on Psychoanalysis*, *PFL*, vol.2.
5. S. Freud [1918], op.cit., p.363.
6. ibid.
7. S. Freud, 'The sexual theories of children', in *On Sexuality*, *PFL*, vol.7.
8. J. Laplanche and J.-B. Pontalis p.24ff; J. Laplanche, *Life and Death in Psychoanalysis* (trans. and intro. by J. Mehlman), Baltimore, Johns Hopkins University Press, 1976.
9. S. Freud, *PFL*, vol.7, p.318.
10. S. Freud, 'The Ego and the Id', in *Metapsychology*, *PFL*, vol.11, p.368.
11. Francesco Orlando, *Toward a Freudian Theory of Literature*, Baltimore, Johns Hopkins University Press, 1978, p.138.
12. J. Laplanche, 'To situate sublimation', *October*, no.28 (spring 1984), p.8.
13. ibid., editorial note, p.7; J. Laplanche (1976), op.cit., p.127.
14. Shoshana Felman gives a psychoanalytically motivated account of reading-effects as the uncanny repetition and transference of seductive scenarios within the text in 'Turning the screw of interpretation', *Yale French Studies*, no.55/56 (1977).
15. In *The Political Unconscious* (London, Methuen, 1981), Fredric Jameson gives an account of different structural levels in the literary text that has close parallels with Laplanche and Pontalis. The primal fantasies would be something like a set of 'ideologemes' in Jameson's sense, 'an amphibious formation whose essential structural characteristic may be described as its possibility to manifest itself either as a pseudoidea ... or as a proto-narrative ... susceptible to both a conceptual description and a narrative manifestation all at once' (p.87). Jameson insists on the profoundly narrative character of the ideologeme and its necessary character as both binary opposition (*langue*) and libidinal fantasy (*parole*), virtually repeating Laplanche and Pontalis' double characterization: 'a kind of language and a symbolic sequence but loaded with elements of imagination; a structure but activated by contingent elements' (p.18).
16. V. Beechey, 'On patriarchy', *Feminist Review*, no.3 (1979); A. Kuhn and A. Wolpe (eds.), *Feminism and Materialism*, London, Routledge & Kegan Paul, 1978; R. Coward, *Patriarchal Precedents*, London, Routledge & Kegan Paul, 1983.
17. C. Belsey, 'The Romantic construction of the Unconscious', in F. Barker et al. (eds.) *1789: Reading, Writing, Revolution*, Essex Sociology of Literature Conference, 1982, pp.68 and 78.
18. C. Kaplan, 'The indefinite disclosed: Christina Rossetti and Emily Dickinson', in M. Jacobus (ed.), *Women Writing and Writing about Women*, London, Croom Helm, 1979, p.61.
19. W. Blake, *The Poetical Works of William Blake* (ed. John Sampson), 1913; rpt. Oxford, Oxford University Press, 1960, p.98.
20. ibid., p.110.

21. W. Blake, *The Marriage of Heaven and Hell*, in ibid., p.249.
22. ibid., p.110n.
23. W. Blake, *The Complete Poems*, (ed. Alicia Ostriker), Harmondsworth, Penguin, 1977, p.136.
24. W. Blake, *Poetical Works*, op.cit., p.116.
25. J. Milton, *The Poems of John Milton* (ed. Helen Darbishire), London, Oxford University Press, 1958, p.58.
26. Romans, chs.2–6.
27. E. Barrett Browning, *The Poetical Works of Elizabeth Barrett Browning* (ed. Henry Frowde), Oxford, Oxford University Press, 1911, p.570.
28. S. Freud, *The Interpretation of Dreams*, PFL, vol.4, ch.6.
29. 'The Garden' in *The Poems of Andrew Marvell* (ed. Hugh Macdonald), Muses Library, 1952; rpt. London, Routledge & Kegan Paul, 1963, p.52.
30. E. Barrett Browning, op.cit., p.214.
31. J. Mitchell and J. Rose, *Feminine Sexuality: J. Lacan and the École Freudienne*, London. Macmillan, 1982, pp.144–5.
32. E. Dickinson, *The Complete Poems of Emily Dickinson* (ed. T.H. Johnson), London, Faber & Faber, 1975, p.254.
33. ibid., p.350.
34. Kaplan, op.cit., p.76.
35. J. Derrida, *Positions* (trans. Alan Bass), Chicago, University of Chicago Press, 1981, p.41.
36. E. Cowie, 'Fantasia', *m/f*, no.9 (1984), p.102.

Cora Kaplan

# THE THORN BIRDS:
## fiction, fantasy, femininity

### Autobiography

Reading, dear reader, is a sexual and sexually divided practice, a fact I discovered in puberty when the erotic possibilities of an already compulsive activity began to appear. Narrative pleasure lost its innocence; adult fictions with their gripping scenarios of seduction and betrayal held me captive. I read with heart pounding and hands straying, reducing the respectable and the popular to a basic set of scenarios. *Peyton Place*, *Jane Eyre*, *Bleak House*, *Nana*: in my teens they were all the same to me, part of my sexual and emotional initiation, confirming, constructing my femininity, making plain the psychic form of sexual difference. In my bookish, left-wing but rather puritanical household I kept the secret of my reading practice pretty well. After all, it was precocious and respectable, was it not, to read all of Dickens at 13, to have a passion for Zola a year later? Only I knew that I read them for the sentimental and sexual hype. Physically I developed late; before I swelled, curved or bled I had, psychically speaking, read myself into womanhood. The difference in me as a *reader* was perhaps the first and most significant sign of the social and psychic implications of being female.

It was confirmed through an incident, when I was at least 14, when I read Margaret Mitchell's *Gone with the Wind*. Like many readers of this early blockbuster romance I read it in what seemed like a single session, unwilling to break engagement with the story to eat or to sleep. I was a fast reader, but it must have taken me two days; no skipping here for the romance takes up most of the text. My compulsion was observed for the book itself was not approved of. Pro-Southern and unashamedly racist, as well as without literary merit in my parents' eyes, it brought together a reactionary political narrative with a reactionary emotional one.

I finished the book late in the night and the ending left me in despair and near hysteria. How could the author refuse a happy resolution? How could Scarlett's moral, sexual and emotional awakening 'come too late'. In the register of psychic melodrama *Gone with the Wind* brought home to me what I already knew at a social and political level, had felt powerfully the day the Rosenbergs were executed – that life was, could be, unfair – and I met this realization with howls of rage and pain. My mother took me into the bathroom and in my memory, though not in hers, threw cold water over me to stop my sobs. And I was ashamed at being so uncontrolled, so held by such a 'bad' book, for this was America in the mid-fifties and my passion for social justice, my political loyalties were well developed. As a political subject I knew what side I was on. In these same years I came home in the afternoon from school and listened to the Army-McCarthy hearings on the radio with my milk and cookies, cheering when the Right was challenged and lost points. I was an optimistic child; I believed even in those dark years that progressive forces would triumph eventually, and in the same way I hoped for the future realization of my sexual and emotional fantasies, though this reward seemed as distant as the revolution.

Both my parents found my slavish addiction to fifties femininity, its fashions which harnessed, thrust and spiked us and its macho-femme versions of sexual difference, regressive and worrying. For me, however, my political and sexual desires, utopian and transgressive, were bound together, which made my passionate response to *Gone with the Wind* even more contradictory. It was not only, not even primarily, Scarlett that drew me to the book, but the whole scenario of lost causes, sexual and political and Rhett Butler above all as the knowing and desiring protagonist. I loved the book, I think, because it was a transgressive read in a house where there was no censorship, only waves of disappointment. The deep South and its fake aristocracy, imitation feudalism (which Mitchell both deplores and celebrates) was an imaginary historic site where traditional femininity could be lived in an unashamed way, at one level at least. It probably met my fantasy that in less politically radical households fifties female adolescence was given more space and approval.

Yet *Gone with the Wind* is not a conventional piece of romance fiction, or Scarlett a conventional heroine. Her femininity is masquerade, for behind it lies a scheming active masculine ambition to survive and get ahead. Only her hopeless passion for the hopeless Ashley Wilkes marks her out as conventionally feminine. Unsentimental and asexual in most of her dealings with men, an unwilling mother, Rhett must convert her to sexuality and, by taking the child away, to some measure of maternal feeling. For all his macho qualities it is Rhett, not Ashley, who is the maternal man, taking over when Scarlett's parents die and the social relations of the South disintegrate, educating and protecting Scarlett, proud involved father to his daughter, a man who values women more than men. When he abandons her she is truly abandoned, and must go back to her childhood, to Tara, to start again. For me personally it was a resonant and painful text, for I was engaged in a long and bitter struggle with my father in these years, for my autonomy, for his love and approval.

But it spoke, I think, to a much wider audience of American women readers for whom the pre-Civil-War South did serve as a sort of pre-capitalist site of family romance, a mythical moment of settled, traditional social relations which the Civil War destroys for ever. In terms of its connotations for twentieth-century readers, both north and south, that imaginary historical landscape was both Edenic and poisoned – by slavery, by illusion – and its disruption necessary, if violent, so that the South could enter modern industrial capitalist society. Sherman's rape of Georgia, Rhett's violent seduction of Scarlett are analogous events in the text, progressive events if you like, which take place in a world tinged with unbearable emotional nostalgia. *Gone with the Wind* encourages the reader to regress, insists that they move on. As a parable of Southern history, as a romantic narrative with incestuous overtones, it is history and fantasy spoken from the position of the women. It remains so today.

My reading of romance didn't stop, of course, with the cold slosh of maternal reality. But I was internally cautious about being so profoundly 'carried away' by my romance reading after that. I read and reread certain texts regularly which spoke to me in the same register of desire as *Gone with the Wind* and these significant fictions crossed the boundaries of high and popular genres. So the two other books I remember from my teens as affecting me in similar ways were Anya Seton's historical novel *Katherine* and *Anna Karenina*. It was over twenty-five years before a novel triggered the uncontrolled level of fantasy response that I had experienced with *Gone with the Wind* and, not surprisingly, I encountered it first as a television serial. Colleen McCullough's *The Thorn Birds*[1] seduced me away from *The Jewel in the Crown*, a more respectable piece of viewing adapted from Paul Scott's *The Raj Quartet*, and so profoundly affected was I by the first episode I saw (not the first in the series) that I rushed out to buy the paperback. A matriarchal family saga which starts in Australia between the wars, it is overtly transgressive where *Gone with the Wind* is subtle. The first two-thirds of the book centre on the growing attachment for, and eventual seduction of, a Catholic priest, Ralph, by a much younger woman, Meggie, whom he meets when she is only 9. Incest is the slightly displaced theme of the book. In the character of Ralph the author constructs an ideal maternal man, even a feminine man, to whom sexual access is of course taboo.

Deeply conservative politically in ways I shall go into later, the book appropriates contemporary feminist discourses on sexuality in an interesting form. I don't know a single man who has read it, except to engage with it professionally; yet like *Gone with the Wind* it has broken sales records internationally. Like *Gone with the Wind*, too, it is a fantasy about both history and sexuality imagined from the women's position and it speaks powerfully to the contradictory and unreconciled feelings about femininity, feminism and fantasy which marks out that position for, at the very least, First-World white female readers. Unlike mass market romance, Mills and Boon and Harlequin, these long blockbuster romances do not solicit the reader to identify with a single female protagonist. Rather they evoke powerful overlapping scenarios in which the relation of reader to character is often deliciously blurred. They invite, I would argue, the female reader to identify across sexual difference and to engage with narrative fantasy from a variety of subject positions and at various levels. *The Thorn Birds* confirms not a conventional femininity but women's contradictory and ambiguous place within sexual difference. Feminist cultural criticism has initiated a very interesting debate about the meaning of reading, and watching, romance. What follows is a contribution to that discussion which tries to see how, in historical, political and psychoanalytic terms, texts like *Gone with the Wind* and *The Thorn Birds* come to have such a broad appeal for women, centering the female reader in a particular way, and reworking the contradictory elements which make female subjectivity such a vertiginous social and psychic experience.

## History

Fiction, fantasy and femininity. Since the rise of the popular novel directed at a female audience, the relationship between these three terms has troubled both progressive and conservative analysts of sexual difference, not least those who were themselves writers of narrative. The terms of the debate about the relationship between 'reading romance' and the construction of femininity have remained surprisingly constant in the two hundred years since Mary Wollstonecraft and Jane Austen first engaged with the issue as a response to the expansion of sensational literature directed at the woman reader.[2]

Both Wollstonecraft and Austen agreed that the 'stale tales' and 'meretricious scenes' of the sentimental and gothic novel triggered and structured female fantasy, stirring up the erotic and romantic at the expense of the rational, moral and maternal. Both thought that such reading could directly influence behaviour – inflamed and disturbed readers might, in Wollstonecraft's evocative phrase 'plump into actual vice'. But Wollstonecraft's main concern was not with junk reading as the route to adultery but as the path to conventional, dependent, degenerate femininity – to the positioning of the female self in the degraded, dependent role as 'objects of desire'. At the time she was writing *A Vindication of the Rights of Woman* Wollstonecraft was defending a relatively conventional sexual morality. Even so, she was much less concerned with the danger to women's sexual virtue which romance reading might breed than with the far-reaching political effects of such indulgence. As the narrative of desire washed over the reader, the thirst for reason was quenched, and the essential bridge to female autonomy and emancipation, a strengthened 'understanding' was washed out. The female psyche could not, it seemed, sustain or combine two mental agendas; for them it must be either reason or passion, pleasure or knowledge. Austen's version of this libidinal economy was perhaps slightly less punitive, but this was only because her ambitions for her heroine/reader were a less radical and more limited moral autonomy within the dominant convention as wife, mother and lover. Moral and spiritual integrity and, to some extent, independence for women were essential, but an independent life and an independently productive life were not unthinkable within her novels. Both Wollstonecraft and Austen assumed, as most analysts of romance reading do today, that romance narrative works on the reader through rather simple forms of identification. The reader aligns herself with the heroine and suffers her perils, passions and triumphs. The narrative structure of the fiction then 'takes over' everyday life, and gender relations are read through its temptations, seductions and betrayals. Alternatively romance provides an escape from the everyday realities; the pleasure of fantasy numbs the nerve of resistance to oppression.

Wollstonecraft's implicit theory of reading assumed the reader would identify herself with the female heroine. The reading of popular fiction and the fantasy induced by it depend at one level on the identification of reader and heroine, and the subsequent acting-out of a related narrative trajectory. Late-eighteenth-century theories of reading, as they appeared in both aesthetic and political discourses, assumed a fairly direct relationship between reading and action, especially from the naïve reader, i.e. the barely literate, uneducated working-class person – and women. In this period of expanding literacy and political turmoil, the question of the ability to read is at the centre of both progressive platforms of radicalization and transformation of the mass of people, and conservative fears of revolution. A great deal of attention was given to not only the dynamic effects of reading on the unschooled subject but also to the distinction between reading as a social act (a pamphlet read to others in a coffee house or village square, books read at the family hearth) and reading as a private act, unregulated and unsupervised by authority. Both forms of reading could be subversive, but the latter, less open to surveillance and control, more defiantly announcing the mental autonomy of individual subjects whose 'independence' is not acknowledged by the dominant social and political order, offered a particularly insidious form of subversion.

The question of women's reading, as it was understood in the 1790s was situated within these wider anxieties about reading and revolution, literacy and subjectivity.[3] Accordingly both Wollstonecraft and Austen knew women must read to achieve even minimal independent status as subjects and were, in somewhat different ways, concerned with something more intangible and complex than a simple incitement, which sensational novels may produce, to misbehave. Private reading is already, in itself, an act of autonomy; in turn it sets up, or enables, a space for reflective thought. Fiction gives that reflection a narrative shape and sensational fiction produces a sort of general excitation, the 'romantic twist of the mind' that concerned Wollstonecraft. The desire to inhabit that provocative landscape and mentally live its stories rather than those of the supposed social real was as worrying as any specific identification with romantic female protagonists. In fact Wollstonecraft's analysis of the construction of a degraded and dependent femininity in *A Vindication* insists that although female children have no innate sexuality – she bitterly rejected Rousseau's insistence that they did – women come to see themselves narcissistically through the eyes of men. Through the gaze of the male rake, they become 'rakes themselves'. Female subjectivity was characterized in this account by its retrograde tendency to take up other subject positions and identify self as object. It was this already unstable, degraded subject (constructed in childhood and early adolescence) that reads romance and fantasizes about it. For Wollstonecraft and Austen popular sensational literature both reinforced and evoked a set of romantic scenarios which the reader will use at once to interpret, act through and escape from ordinary lives. Each part of this reading effect is 'bad', each involves different elements of projection and displacement and together they constitute the negative effect of fiction and fantasy.

There was very little possibility in late-eighteenth-century progressive or conservative thought for a positive account of fantasy for women, the lower classes or colonial peoples. For all of these lesser subjectivities the exercise of the imagination was problematic, for the untutored, 'primitive' psyche was easily excited and had no strategies of sublimation; a provocative narrative induced imitation and disruptive actions, political or social. When radicals supported the subjective equality of any of these groups, they generally insisted that their reasoning capacity was equal to that of a bourgeois male. The psyche of the educated middle-class male was the balanced psyche of the period: reason and passion in a productive symbiosis. Men of this class were felt to have a more fixed positionality. Radical discourses presented them as the origin of their own identities, as developing independent subjects, the makers and controllers of narrative rather than its enthralled and captive audience. This capacity to produce a master narrative like their rational capacity to take civic, political actions remained latent in them as readers. Men of the ruling class, so went the dominant mythology, read critically, read not to imitate but to engage productively with argument and with narrative. They understood the difference between fiction and fact, between imagination and reason. The normative male reader, unlike his credulous female counterpart, could read a gothic novel for amusement and pleasure. Like the poet whose writing practice used 'emotion recollected in tranquility', the two modes of reason and passion were ever open to him; in the same way he could inhabit both a public and private sphere and move between them. The enlightenment asked man to subordinate passion to reason. Romanticism argued for a productive interaction between them, assuming optimistic- ally that the rational would act as a check to passion, and that passion itself would be transformed, sublimated through the imagination.

As literacy spread and reading became one of the crucial practices through which human capacity, integrity, autonomy and psychic balance could be assessed, reading habits and reading response were increasingly used to differentiate readers by class and sex. By the 1790s reading by the masses was being argued *for* as a necessary route to individual and group advancement, as the crucial preparation for social and political revolution, and, at the same time, argued *against* as the significant activity which might stem the revolutionary tide. Thomas Paine pushed the polemic furthest, conflating reading with civil liberty itself – prophesying that censorship would breed its own revenge – that it would become dangerous to tell a whole people that 'they shalt not read'. Reading, both as an activity and as a sign of activities it may engender, became a metonymic reference to forms of good and bad subjectivity, of present and potential social and psychic being. So Wollstonecraft in 1791 ends her diatribe against romance reading on an uncertain note, insisting that it is better that women read novels than not read at all.

## Fantasy

In the preceding two sections I have been deliberately using the term fantasy in its contemporary everyday sense: as a conscious construction of an imaginary scene in which, it is invariably assumed, the fantasist places him/herself in an easily identified and constant role in the narrative. This common-sense working definition has been undermined at various points in the discussion of autobiography and history, but it is more or less adequate for a preliminary account of fantasy as 'daydream', as a conscious, written narrative construction, or as an historical account of the gendered imagination. Yet fantasy used solely or unreflectingly in this way invokes a notion of the relation between dream and fiction, without actually theorizing that connection. Unless we actually do work through that relationship and distinguish between fantasy as an unconscious structure and as forms of social narrative, we are unlikely to break free from the stigmatizing moralism which taints most accounts of romantic fantasy and gender, representing romance as a 'social disease' which affects the weaker constitution of the female psyche.

Psychoanalytic discussions of fantasy are not wholly free of elements of moralization but, as Alison Light has commented in her illuminating discussion of romance fiction, sexuality and class, psychoanalysis at least 'takes the question of pleasure seriously, both in its relation to gender and in its understanding of fiction as fantasies, as the explorations and productions of desires which may be in excess of the socially possible or acceptable'.[4]

Freud began his work on fantasy by appealing to the relationship between fantasy and day-dream: 'scenes, episodes, romances or fictions which the subject creates and recounts to himself in the waking state'.[5] But as he develops his concept of fantasy, it becomes clear that fantasy operates at three different registers at least – at unconscious, subliminal and conscious levels. At each level fantasy expresses social content, but is, at the same time, separate from it. Indeed Juliet Mitchell, in an interesting discussion of the origins of fantasy, specifies its moment of genesis as the moment when the baby deprived of the breast fantasizes sucking, transforming the external world and its '"things" – the people, sounds, sights and smells and so on' into representation. This moment is identified in psychoanalysis as the moment of the foundation of desire and, according to Mitchell again, as the moment when the 'human animal' becomes a 'human being'. Thus the experiences of the external world provide 'the support (or underpin) for the phantasy scenario which comes into being with their absence'.[6]

Sexuality, representation, fantasy and subjectivity. In psychoanalytic theory, the infant's fantasy is the mode through which sexuality (desire) is constituted, and equally the ability to represent the missing activity or pleasure is the process through which subjectivity – social and psychic identity – is formed. A psychoanalytic theory of fantasy not only takes 'pleasure seriously' but places the ability to think about pleasure at the centre of what constitutes us as human subjects. If we accept that fantasy has this crucial place in mental life, and if we emphasize it for the moment as a process rather than a particular scenario or set of scenarios, then perhaps we can make more sense of the problem it has posed for feminism. For the advocacy of stern prophylactic measures to 'cure' women of romantic fantasy has, in this recent wave of feminism as in the ones that have preceded it, produced its own backlash and internal unease. Letting go of romantic and sexual fantasies of an 'incorrect' kind has proved very difficult; perhaps because their obstinate presence in women's imaginative life can never simply be a sign of their psychic subordination to patriarchal relations, but is always, simultaneously, the mark of their humanity.

In a few pages we shall look at *The Thorn Birds* as an example of how fictions, written in the past fifteen years for and by women, can remap the insistent scenarios of fantasy in relation to feminist discourse. First, however, something needs to be said about the specifically Freudian elaboration of a theory of fantasy. It is helpful to isolate three important elements of Freud's use of fantasy: first, how it specifies the relationship of classic fantasy scenario to the place of the subject within it; second, how it describes the relationship between the different psychic registers in which fantasy occurs; and third, its problematic perspective on the origins of primal or unconscious fantasy.

My understanding of Freud's deployment of fantasy is heavily dependent on two interpretative texts, the entry on 'Phantasy (or fantasy)' in J. Laplanche and J.-B. Pontalis' *The Language of Psychoanalysis* and the essay by the same authors 'Fantasy and the origins of sexuality' (1968).[7] The latter piece in particular explores the question of the positionality of the subject in fantasy. The authors begin by emphasizing that 'the primary function of fantasy' is to provide 'a setting for desire'. Scenario thus takes precedence over any fixed identification of the subject with any one character in the scene, and indeed such identification may shift in the course of a fantasy scenario (the example from Freud is his brief and suggestive essay 'a child is being beaten').[8] More radically, Laplanche and Pontalis suggest that the 'fixing' of subject identification is not the point of fantasy anyway. Insisting on the close relationship between the initiation of desire in the psychic subject and the origin of fantasy they argue that:

> Fantasy is not the object of desire, but its setting. In fantasy the subject does not pursue the object or its sign: he appears caught up himself in the sequence of images. He forms no representation of the desired object, but is himself represented as participating in the scene although, in the earliest forms of fantasy, he cannot be assigned any fixed place in it. . . . As a result, the subject, although always present in the fantasy, may be so in a desubjectivized form, that is to say, in the very syntax of the sequence in question (p.26).

Moreover, the point at which desire originates, the point of separation of the subject from the sensory objects of satisfaction, becomes soon enough in psychic development a point of prohibition. Fantasy thus becomes the 'favoured spot', the Nile Valley for the articulation of those defensive mechanisms through which the psyche deals with such prohibition. Fantasy scenarios and the subjectivity they end up representing are rarely straightforward narratives in which the 'wish' they embody is simply represented in the pursuit of an object by a subject-protagonist. Yet this is, on the whole, how it is assumed fantasy works when it is induced or provoked by visual or written fictions. In particular, analyses of mass-market romances of the Mills and Boon and Harlequin type have emphasized the congruence between reader and heroine and the coherence between socially normative models of heterosexual romance and romance narrative. Moreover, mass-market romance is frequently assumed to embody the basic schema or scenario of romantic fantasy which is then elaborated in more sophisticated or complex narratives. These latter may be novels in the high art canon, like Ann Radcliffe's gothic masterpiece, *Mysteries of Udolpho*, or Bronte's *Jane Eyre*, or they may be slightly up-market modern popular texts – blockbusters, bodice-rippers, historical romances, family sagas.

In *Loving with a Vengeance*, which focuses on the Harlequin, gothic and soap-opera genres, Tania Modleski argues convincingly that it is useful to distinguish between types of romance in thinking about the relationship of different kinds of narrative to female subjectivity. Modleski, however, sees the lack of an easy identification of reader to protagonist in the text as a 'problem' and one which points towards a critique not of the novels but 'the conditions which made them necessary'.[9] Although her analysis of the revenge narrative beneath the narrative of seduction contests, in persuasive ways, the notion of the simple scenario of mass-market romance, her discussion of the identification of the reader with the heroine is disappointing. Her strategy is to associate the 'schizophrenic' and 'apersonal' effect of reading Harlequins (where the reader is always more knowledgeable and in control than the heroine) with the situation of the hysteric, as if seeing oneself from outside in the dramatic script were only a sign of female distress about femininity, a form of splitting which a reformed social world could and ought to remedy.[10] In a similar way, her comparison of the gothic formula with paranoia, while not falling into the trap of pathologizing either reader or text, tends to set up certain narrative elements – the use of the feminine man in gothics, for example – as subject/object relations. *Loving with a Vengeance* uses Freud but tends to read him through psychoanalytic theory and feminist appropriations which emphasize 'object relations' in the formation of subjectivity, rather than fantasy as a scenario in which the shifting place of the subject is a characteristic part of the activity.[11] Accordingly, her analysis is quite gender bound. The female subject/reader has, as she suggests, a great deal of active psychic process in relation to the texts in which heroines are posed as passive, but she must be situated in the text *as* female subject. Crossing the boundaries of gender as part of the act of reading and fantasizing plays no significant part in her analysis.

For Laplanche and Pontalis, however, the variability of the subject's place in fantasy is a key to the heterogeneous nature of fantasy itself, the mixed form in which it mostly appears to us in reverie, reminiscence and dream. The lack of subjectivization of fantasy in original fantasy scenarios – the primal scene, seduction and castration – cannot be clearly contrasted with the presumed place of the subject in daydream as a 'first person' narration in which the subject's place is 'clear and invariable'. For, although 'the work of our waking thought' which organizes and makes dream scenes coherent, may impose a day-dream form on the incoherence of dream, and so rationalize the material in relation to a fixed subject position, certain characteristic fantasies of a waking kind refuse the imposition of this kind of narrative realism. To support their argument Laplanche and Pontalis cite especially 'A child is being beaten', in which Freud notes that both the sex of the child and the figure of the beater oscillate in the course of the fantasy, and 'Screen memory', where the subject sees the self as a character in the narrative reconstruction. They go even further in analysing the instability of subject position in seduction fantasy:

> 'A father seduces a daughter' might perhaps be the summarized version of the seduction fantasy . . . it is a scenario with multiple entries, in which nothing shows whether the subject will be immediately located as *daughter*: it can as well be fixed as *father*, or even in the term *seduces* (p.22–3).

Freud asserts the 'profound kinship' of original, unconscious fantasy and conscious fantasy and their persistence through very different modes and stages of psychic life by emphasizing that:

> The contents of the clearly conscious fantasies of perverts (which in favourable circumstances can be transformed into manifest be-haviour), of the delusional fears of paranoiacs (which are projected in a hostile sense on to other people), and of the unconscious fantasies of hysterics (which psychoanalysis reveals behind their symptoms) – all these coincide with one another even down to their details.[12]

The persistence and repetition of certain fantasy scenarios in the psychic life of men and women with very different psychological disturbances, and the ambiguity of subject positions in the elements of original fantasy which are supplied in dream, acting-out and waking reverie, these aspects of Freud's work on fantasy, highlighted by Laplanche and Pontalis, can lead to a very different 'take' on both the textual fantasy inscribed in romance fiction and the reader's mode of appropriating such fantasy. Freud's development of his ideas about fantasy was, as Laplanche and Pontalis suggest, marked by an 'ambiguity of conceptions as new avenues open out to him with each new stage in his ideas'. If we follow Laplanche and Pontalis' way through this conceptual underbrush, however, it is clear we are moving away from fantasy as an activity which mainly serves to fix subject positions, without moving towards some form of reversal in which female fantasy, because it is active, as psychic process becomes a morally liberating activity for women. Fantasy, as Modleski suggests, has utopian elements in it; indeed, without fantasy we could not imagine utopias. But fantasizing *as such* is a crucial part of psychic life, a process required for human sexuality and subjectivity to be set in place and articulated, rather than a process that is either good or bad, or of which we can have too much or too little. How fantasy, with its aggrandizing narrative appetite, appropriates and incorporates social meaning and, structuring its public narrative, forms the historically specific stories and subjectivities available – that aspect of fantasy is open to political analysis and negotiation. But the ways in which the subject/reader engages with textual fantasy which combines original or primal fantasy in which desubjectivization is characteristic, with reverie and daydream in which 'first person' identification is more common, is clearly more complex than most accounts of reading romance have allowed.

The least satisfactory element in Freud's exploration of fantasy is his phylogenetic solution to the question of the 'origins' of the basic fantasy scenarios, the witnessing of sexual intercourse between parents, seduction and castration. The search for a prehistory of origins for these fantasies which themselves pose the question of origins is, as Laplanche and Pontalis note, only one aspect of Freud's many-sided discussion of fantasy. Phylogenetic explanation places the 'acts' and 'scenes' of primal fantasy as 'real occurences in the primaeval times of the human family . . . children in their phantasies are simply filling in the gaps in individual truth with prehistoric truth'.[13] In fact, phylogenetic explanation itself fills in, to some extent, the gap left when Freud abandons the seduction theory and, with it, the notion that the analyst can uncover a verifiable real event behind the adult history. Phylogenetic explanation both works in tandem and competes with Freud's concept of 'psychical reality' which gives psychic life an autonomous identity. Its presence indicates how much it mattered to Freud that a 'bedrock of the event' be located somewhere outside the recounted fantasies of the adult patient, in primal fantasy first, and then, if necessary, in 'the history of the species'. The search for the true story in the history of an individual subject can be found in Freud's work many years after he rejected the seduction theory and speaks to his desire to found the theory on a reality principle of some kind, even if its register is mythic rather than historic, metaphysical rather than material.

Modern psychoanalytic theory is, understandably, unhappy with mythical prehistories. Its tendency is to ignore or displace the search for the origin of primal fantasy or simply to confess, with Laplanche and Pontalis, that it is a project for 'philosophers'. Nevertheless, Freud's own need for such a theory, and its literal embodiment in notions of the 'primitive' and 'archaic' as a set of social practices, suggests the ways in which primal fantasy remains morally and ethically ambiguous. Not only are its scenes dramas of prohibition, but they remain tainted with the taboo they enact. The foundation of sociality and identity, they are also, always, scripts which define otherness and exclusion. Imagining a mythic prehistory for the classic primal scenarios, in which fathers *actually* castrated children, evokes contemporary ideas of 'primitive' practice, invites us to think synchronically, across cultures, as well as diachronically back through history. In short, phylogenetic explanation calls on other systems of difference, the difference between cultures or between subjectivities, to account for the foundation of sexual difference. It intrudes into the discussion of fantasy as the colonial discourse of 'otherness' in which degraded subjects act out the prohibited scenarios of European cultures.

The subliminal moralizing of the different levels of fantasy via the invocation of racial hierarchy is expressed very directly at one point in Freud's discussion of the 'hybrid' nature of fantasy as conscious and unconscious forms, in day-dream and dream facade. In 'The unconscious' (1915) Freud uses the example of 'individuals of mixed race' to illustrate the way in which primal fantasy both hides and reveals its origins when it is embedded in apparently coherent, sophisticated, fantasy narrative. This educated fantasy which presents itself as 'highly organised, free from self-contradiction' seems, at first glance, part of the rationally integrated system of consciousness. But, Freud notes, intepretation unmasks them:

> The origin is what decides their fate. We may compare them with individuals of mixed race who, taken all round, resemble white men, but who betray their coloured descent by some striking feature or other, and on that account are excluded from society and enjoy none of the privileges of white people.[14]

In his comparison Freud uses a biological basis of racial difference. His assumption that the social recognition of difference will automatically lead to exclusion maps the politics of racism over the rules which govern the hierarchy of psychic discourses. Less metaphor than metonym, this disturbing image invokes both biological and social notions of degraded subjectivity and social forms of exclusion as a way of indicating the incomplete integration of fantasy discourses. The imbrication of sexuality and race in Freud's example is complete when we learn that it is through the tell-tale shape of 'nose' and kink of 'hair' that the outlaw primitive will be identified. More than anything else this passage reveals the insistent connection between fantasy, social law and the related forms of degraded and excluded subjectivity, a connection which remains politically opaque and therefore ambiguous in Freud's own writing.

## Text: The Thorn Birds

In 'Returning to Manderley' Alison Light reclaims Daphne du Maurier's *Rebecca* as a text which provides 'a classic model of romance fiction while at the same time exposing many of its terms'.[15] I would like to adopt a similar critical strategy towards Colleen McCullough's *The Thorn Birds*, a family saga whose events start in 1915 in rural New Zealand and end in 1965 in a London town house. Written by an Australian emigrée living in America in the mid-seventies, the novel subtly appropriates elements of feminist discourse, integrating the language of romance fiction with new languages of sexuality and sexual difference. Fantasy is quite unashamedly mobilized in *The Thorn Birds* both at the level of content – the narrative scenario – and at the level of rhetoric – the various styles which mark out its different registers within the story. Through these means the novel weaves a seeming social realism together with a series of original fantasies so that the text resembles the heterogeneous or hybrid form of fantasy described by psychoanalysis. Although, like a retold dream, the text rationalizes fantasy scenes into a coherent narrative sequence, the plot is in fact full of unlikely incident and coincidence which characters and authorial voice are constantly trying to justify. The implausible elements of the plot and their elaborate rationalization signals the presence of original fantasy in the text. Like many family sagas, *The Thorn Birds* inscribes all of the generic original fantasies, often mapping them over each other and repeating them with variations in the experience of different generations. Laplanche and Pontalis describe these fantasy categories as:

> Fantasies of origins: the primal scene pictures the origin of the individual; fantasies of seduction, the origin and upsurge of sexuality; fantasies of castration, the origin of the difference between the sexes.

Ambiguities about paternity run through the text. Intimations of incest affect almost all the familial and extra-familial relations, as father–daughter, mother–son and brother–sister ties. These fantasy scenes are structured and elaborated from the women's position, which sometimes means only that they offer a mildly eccentric elaboration of the classic fantasy scripts. For example, castration fantasy in the narrative emphasizes both lack and power in women and mothers, on the one hand, and retribution by that eternally absent father, God, on the other. The third-person narration, typical of family saga romance, allows a very free movement between masculine and feminine positions, and different discursive genres and registers. It also permits the narrative as a whole to be contained within a set of determinate political ideologies for which the characters themselves bear little responsibility. Like *Gone with the Wind*, but with significant differences, *The Thorn Birds* pursues an interesting and occasionally radical interrogation of sexual difference inside a reactionary set of myths about history.

At the heart of *The Thorn Birds* lies a scandalous passion between a Catholic priest, Ralph de Bricassart, and Meggie Cleary, whose family are the focus of the novel. Ralph meets Meggie when she is 9 years old, the only and somewhat neglected girl child in a large brood of boys. Ralph himself is a strikingly handsome and ambitious Irish-born priest in his late twenties, sent into temporary exile in this remote bit of rural New South Wales because he has quarrelled with his bishop. Ralph loves the child for her beauty, and for her 'perfect female character, passive yet enormously strong. No rebel, Meggie: on the contrary. All her life she would obey, move within the boundaries of her female fate' (p.105).

The whole first half of the novel follows the Clearys' fortunes on Drogheda, the vast Australian sheep station, which belongs first to the widowed millionaire matriarch, Mary Carson, and after her death to the church, with Ralph as its agent. Its narrative moves in a tantalizingly leisurely fashion towards the seduction of the proud, virginal Ralph by Meggie, whose female fate seems to include some fairly fundamental disobedience to church and state. Ralph 'makes' Meggie, as he tells his Vatican superior and confessor later in the text, shaping her education and sensibility from childhood. She, like a dutiful daughter in someone's fantasy, returns his seemingly non-sexual love with a fully libidinized intensity.

The text plays with great skill on the two narratives of prohibition, familial and ecclesiastic, that are bound together in Meggie and Ralph's romance. 'Don't call me Father', he keeps insisting, while disentangling himself reluctantly from the arms of the teenage girl who assaults him at every opportunity. Ralph is represented as mother, father and lover in relation to Meggie. Somehow it is Ralph, in the confessional, who has to tell the 15-year-old Meggie about menstruation, because mother Fee is too busy with the boys. Somehow it is Ralph, not Meggie's negligent macho husband, who arrives in a distant part of the outback to hold her hand in her first painful experience of childbirth.

The ideal feminine man – he has a way, he tells us, with babies – Ralph is bound to the church by pride and ambition, sure that it will give him a transcendent identity: 'Not a man, never a man; something far greater, something beyond the fate of a mere man' (p.355). Losing his virginity at 40 odd, Ralph discovers *in media res* that he is a 'mere man' after all, while Meggie finds out that only symbolic incest and transgression can make a woman of her. Their brief week's consummation takes place on a remote South Sea island. After an Edenic interlude, Ralph leaves for Rome and his rising career in the church. Meggie, gestating his son, returns to the Cleary family base at Drogheda with Justine, her daughter, by her husband Luke. Here, under her mother's benign matriarchy (her biological father, significantly dies before her marriage and adultery), she will raise her children and even enjoy a short second honeymoon when Ralph comes to Drogheda to visit years later.

The novel, 591 pages long, deals with major events in the life of three generations of Clearys as well as Ralph's trajectory from country priest to cardinal via his broken vows. Like *Gone with the Wind* and other family saga romances, part of its pleasure is in the local, historical detail. Most of the energy of the text, however, is reserved for the emotional encounters. Its power to hold the female reader, in the first half anyway, is linked to the inexorable unfolding of Meggie and Ralph's story, the seduction scenario played through the narrative of another durable fantasy – the family romance in which a real-life parent is discarded as an imposter and a more exalted figure substituted.

The incest motif is everywhere in the novel, saturating all the literal familial relations as well as the metaphorical ones. Within the Cleary household all the boys remain unmarried; they are, as Meggie tells Ralph during their island idyll 'terribly shy . . . frightened of the power a woman might have over them . . . quite wrapped up in Mum' (p.358). Most wrapped up in Fee Cleary is her eldest son Frank, the illegitimate child of a New Zealand politician, half Maori. Through her affair with him Fee has lost her social position; her upper-class Anglican family marry her off to their shy dairy hand, the Irish Catholic immigrant Paddy Cleary, and then disown her. Frank acts out an Oedipal drama with Paddy who he believes is his real father, until he goads Paddy into revealing his illegitimate status. They quarrel. Frank calls his father 'a stinking old he-goat . . . a ram in rut' for making his mother Fee pregnant yet again. The father, stung, calls the boy 'no better than the shitty old dog who fathered you, whoever he was!' (p.119). This quarrel takes place in front of the child Meggie and Father Ralph. After it Frank leaves home, eventually commits murder and is given a life sentence. His fate is seen in the text quite specifically as Fee's punishment for her sexual transgression. In the second half of the novel, Meggie too will lose her much loved son by Ralph, first to the church and then by death.

These symmetrical events are reinforced by the deep but sexually innocent attachment of brother–sister pairs in each generation: Frank and his half-sister Meggie; Justine and her half-brother Dane. Within the male Cleary brood there are homosocial attachments too, the twin boys Patsy and Jims are represented as a symbiotic couple. And *The Thorn Birds* extends and elaborates the homosocial, homoerotic themes, though never in a very positive way, through Meggie's husband Luke's preference of his

workmate Arne, and, within the church, through Ralph's friendship with
his Italian mentor. Male bonding is seen as something of a problem in the
book, a problem certainly for Meggie who, as she says, seems drawn to
men who don't have much need of women and fear too much closeness
with them.

Meggie (and Ralph) witness two primal scenes – in discursive form
to be sure – in watching and hearing the revelations in the argument
between Paddy and Frank. They hear a graphic, animalized account of the
act between Paddy and Fee, and between Fee and some unknown lover,
whom we later discover to be the half-caste politician. (Children often
interpret parental coitus as a fight.) Ralph fears that Meggie will be
psychologically damaged by witnessing the argument. The text doesn't
follow this up with any reflexive comment. At a narrative level, in relation
to the sequence of the fantasy scenes involving Meggie which now begin
to move inevitably towards the seduction scenario, the fight, as a stage in
the destruction of her innocence and perhaps an erosion of her father's
authority, is certainly important.

Having sorted out in one part the question of the origin of babies,
the next fantasy sequence is the one in which Ralph tells the super-
innocent 15-year-old that she is menstruating, not dying of cancer. Meggie
is presented as peculiarly ignorant of the facts of life for a girl who lives on
a working farm. The author has to insert a long justifying didactic passage
(p.144) which claims, incredibly, that the sexual division of labour on the
station, together with the patriarchal puritanism of Paddy Cleary, has kept
her wholly innocent. Even this touching moment of instruction stops short
of full knowledge. When Ralph asks Meggie whether she knows how
women get pregnant her answer is wholly within the register of fantasy:

> 'You wish them.'
> 'Who told you that?'
> 'No one. I worked it out for myself,' she said (p.151).

The next scene in the seduction sequence is the first unintended kiss
between Ralph and Meggie, aged 16, which she half initiates. Ralph then
leaves Drogheda for some time. In his absence Meggie has a conversation
with her father in which it is clear that she believes that Ralph will, when
she tells him to, leave the church and marry her. Paddy tries, without
much luck, to disabuse her of this illusion:

> 'Father de Bricassart is a *priest*, Meggie. . . . Once a man is a priest
> there can be no turning away . . . a man who takes those vows knows
> beyond any doubt that once taken they can't be broken, ever. Father
> de Bricassart took them, and he'll never break them. . . . Now you
> know, Meggie, don't you? From this moment you have no excuse to
> daydream about Father de Bricassart' (p.209).

But Paddy is unconvincing as bearer of the reality principle, either to the reader or to Meggie.

After one more unsuccessful attempt to seduce Ralph in the hours after her father's death, Meggie is temporarily persuaded to give him up. She marries Luke, one of the seasonal sheep shearers, because he reminds her of Ralph physically. The substitution is an abominable failure, although it gives McCullough a rich opportunity to expand on the incompetent sexual style and homosocial tendencies of working-class Aussie males. Luke is like Ralph in that he can do without women, preferring the world of work and men, but he is unlike Ralph in that he has no nurturant qualities whatever. The text records Meggie's painful, incompetent deflowering in graphic and ironic detail which combines the style of a sixties sex manual with a feminist debunking of heterosexuality. Luke sets her to work as a servant for a crippled farmer's wife and goes off with the boys to cut cane.

Although the book's account of their brief marriage is convincingly realistic in its local incident, the extremity of Luke's punitive treatment of Meggie actually extends the fantasy register of the narrative. Ralph's accidental arrival during Meggie's difficult labour is the penultimate scene in the seduction sequence. He takes her through the menarche and childbirth and will, on Matlock Island, answer her wish at last and take her sexually.

Through the novel sexuality is discussed in at least two different languages. Sex which is pleasurable for women is narrated in the generic style of historical romance – steamy, suggestive and vague: 'It had been a body poem, a thing of arms and hands and skin and utter pleasure' (p.356). Bad sex is exposed in the new pragmatic realism of post-war prose: 'with a great indrawn breath to keep her courage up she forced the penis in, teeth clenched' (p.317). Ralph fucks Meggie in Barbara Cartland's best mode. In the process of losing his virginity he also forgoes his exalted notion of himself as above sexual difference. In sexual pleasure Meggie's femininity is confirmed. Meggie and Ralph conceive a male child, though Ralph's punishment is to be ignorant of this fact until after his son's death, since this is a fantasy from the women's position. Keeping men in ignorance of their paternity can be seen a female prerogative. The question of origins is thus reopened for the next generation in the final seduction, but the question of identity, sexuality and difference is temporarily resolved for Ralph, Meggie and reader.

Narrative rationalization binds the fantasy scenarios together. No amount of tricky discursive justification really explains why Meggie should witness Frank and Paddy's quarrel, need to be told by a priest about menstruation, time her labour for Ralph's visit – and so on. Yet all these events are necessary to construct a complex fantasy, a series of scenarios in which the reader's position *vis-à-vis* Ralph and Meggie is constantly shifting. Until the sequence reaches its penultimate moment, it is fair to say that the reader oscillates from the woman's position to the man's position – represented as poles of subjectivity rather than fixed, determinate identities. For it is wholly unclear that these subject positions can be actually identified with the gendered characters Ralph and Meggie.

What, in text and context, creates this reading effect which is responsible in great part for the pleasure of the novel? *The Thorn Birds* is directed at a female audience, one that by the late seventies has certainly been affected by debates around feminism, if only in their most populist and watered-down form. Even through media representations of feminist discourse there had developed among women a more inquiring attitude towards traditional masculinity and femininity. The acceptable social content of daytime fantasies had shifted enough to allow the woman to be the sexual initiator, especially if, like Meggie, she is also the model of femininity who only wants marriage and babies, content to stay out of modern, urban public space, down on the farm. Within the terms of the fantasy Meggie is allowed to be both active *and* feminine. With certain fundamental reservations about her social role *The Thorn Birds* offers the female reader a liberated de-repressed version of the seduction fantasy, a written-out, up-front story of 'A daughter seduces a father' in place of that old standard 'A father seduces a daughter'.

Most mass-market romance, as Modleski and others point out, has stuck with the conservative androcentric version, counting on the third-person narrative which looks down on the woman in the text to inscribe the active female as the knowing reader in the narrative 'a man seduces a woman'. Shifts in the public discourses about sexuality, specifically feminist discourse, permit the seduction fantasy to be reinscribed in a more radical way in popular fiction. They allow the narrative itself to express the terms of original fantasy from the place of the woman, while reassuring us through Meggie's character that such a fantasy, however transgressive in social terms, is perfectly feminine. If the text stopped there it would still be disruptive for, if we put the relationship between femininity and transgression another way, the fantasy sequence suggests also that, in order to be perfectly feminine, a woman's desire must be wholly transgressive. But the role reversal of the seduction fantasy is only the first and simplest stage in the transformation of the seduction story.

More unexpected and eccentric is the way in which Ralph as the feminine man and virgin priest is mobilized within the fantasy. Critiques of traditional macho masculinity abound in the popular fictions of the seventies, especially perhaps in Hollywood film. Decentred masculinity can be represented through a figure like Ralph, whose maternal characteristics are balanced by his public power. Ralph's feminine side is also signified, however, by his great personal beauty, to which he himself calls attention in the early scenes, and his prized virginity. As a beautiful and pure object of desire he stands in the text in place of the woman, often obscuring Meggie. As decentred man, Ralph displaces Meggie as the object to be seduced. This blurring of masculine and feminine positions is worked through in all but the last seduction scene.

Meggie's passion is usually straightforwardly expressive; Ralph's is held back by taboo. His desire is accompanied by shame, disgust and horror at his own wayward libido on whose control he so prides himself: 'I can get it up. It's just that I don't choose to' (p.166). 'Spider's poison', 'snakes', 'ghastly drive' are the phrases used to describe Ralph's illicit desire for Meggie. Yet Ralph is at last moved by his love for her, and his suppressed desire, to consummate the relationship. In the final scenario it is Ralph who pursues and takes action, restoring the initiatives of sexual difference to their right order. The moment of absolute transgression, when Ralph breaks his vows to the church, is later described by him as another kind of 'sacrament'. It is also the moment when the even more transgressive definitions of sexual difference that have been offered the reader are withdrawn. Incest makes real men and women of us all.

It is not simply plot and character that structure the text's unstable inscriptions of sexual difference. The narrative strategy and the language of the novel contribute centrally to this effect. Third-person narration helps a lot. Although the novel starts out with Meggie's early childhood traumas, setting her up as a figure who endures loss and punishment at an early stage, her psyche is always held at one remove. The authorial voice is adult and knowing about her, its tone sympathetic and realistic but never really intimate. Ralph's consciousness, on the other hand, especially where it touches on his feeling for Meggie, is presented consistently in lyrical and philosophical terms. Long paragraphs speculate on Meggie's attraction for the priest:

> Perhaps, had he looked more deeply into himself, he might have seen that what he felt for her was the curious result of time, and place and person . . . she filled an empty space in his life which God could not . . . (p.105).

Ralph 'redecorates' a room for Meggie at the presbytery in which she is installed as surrogate daughter. The text 'decorates' Ralph's feelings for her, offering us a running inner narrative on them, while Meggie's growing feeling for Ralph is rarely given such discursive space. The text gives us a 'natural' identification with Meggie because of her initial priority in the story and because she is the woman in the novel, but it also offers us a seductive alternative identification with Ralph, as a more complex and expressive subjectivity. The oscillation between the realistic and lyric modes, the disruption of the terms of sexual difference, is both titillating and vertiginous. It makes obvious what is perhaps always true in romance reading for women: that the reader identifies with both terms in the seduction scenario, but most of all with the process of seduction. In *The Thorn Birds* sequence the term in which subjectivity is most profoundly inscribed is the verb: *seduces*. It is both disappointing and a relief when the scenario reverts to a more conventional set of positions:

> Go, *run*! Run, Meggie, get out of here with the scrap of pride he's left you!

> Before she could reach the veranda he caught her, the impetus of her flight spinning her round against him. (p.354)

It is as if the act itself, so long deferred, textually speaking, so long the subject of daydream within the narrative, stabilizes the scandalous encounter in terms of socially normative gendered activity and passivity.

There is a whole further generation of things to say about the rewriting of sexual difference in *The Thorn Birds*, but for the purposes of this argument it is perhaps enough to note that Meggie's 'liberated' 'bitchy' actress daughter makes, in the end, a typically feminine match with a macho German financier into whose hands Ralph delivers the stewardship of the Cleary family estates. The novel ends in the moment of European modernity with the union of Rainer and Justine. Twin 'stars' in public life, they also represent socially acceptable and highly polarized versions of late-twentieth-century masculinity and femininity in which tough public men are privately tender and ambitious, successful women are little girls at heart. There are fantasy elements in the 'European' part of the novel, but they are relatively superficial ones. And the seduction scenario between Rainer and Justine is definitely the right way round: 'A man seduces a woman.' Modernity turns out to be pretty old-fashioned after all.

The most daring interrogation of gendered subjectivity is located in the story of Meggie and Ralph and articulated through original fantasy. The English-speaking sub-continent, New Zealand and Australia, before World War II, and especially its idealized rural locations, Drogheda and Matlock Island, stand in as the 'archaic' and 'primitive' setting for the origins of modern sexuality and difference. They work in this way *historically* for the Australian reader, just as the pre-Civil-War American South does for the American reader, or early nineteenth-century Yorkshire for the British reader. But for the 'foreign' reader – and *The Thorn Birds* is written with an international reading market in mind – the setting is doubly displaced and mythologized through distance and history. It is as if, to paraphrase John Locke's famous colonial metaphor about America, 'In the beginning, all the world was down under'.

Myths of origin need actors as well as settings. *The Thorn Birds* does not revise biblical wisdom in this respect; transgression and sexuality are set in motion by Fee's adulterous, cross-racial affair with the half-Maori Pakeha. And I must admit, dear reader, that I have been an unreliable narrator and have held back a crucial piece of information from the text so that it can round out my argument. When Fee and Meggie confess their transgressions to each other, Fee lets slip an important piece of information.

> I have a trace of Maori blood in me, but Frank's father was half Maori. It showed in Frank because he got it from both of us. Oh, but I loved that man! Perhaps it was the call of our blood. . . . He was everything Paddy wasn't – cultured, sophisticated, very charming, I loved him to the point of madness . . . (pp.421–2).

How does this 'trace' of 'Maori blood' – McCullough, like Freud, chooses a racist definition of race – work to explain an heredity of transgression in the text? In the first place the inscription of sexual difference at any historical moment not only requires an 'original' myth of a primal scene, it frequently takes on a third term of social difference and prohibition. This acts as defence, perhaps, against the scandal of the child watching the scene of its own origins or, in castration and seduction fantasy, the scandal of sexual difference itself. In any case, it is interesting that in modern Western myth this social difference frequently takes both a racial and specular form, projecting and displacing sexual taboo and illicit desire into cultural taboo and hierarchy. In *The Thorn Birds*, racial and religious taboo serve to express the transgressive and asocial character of original fantasy, just as class, race and symbolic incest do in *Wuthering Heights*. Although the men in these texts may threaten social coherence by their 'hybrid' nature and their deceptive veneer of civilization, it often turns out to be the 'savage' nature and original taint of the women who love them that are most profoundly disruptive. It is Cathy, not Heathcliff, who stands most absolutely outside the social, knocking at the window in vain. In these texts written by and for women, women nevertheless end up responsible for the scandalous origins of sexuality and difference. *The Thorn Birds* makes this point quite explicitly, adding Fee's own drop of 'primitivism' as a gratuitous racialist confirmation. These two anarchic women are contained in the narrative by the chosen role as mothers and matriarchs. Kept on the plantation, they are not allowed to affect the modern resolution of sexual difference and invade the public sphere. '. . . where *do* we go wrong?' Meggie asks Mum, 'In being born,' Fee replies (p.422).

The second half of the novel disappoints in terms of its normalization of sexual difference, rather like the last section of *Wuthering Heights*. But the really worrying elements of the European portions of the narrative reside in their overt politics. I have said very little about the novel's lengthy and interesting treatment of the Catholic church and the priesthood, a treatment which was in dialogue, no doubt, with elements of the reformist debates within the Catholicism in the seventies. Although the author takes a liberal Catholic line on the chastity of priests, the rest of her views on the church are anything but progressive. Despite acknowledging its economic opportunism and political infighting, the novel is largely uncritical of the church's international influence. Indeed, it openly defends the Vatican's record in relation to fascism and endorses its steadfast opposition to revolution. When Meggie and Ralph's son Dane becomes the perfect priest, he goes on holiday to Greece where his visit is shadowed by a threatening crowd which is 'milling' and 'chanting' in support of 'Pap-an-dreo'.

Although the story contains a rags-to-riches element, the origins and morality of wealth are never questioned. Rainer's rise to fortune and power endow him, in the novel, with wholly admirable and desirable qualities. With Ralph and Dane dead, he becomes the secular inheritor of the power which the church held earlier in the narrative. Fantasies of wealth and power find a lot of scope in family sagas, where they intersect with and support the original fantasies which are represented there. Like *Lace*, *Dallas* or *Dynasty*, *The Thorn Birds* masks the origins of wealth, naturalizing and valorizing it even as it exposes and, up to a certain point, reflects upon the nature of social myth and psychic fantasy about the origins of sexuality and sexual difference. It is this appropriation of fantasy, not fantasy itself, that is implicitly dangerous.

Reading *The Thorn Birds* should warn us away from those half-baked notions embedded in certain concepts of 'post-modern' culture and 'post-feminism' which see the disruption of subjectivity and sexual difference as an act which has a radical autonomy of its own and a power to disrupt hierarchies beyond it. *The Thorn Birds* is a powerful and ultimately reactionary read. In its unashamed right-wing bias the text assumes that its millions of women readers have become progressively reflective about sexuality, but remain conservative, uninterested and unreflective in their thinking about other political and social concerns. Indeed, to return to my initial analysis of the pleasure of reading *Gone with the Wind*, the reactionary political and social setting secure, in some fashion, a privileged space where the most disruptive female fantasy can be 'safely' indulged.

If we ask why women read and watch so much popular romance, the answers seem at one level mundane and banal. Still excluded in major ways from power (if not labour) in the public sphere, where male fantasy takes on myriad discursive forms, romance narrative can constitute one of women's few entries to the public articulation and social exploration of psychic life. It is wrong to imply, as many studies of romance reading seem to, that fantasizing is a female speciality. On the contrary fantasy is, as Freud's work suggests, a crucial part of our constitution as human subjects. It is neither the contents of original fantasies nor even necessarily the position from which we imagine them that can, or ought, to be stigmatized. Rather, it is consciousness of the insistent nature of those fantasies for men and women and the historically specific forms of their elaboration that need to be opened up. Our priority ought be an analysis of the progressive or reactionary politics of the narratives to which they can become bound in popular expression. Those narratives – which of course include issues around sexual difference as well as around race, class and the politics of power generally – can be changed.

> *The Thorn Birds*, first published in hardcover in America in May 1977, has sold more copies than any other novel of the past ten years, and rights have been sold all over the world for more money than publishers have ever paid for a book before.[16]

## Notes

1. C. McCullough, *The Thorn Birds*, London, Futura, 1977. References to this edition are given in brackets in the body of the text.
2. M. Wollstonecraft, *A Vindication of the Rights of Woman*, C.H. Poston (ed.), New York, 1975, pp.183–6. J. Austen, *Northanger Abbey* and *Mansfield Park*. The following discussion of gendered reading in the late eighteenth and early nineteenth century is drawn from the above text.
3. The debates about reading appear *passim* in the extended pamphlet exchange over the French Revolution and its effects in Britain. See especially the writings of Thomas Paine and Hannah More, the trials of booksellers and publishers in the 1790s as well as letters and papers of various radical figures. E.P. Thompson, *The Making of the English Working Class*, Harmondsworth, Penguin, 1968, part 1, pp.19–293 contains a general discussion of these issues. See also O. Smith, *The Politics of Language, 1791–1819*, Oxford, Oxford University Press, 1984.
4. A. Light '"Returning to Manderley" romance fiction, female sexuality and class', *Feminist Review*, no.16 (summer, 1984) p.7.
5. J. Laplanche and J.-B. Pontalis, 'Phantasy (or Fantasy)', *The Language of Psychoanalysis*, London, Hogarth Press, 1983, p.316. I have chosen to follow the general American usage, and have used a single spelling 'fantasy' for both conscious and unconscious fantasy.
6. J. Mitchell, 'Psychoanalysis: a humanist humanity or a linguistic science?', in *Women: The Longest Revolution: Essays in Feminism, Literature and Psychoanalysis*, London, Virago, 1984, pp.233–47.
7. J. Laplanche and J.-B. Pontalis, 'Fantasy and the origins of sexuality', *International Journal of Psychoanalysis*, vol.49, part 1 (1968), pp.1–17, reprinted in this volume.
8. S. Freud, 'A child is being beaten', *The Standard Edition of the Complete Psychological Works of Sigmund Freud*, London, 1953–74, vol.XVII, p.177.
9. T. Modleski, *Loving with a Vengeance: Mass-produced Fantasies for Women*, London, Methuen, 1984, p.57.

10. ibid. There are, however, many instances of psychic states other than hysteria where subjects see themselves from outside. See, for example, Freud's discussion in 'Screen memories' [1899], *SE*, vol.III.

11. As in the work of Melanie Klein and others. N. Chodorow, *The Reproduction of Mothering*, Berkeley and Los Angeles, University of California Press, 1978, is an example of one kind of feminist appropriation of 'object relations' theory.

12. S. Freud, *Three Essays in the Theory of Sexuality* [1905], cit. Laplanche and Pontalis, this volume, p.20.

13. Laplanche and Pontalis, entry on 'Primal phantasies', in *The Language of Psychoanalysis*, op.cit., p.331.

14. S. Freud, 'The unconscious' [1915], in *On Metapsychology: The Theory of Psychoanalysis*, *Pelican Freud Library*, vol.11, Harmondsworth, Penguin, 1984, p.195.

15. Light, op.cit., p.7.

16. Inside cover blurb, *The Thorn Birds*.

Valerie Walkerdine

# VIDEO REPLAY:
## families, films and fantasy

I am seated in the living room of a council house in the centre of a large English city. I am there to make an audio-recording as part of a study of 6-year-old girls and their education. While I am there, the family watches a film, *Rocky II*, on the video. I sit, in my armchair, watching them watching television. How to make sense of this situation?

Much has been written about the activity of watching films in terms of scopophilia. But what of that other activity, film theory, or, more specifically, what about this activity of research, of trying so hard to understand what people see in films? Might we not call this the most perverse voyeurism?[1] Traditionally, of course, observation – like all research methods in the human and social sciences – has been understood as, at worst, minimally intrusive on the dynamics and interaction unfolding before the eyes of the observer, who is herself outside the dynamic. My argument is that such observation, like all scientific activity, constitutes a voyeurism in its will to truth, which invests the observer with 'the knowledge', indeed the logos. The observer then should be seen as the third term, the law which claims to impose a reading on the interaction. This is offered as an explanation to which the observed have no access and yet which is crucial in the very apparatuses which form the basis of their regulation. In addition, the observer becomes the silent Other who is present in, while apparently absent from, the text. Clearly, I cannot escape the contradictions and effects of my own need here to produce a reading, an analysis, an account of what happened. But in order to insert myself explicitly into the text, I shall attempt to speak also of my own identification with the film I watched with this family.

My concern is therefore not just with the voyeurism of the film spectator, but also with the voyeurism of the theorist – in whose desire for knowledge is inscribed a will to truth of which the latent content is a terror of the other who is watched.

From this perspective, I shall explore, in a preliminary way, the relationship of families to television and video and, more particularly, the effectivity of the films they watch upon the constitution of family dynamics. Within film theory concepts from psychoanalysis do not seem to have been used to examine how specific films have been read in practice, nor how they produce their specific effects. Identification, for example, is often discussed in terms of the effectivity of representation as distorted perception – the viewer is accorded no status which pre-exists the film. Psychoanalysis is used, in the end, to explore the relations within a film rather than to explain the engagement with the film by viewers already inserted in a multiplicity of sites for identification.

The family I shall be discussing did not watch *Rocky II* as ideal, acultural viewers, for example, but in relation to complex and already constituted dynamics. And these dynamics cannot simply be reduced to differences of class, gender and ethnicity – although the question of how these enter into the divided relations of domestic practices is, nevertheless, central.

Such differences themselves exist within a regime of practices, in which 'fantasy' and 'reality' already operate in a complex and indiscernible dynamic.[2] In trying to understand the domestic and family practices in which adults and children are inscribed, therefore, I examine the play of discourses and the relations of signification which already exist. And I approach the viewing of the film in the same way, as a dynamic intersection of viewer and viewed, a chain of signification in which a new sign is produced – and thus a point of production or creation in its own right.

In discussing families watching films, I try to show how aspects of the filmic representations are incorporated into the domestic practices of the family. This explains the themes and emphases in my argument. First, there is the question of how to understand the act of *watching*. I shall describe the watching of families as a surveillant voyeurism, a 'will to tell the truth' about families which contains a set of desperate desires – for power, for control, for vicarious joining-in – as well as a desperate fear of the other being observed. Secondly, I want to challenge the 'intellectualization of pleasures' which seems to be the aim of much analysis of mass film and television. In opposition to the implicit contrast between the masses narcotized by the mass fantasies produced by the consciousness industry and the intellectual unbefuddled by the opium of ideology, it seems to me that we should look at the desire for forms of mastery that are present in our own subjectification as cultural analysts before rushing to 'save' 'the masses' from the pleasures of imaginary wish-fulfilment. Thirdly, therefore, I stress the materiality of power and oppression. Politics, in other words, are central to the analysis.

## Rocky II

The Coles are a working-class family. They live on a council estate and have three children – Joanne, aged 6, Robert, 9, and James, 13 – together with a large Alsatian dog, named Freeway.[3] I am seated in their living room. The video of *Rocky II* is being watched, sporadically, by the whole family. I sit there, almost paralysed by the continued replay of round 15 of the final boxing sequence, in which Mr Cole is taking such delight. Paralysed by the violence of the most vicious kind – bodies beaten almost to death. How can they? What do they see in it? The voyeuristic words echo inside my head, the typical response of shame and disgust which condemns the working class for overt violence and sexism (many studies show, for example, how much more sex-role stereotyping there is amongst working-class families). In comparison with a bourgeois liberalism it seems shameful, disgusting (key aspects of voyeurism) and quite inexplicable except by reference to a model of pathology.

I do not remember if I saw all of the film then. All I recall now is the gut-churning horror of the constant replay. Much later, when beginning to do the work for an analysis, I hired the video of *Rocky II* and watched it in the privacy of my office, where no one could see. And at that moment I recognized something that took me far beyond the pseudo-sophistication of condemning its macho sexism, its stereotyped portrayals. The film brought me up against such memories of pain and struggle and class that it made me cry. I cried with grief for what was lost and for the terrifying desire to be somewhere and someone else: the struggle to 'make it'. No longer did I stand outside the pleasures of engagement with the film. I too wanted Rocky to win. Indeed, I *was* Rocky – struggling, fighting, crying to get out. I am not saying that there is one message or reading here for all to pick up. On the contrary the film engages me as a viewer at the level of fantasy because I can insert myself into, position myself with, the desires and pain woven into its images. Someone else might have identified with Rocky's passive and waiting wife. But Rocky's struggle to become bourgeois is what reminded me of the pain of my own.[4] The positions set up within the film then create certain possibilities, but it seems to be the convergence of fantasies and dream which is a significant in terms of engaging with a film.

One aspect of the popularity of Hollywood films like the *Rocky* series is that they *are* escapist fantasies: the imaginary fulfilment of the working-class dream for bourgeois order. And they reveal an escape route, one which is all the more enticing given the realistic mode of its presentation, despite the very impossibility of its realism.[5] Such are popular films then, not because violence or sex-role stereotyping is part of the pathology of working-class life, but because escape is what we are set up to want, whatever way we can get it. For the majority of women and men, the escape-route open to me, that of the mind, of being clever, is closed. It is the body which presents itself either as the appropriate vehicle

The editors and publishers regret that permission to print an illustration of Sylvester Stallone in *Rocky II* on this page was refused.

for bourgeois wardship (all those women starlets, beauty queens and 'kept' women) or for the conquering champion who has beaten the opponents into submission.

What is important for me about watching a film like this is the engagement, the linking, of the fantasy space of the film and viewer. Watching *Rocky II*, to be effective, necessitates an already existent constitution of pains, of losses and desires for fulfilment and escape, inhabiting already a set of fantasy spaces inscribing us in the 'everyday life' of practices which produce us all. This does not imply a concept of a unitary subject, whose location in a 'social totality' determines the reading of a film, but rather a fragmented subjectivity in which signifying practices produce manifest and latent contents for the inscription of fantasy. Such wishes cannot be understood outside signifying activity – which is itself also discursive and involves aspects of power and regulation.

The magic convergence, therefore, is an act of signification, the fusion of signifier and signified to produce a new sign, a new place, desire leaping across the terminals, completing the circuit, producing the current. These multiple sites of my formation, these dynamic relations, are the diversity of practices in which power and desire inscribe me. The reader is *not* simply in the text, not then the spectator in the film, motivated simply by a pathological scopophilia. The *position* produced for the reader or spectator is not identical with an actual reader constituted in multiple sites and positions. Perhaps the 'desire to look' belongs with the film theorist and social or behavioural scientist who disavow their own engagement and subsume their own fantasies into a move into the symbolic, the desire for the mastery of explanation. Just as there is no 'reader' (simply and exclusively) 'in the text' nor is there a preformed subject whose experience is reflected, biased or distorted in the film. If fantasies of escape are what we are set up for, then any amount of cinematic fantasy posing as realism about the drudgery of our lives will not convince us to abandon our enticing fantasies.

There is, in this watching, a moment of *creation* – if it is effective and successful as a cultural product for the mass market whose desires it helps to form. There is certainly an aesthetic or a pleasure, and yet each of these terms is more redolent of an up-market art movie in which there are taken only to be acceptable, not nasty, pleasures. An aesthetic is cold. What I am talking about is red hot. It is what makes the youths in cinema audiences cheer and scream for Rocky to win the match – including many black youths, even though the Mr Big of boxing, whom he defeats, is black. It is what makes Mr Cole want to have the fight on continuous and instant replay forever, to live and triumph in that moment. And it is what makes me throb with pain.

*Rocky II*, like *Rocky I*, was a great box-office success. It brought in huge cash returns and Sylvester Stallone as Rocky was said to live out the part of the poor Italian-American who makes it in his 'real' life. The films tap into the classic working-class image of boxing as an escape-route for tough young men. Boxing turns oppression into a struggle to master it, seen as spectacle. In Stallone's later films this is transformed into a one-man defence of 'America' (against Russia in *Rocky IV*) and the 'forgotten heroes' of the Vietnam War in *Rambo*. Although it is easy to dismiss such films as macho, stupid and fascist, it is more revealing to see them as fantasies of omnipotence, heroism and salvation. They can thus be understood as a counterpoint to the experience of oppression and powerlessness.

*Rocky II* tells the story of a successful fighter who, after a successful career in the ring, tries to go straight. Despite his attempts to achieve respectability and a 'decent' lifestyle, he can find no way out of the misery of menial manual labour (working in an abattoir) except a return to boxing. Rocky is portrayed as a 'tryer', a 'fighter', a small man who beats the black, villainous Mr Big by dint of his perseverance, his 'sticking power'. The story thus engages the fight for the bourgeois dream of the small man who has 'brawn not brains'. Rocky's attempts to get a clerical job or to become an actor in television commercials are doomed because he cannot read. It is the woman he marries, the quiet girl, who equally struggles for him, who bears and nearly loses 'his' child, who, like the good-enough bourgeois mother, teaches him to read. Yet, failing all else, in order to become respectable, he has to return to fighting and he has to fight to win, nearly killing himself in the process. The struggle to be respectable is therefore also to be able to 'provide for' and 'look after' a wife and child/ren who will not need to work, suffer or go short of anything. The film itself is replete with such fantasies. What is important for Rocky's story is the presentation of the *necessity* of fighting for survival. Certainly here the fight pays off and the hero wins. But it validates trying and fighting and therefore the singular effectivity of bodily strength and the multiple significance of 'fighting'. Understood in this way, 'macho-masculinity' becomes no mindless sexism, but a bid for mastery, a struggle to conquer the conditions of oppression, which remain as terror. It also throws into sharp relief the effects of the bourgeois mastery of the mind. These do not require the *overt* forms of physical violence or shows of strength, which are replaced by symbolic violence and displays of logocentric pyrotechnics.

Intricately tied in with the necessity for fighting, and therefore for aggression, is the necessity to protect a 'good woman'. The wife is both to be protected from other men (with more money and more glittering prizes?) and to be protected from the 'streets' – from being the bad woman, the whore, the tart. She has to be kept pure and virginal. In this respect Rocky is represented as a 'big man' at home. The sets are made especially small so that he looks giant-size and yet remains a 'small man' in the outside world: a man who has to fight and to struggle therefore 'to be' the big man at home. This shift is especially significant for Mr Cole.

As well as being portrayed as bodily big at home and small outside and in the ring, Rocky is also presented as an outer spectacle, hiding inner pain. Rocky is a public hero who provides good entertainment. 'The crowd' and 'the public' do not see the inner suffering and struggle which produce this entertainment; only his wife does. In the opening minutes of the film, when Rocky has won a match after almost being beaten to death, he screams 'Adrienne, Adrienne', like a desperate child; her protector is in reality dependent upon her. Against a musical crescendo on the soundtrack they slowly struggle to reach each other. Finally, when he is safe in her arms, they say 'I love you' to each other. This shot is held for several seconds, before a cut to the titles for *Rocky II* – this narrative image provides the lead-in from, and flashback to, the first film.

Fighting, as a key signifier in the film, is related to a class-specific and gendered use of the body (as against the mind). Masculinity as winning is constantly played across by the possibility of humiliation and cowardice (that he is 'chicken'); Rocky's body is constantly presented as beaten, mutilated and punished. The film always presents this body as spectacle and triumph, triumph over and through that mutilation, which is the desperate fear which fuels it. Although such a reading of masculinity is now common within film analysis,[6] it is the *class-specific* aspects of this masculinity that are important. Physical violence is presented as the only way open to those whose lot is manual and not intellectual labour, and another aspect of this classed masculinity is the wardship of a woman who does not have to work (like a man) but whose domain is the domestic.

The fantasy of the fighter is the fantasy of a working-class male omnipotence over the forces of humiliating oppression which mutilate and break the body in *manual* labour. Boxing as a sport is a working-class-specific development of fighting, in which young poor men break their bodies for prize money. It is a classic working-class spectacle in that sense, in which the boxer's mutilation provides the sport for the spectators. What is to be won is both the symbolic conquering of oppression and monetary gain – although of course, young men are as exploited in boxing as anywhere else.

Echoes of upward mobility recur throughout the film, and not just in Rocky's attempts, despite his wife's protests, to display the 'proletarian flash' of cars, jewellery and clothes. Particularly significant is the way his attempts at respectability are seen to be thwarted by his failure at school.

Asked what he was thinking about in the last round of his fight as he is loaded into an ambulance, he replies, 'I don't know – that I should have stayed at school or something.' His interview for a clerical job goes like this:

> INTERVIEWER: How far did you go in high school, Mr Balboa? . . . Do you have a criminal record? Would you be interested in manual labour?
>
> ROCKY: Well, I've got nothing against honest manual labour, it's just that I'd like to see if I can make a living sitting down, like you're doing over there.[7]
>
> INTERVIEWER: Can I be honest? No one's going to offer you an office job: there's too much competition. Why don't you fight? I read somewhere that you're a very good fighter.
>
> ROCKY: Yeah, well, when you're punched in the face five hundred times, it kind of stings after a while.

And at a later interview, he is told:

> Hey, look, pal, you've got to be realistic. You've got no high school diploma, no qualifications, wouldn't you be better with a good paying menial job?

'Adapting to reality' is presented as the most punitive of options, for it condemns him to a life of misery and poverty. It is bourgeois dreams which provide a way out, and the body which is the vehicle, given an absence of 'brains'. Constantly, the 'assurance' of a secure gender, and class identity is subverted by Rocky's terror, struggle and failure – in fighting and reading for example. A coherent identity, a sense of having 'made it', is presented as a sham, not anything easily achieved.

Meanwhile Adrienne works and suffers in silence, having got a job in a pet shop to help out. She gives birth prematurely through overwork and goes into a coma. No wonder that Rocky needs to box, because he is saving her from death through overwork. She is a key figure: she simultaneously prevents Rocky from boxing and spurs him on to win. The struggle is thus also a specifically gendered struggle, in which positions relating to domestic and waged work are played out.

## The Coles

I have chosen to explore the term 'fight/ing/er' because it figures centrally in the *Rocky* films, not as a celebration of masculinity in a positive sense, but as something Rocky is 'driven to', a last resort.[8] I now want to consider how 'fighting' enters as a relation into domestic discursive practices and produces a certain effectivity with respect to the family members, linking this to my presence as an observer and thus to the monitoring of pathology (correct language for example) and to moral regulation.

Let me begin by outlining briefly how the observation was experienced as my surveillance of them. When I entered the house for the first recording, Mr Cole shouted to his daughter, 'Joanne, here's your psychiatrist!' I had never mentioned psychiatry, let alone psychology, and yet it was evident to him that I was monitoring normality/pathology. In addition to this, on several occasions he made reference to the monitoring of 'correct language'. Joanne would at first not wear the microphone and Mr Cole was quite clear that, if nothing was said into it, 'they' would think she had nothing to say. Quite.

> Do you know you're wasting the tape, you are missy. Gonna go back to school and say what did Dodo do at home? And they'll say 'nothing'. Here's the proof – a blank tape.

In addition, he tells his daughter to 'do nothing, just act normal' and yet tries to encourage her to speak by saying 'The rain in Spain falls mainly on the plain' or 'How now brown cow' (phrases often used in elocution lessons, of course) into the microphone. On other occasions, moral regulation centres around the dichotomy 'rude vs. respectable' behaviour.

How did the family watch *Rocky II*? I shall begin with the final, bloody rounds of the boxing match at the end of the film. At this time Mr Cole (F), Joanne (J), or Do, and her brother, Robert (R), were watching, together with the 3-year-old child of a friend, called Jonas. Mrs Cole (M) was in the kitchen, working, and 13-year-old James was elsewhere in the house. I reproduce below an annotated transcription of the sequence.[9]

### *Rocky II*, the video

Fight scene, possibly the 15th round.

000

R: (untranscribed)

F: Watch, watch. Cor he ain't half whacking him, ain't he, Do?

Watch, here.

010

F tells J to go and ask M to make some tea. J goes to the kitchen. M's friend is with her – Scottish accent – with her young child. They talk about karate.

050

J is back in the TV room. She brings in the doughnuts. Film is on in the background.

J goes out again. She talks to M in kitchen.

090

J is back in TV room. There is general conversation going on, 'Do you want a doughnut', etc. J is not saying much.

M's friend comes in with younger child.

112

J is sitting on the settee, eating a bun.

115

No one is saying much.

118

F: Hey, watch this, Rob.
R: Does he kill him?
F: Watch.

125

F pauses video or winds back to the closing round, because M is handing out the tea and cakes.

R: Mum, hurry up.
F: You ready?
M: What?
F: We've yet to see the end of this.

R: This is the 5th round.
F: Fifteenth, watch it.

Rocky fighting championship round, pitched against huge black opponent. Things aren't looking good. Rocky is taking a beating. The crowd is going wild, cheering, shouting.

Rocky is in his corner with his trainer, Chris, who is warning him.
ROCKY: I know what I'm doing.
CHRIS: Listen. You're getting killed out there.
ROCKY: It's my life.

Both fighters are in their corner with coaches. They are both badly beaten.

The commentator favours Rocky's opponent. He says 'All he has to do is stay awake to steal the title'.

There is talking in the background. M asks R to get something for her (?her slippers). R is put out.

R: Dad, stop it for a minute.
F: Ohhh, June.
M: Well, I wasn't to know. I thought you'd stopped it just for me.
F: No, we didn't stop it just for you. He's been trying to watch it.

The video is stopped again and wound back to the 15th round.

145
M and F are talking.

148
Getting ready to switch video back on.
F: Are you ready? (? to R or M)

149
Video is switched on.

This is the 15th round again. Rocky takes lots of punches from opponent. Then he fights back for a bit.
The crowd is shouting and cheering. Who for?
Both fighters are in a bad way – no one seems to be winning at the moment.

J talks about Jason.

J: He's got all jam down him.

155
Everyone is quiet, all watching the film.

Rocky begins to punch opponent who is too weak to retaliate by this time.
Both men's faces are a bloody mess. They both stagger round the ring, exhausted, but Rocky just has the upper hand.

161
The crowd chants 'Rocky, Rocky'.

F ask J if she likes her cake.

Suddenly the film switches to slow motion.

There is slow, dramatic music. Rocky and his opponent fall.

All the while Rocky's wife has been watching the fight at home with her brother.

She seems to feel every punch herself, she looks distressed. Her brother is enjoying the fight, cheering and jumping up and down. Rocky's wife gasps 'Oh'. She has her hands up to her face.

In the ring everyone is shouting for Rocky and opponent to get up. The crowd is still going wild. Rocky's coach is yelling for Rocky to get up.
Rocky just about manages to stagger to his feet before the countdown ends.
Film cuts to wife and her brother at home. They are both jumping up and down with joy.

Crescendo of triumphant music.

Rocky's face is a bloody mass as he accepts the prize.
He is very emotional.
He speaks to the TV cameras.
ROCKY: Thank you, thank you, I can't believe this is happening.

Rocky says that this is the greatest moment of his life, 'apart from when my kid was born'.

F hands round custard tarts.

172

R: They both fall down.

All very quiet in TV room.

175
Author and M talk about cakes.

179
F says something to R about the film (untranscribed)

185
Child (unidentified) talking.

190
M and author are talking.

He begins to cry.
He says to his wife at home 'I did
it'.

We see her crying as she quietly
says 'I love you, I love you.'

199

R: (? to F) I've gotta see, err, *Rocky
I*.

F: So have I. You saw *Rocky II*
today.

201

F: (untranscribed) ... after the
last film (laughs).

M(?): They're only messing.

There is much triumphant cheering and music.
End of film.

208

M: He says to Paul (untranscribed) ... no, he said, you're
Rocky II and I'm (untranscribed) ...

F: Paul said that? (laughs)

214

Turn over to television.

I would like to pick up several points from this. First, there is the specific
way in which a videotape is watched. This differs from the fascinated
concentration of the spectator in the darkened cinema, and also from the
way that television is often used as a backdrop to domestic routines. The
video has been deliberately selected and hired. More important, because –
as here – it can be stopped and replayed, it allows for more overt
connections to domestic practices and relations. Thus, secondly, Mr Cole
is able to point excitedly to the fighting – once to Joanne ('He ain't half
whacking him . . .'), later to Robert. Thirdly, Mr Cole both 'sends out for'
tea from Mrs Cole, who has to service the family, and also emphasizes that
they have not stopped the video to replay it for her. She is told in no
uncertain terms that 'we didn't stop it just for you', but for Robert who's
'been trying to watch it'. The fighting (linked to control of playback on the
video machine) is in this way most clearly presented as masculine, and
something from which women are excluded.

The theme of fighting came up many times in my recordings and interviews with the family. Fighting is the key term for Mr Cole in particular. He sees himself as a 'fighter' – against the system and *for* his children, whom he also encourages to fight. In my second recording, he urged Robert and Joanne to fight each other, telling Joanne to give as good as she gets: 'Well, bash him hard . . . You've been told, you whack him as hard as him.' Mr Cole also commented to me: 'It's surprising really, they're like this at home, but in school, if someone's whacked her, she's crying for about an hour after.'

In an interview with me, Mr and Mrs Cole also referred to Joanne as a tomboy, relating this to fears for her feminity. As Mr Cole observed: 'Obviously, she plays with dolls . . . (untranscribed) with any luck . . . (untranscribed) . . . she might get married and away we go . . . if we can find somebody.'

This concern for her future in terms of femininity is cross-cut by issues about class, in which fighting is a key term. When I commented that Joanne is quiet at school, Mr Cole saw the solution in terms of standing up for herself: 'Well, I think she needs to have a good row with one of the kids in school, give them a good hiding', adding that the two boys were 'the same, until they started like'. The fear would disappear if she could 'hit just as hard or harder'.

Other aspects of Mr Cole's relation to Joanne are salient here. His nickname for her is 'Dodo'. In this instance, although 'Dodo' might relate to an infantile mispronounciation of Joanne (Jo-Jo: Dodo), it also has links with infantilization and death. Dodo, says Mr Cole, is an extinct bird. Dodo is therefore an anachronism, something which no longer exists (a baby?) but which is kept alive in Mr Cole's fantasy of his daughter as dependent. It may also keep alive for Mr Cole a feminine which is opposite from, and Other to, himself.

Mrs Cole revealed her own reticence and similarity to Joanne when I questioned her about her own activities as a shop steward for NUPE. 'Well, I wouldn't have done it, not less I got roped into it,' she says; and 'I think if I had to stand up there and talk in front of a whole load of people I'd crack . . .' Mr Cole systematically encourages and undermines her, commenting that 'we're not talking about thousands of people'. He, conversely, is on the executive of the local Labour Party. He also 'fights for his children'. Mr Cole is the 'big man' at home. He 'talks for' his wife and systematically stops her talking. He is the 'fighter'. Like Rocky, he is a 'big man' at home who is 'small' and has to 'stand up for himself' in the world outside. Mr Cole is physically very small and the necessity for a fighting masculinity might therefore relate here to a terror of femininity (invested in Dodo?)

Two incidents illustrate this combativeness. The first was the Coles' successful struggle with their local education authority to get the elder son, James, into a prestigious school. The other was their campaign for the removal of asbestos from their daughter's school. For Mr Cole 'The point of fact is though, as any layman knows, asbestos kills'; unlike other parents and teachers he would not put education above physical health and life. The Coles were the only parents to keep their daughter home until the asbestos was removed – the only ones who 'had enough fight'. According to Mr Cole: 'we're Evil . . . We like to go against the system . . . I think they've got a little black book on me somewhere.' Indeed, the Coles are not liked by the school, for whom their fighting is perceived as 'trouble-making'. The notions of fighting stressed by the Coles also make Joanne's 'nurturant' teacher see her as a problem child.

Here the signifier 'fighting' enters into a different relation as it forms for the teacher a characteristic of combative and troublesome parents. It is read as a threat to her position and therefore relates to her reading of the Coles and her own fears of professional powerlessness. Joanne, for her part, stresses the need to 'work hard' and not to 'jaw'. She is largely silent in her interview with me and wants to go and 'get on with her work'.

Mr Cole also encourages his sons to fight and had Robert tell me a story of how he was banned from the school coach because he 'beat up' another boy. In addition, during one recording, he stopped the play-fight between Robert and Joanne with 'no fighting downstairs, eh? . . . Yes, sir, I'll kill you'. At the end of the recording, because of my presence, James managed to go off swimming without really getting permission. Mr Cole's response was, 'Wait till this lady goes, you've had it.' Here, 'fighting' is both an aspect of a bid for power over the body and yet a desperate struggle in relation to it. Fighting can be turned into a celebration of masculinity, but its basis is in oppression. This should also be understood, as in *Rocky*, as the desperate retreat to the body, because the 'way out', of becoming bourgeois through the mind is not open to Mr Cole.

Talking (saying 'the right thing', surveillance) is also crucial to aspects of power and regulation. As in *Rocky*, it establishes the place of the body and its place in relation to class and gender. Always there is a sense of surveillance of what is said, what can be said outside my hearing, its wrong and pathologized character, as well as the silence and silencing of Mrs Cole and Joanne, the combatative talk and fighting. Fighting and power/powerlessness therefore seem to me especially related to an experience of oppression and present a picture of the very 'failure' in covert regulation, the reasoned/reasoning avoidance of conflict which is the object of psycho-educational discourse and which therefore pathologizes them.[10] Although Mr Cole stressed his concern that Joanne should fight (like the boys), fighting remains an aspect of a gendered practice. It is the masculine body which is invoked even when Joanne fights, as a 'tomboy'. Mrs Cole's only role in this is to service. She performed domestic labour throughout the recordings and very rarely spoke. Mr Cole 'ordered' cups of tea and stressed that he likes times when his wife is on holiday best because 'she bakes every day'. Robert picks up Mrs Cole's status as a 'servant' in relation to Joanne, at one point calling her his 'slave'.

Fighting enters into the Coles' domestic practices as a relation in a way which is totally consonant with its presentation in *Rocky II*. That relation was crystallized in the watching of the film and the repetition of the final round. In terms of 'forwards' movements therefore, I am placing the relations of signification within history, and within an experience of gendered and class-specific lived oppression. Fighting is a key term in a discourse of powerlessness, of a constant struggle not to sink, to get rights, not to be pushed out. It is quite unlike the pathological object of a liberal anti-sexist discourse which would understand fighting as 'simply' macho violence and would substitute covert regulation and reasoning in language as less sexist.

It is in this way that I am aiming to demonstrate the *fixing* of fighting in that lived historicity – the *point de capiton*. I am stressing too that 'fight/ing/er' as a relation is quite specific in its meaning and therefore *not* co-terminous with what fighting would mean in, for example, a profes-sional middle-class household where both the regulation of conflict and the relation to oppression are quite different. This is an argument *against* a universalism of meaning, reading and interpretation. However, having examined the manifest content in which the relations of signification are historically fixed, this is not all there is. If we are to explore the latent content, it is necessary to ask what is suppressed/repressed/forgotten beneath the term? The working-class male body is a site of struggle and of anxiety, as well as pleasure. Mr Cole is a very small man. Fighting is a way of gaining power, of celebrating or turning into a celebration that which is constituent of oppression. Power in its manifest content covers over a terror of powerlessness, an anxiety beneath the pleasure.

Mr Cole is afraid of being 'soft', of a femininity lurking beneath the surface. This is referred to while the family watch the musical film *Annie* on video. It is seen as a 'women's film', and its fantasies, its dancing and singing, are constantly held up for ridicule. It is as though Mr Cole cannot bear to be seen (by me?) as liking such a film, as having passive, romantic fantasies. In this analysis, masculinity as fighting is a defence, a defence against powerlessness, a defence against femininity. The backwards movement can be articulated in relation to several points. The fear of being watched or monitored (counterpointed by my voyeurism), the expectation of female servicing (when his wife is at home), the *struggle* to fight against a fear: all these suggest that fighting represents a triumph over, repression of, defence against, the terror of powerlessness. This powerlessness, as in *Rocky II*, is presented as the humiliation of cowardice – of the man who cannot work, fight, protect women, and who is therefore feminized. Latent beneath Mr Cole's conscious self-identification as a fighter may lurk the fear of a small man whose greatest fear is his cowardice and femininity. It is this which has to be displaced by projection on to, and investment in, others (his wife, Joanne) who can be the objects of his protection and for whom he fights.

In psychoanalytic terms, such a reading keys into the necessity for – but also the fraudulence of – the phallus as a sign of power. Whether one finds in this an Oedipal struggle or an omnipotent, pre-Oedipal one, might be a point of dispute. However, my aim is not to suggest that the historical 'fighting' is really about a psychic relation. Far from it. It is to demonstrate the centrality of sexuality and power in the lived historicity of current struggles and the interminable intertwining of present and past, of material conditions and psychic relations. What is being fought for and fought against by Mr Cole can therefore be understood as having a manifest and latent content. But, since Mr Cole's (childhood) anxieties were and are produced in specific historical conditions, it is quite impossible and indeed dangerous to separate the one from the other.

**Psychical reality**

In suggesting that the practices in which Mr Cole is inscribed locate him as a 'fighter', I have argued for a reading of the manifest and latent content of the term. In understanding the relation between the manifest content of *Rocky II* and that of the Coles' domestic practices, it is necessary to examine the chains of signification produced which link the two. This is particularly possible with a video-recording, since it is watched partly as a backdrop to other practices rather than in a darkened cinema.

Identifications, like those of Rocky and Mr Cole as fighters, may be fictions inscribed in fantasy, set and worked out in the film itself, but they are also lived out in the practices in which Mr Cole is inserted. There is no 'real' of these practices which stands outside fantasy, no split between fantasy as a psychic space and a reality which can be known. If such fictional identities become 'real' in practices, they must have a psychical reality which has a positive effectivity in the lived materiality of the practices themselves. Such fictional identities must be created in the plays of power and desire. They are also therefore created in relational dynamics in which others can project fantasies on to, and invest them in, subjects within the family and other relations. I want to point up the psychical reality of such projections by dwelling for a moment upon Mr Cole's nickname for his daughter, Joanne: Dodo. Although I have suggested that this may well be derived from a childish mispronounciation 'Jo-Jo', it has other associations, which Mr Cole makes, of the Dodo as an extinct bird.

It is not uncommon for men to give baby names such as Dodo to women and girls in their wardship. Deborah Cherry and Griselda Pollock, for example, have analysed Rossetti's use of 'Guggums' for his model and mistress, Elizabeth Siddall.[11] They make reference to Lacan's statement that 'woman does not exist' except as a symptom and myth of a male fantasy. Like his later statement that the 'phallus is a fraud', Lacan sets up there the possibility that subjectivity is created not in a fixed and certain gender-identity, but in shifting and uncertain relations. The desire of the Other, the fears and fantasies inscribed in and projected on to that Other, help to fix what 'woman' and 'man' are taken to be, not the essentiality of their nature. In addition, actual men and women strive and struggle to be 'man' and 'woman' within specific regimes of representation.

Cherry and Pollock's concern is to demonstrate that Elizabeth Siddall, as the object of a regime of representation (i.e. Rossetti's paintings), is a fiction. They make a strong distinction between Rossetti's representations and the historical individual, Elizabeth Siddall, suggesting, for example, that, renamed Guggums by him, this fiction itself constituted the object of a male fantasy.

In using the idea of a 'historical individual', however, they seem to me to elide the issue of psychical reality and the material effectivity of such fantasied representations. It is as though they understand this fictional identity as, in some sense, not claiming a part of her lived historicity. This tends to deny the issues of wardship and patronage in which poor women became 'kept' women and in which their objectification consisted in the utilization of their bodies to keep them, as it were, from the streets. Elizabeth Siddall, like many other women of her class, used her body as her means of survival. Her infantilization as Guggums by Rossetti was a fantasy of protection played out right to the point of the romanticization of her death as a consumptive.

Let me take this further by taking as an example a number of representations from my own history. The first image is of Valerie Walkerdine, dressed as a bluebell fairy in a local carnival. There are a number of similar representations: a press photograph, from the local evening paper, *The Derby Evening Telegraph*; another press photograph (possibly from the same edition) in which Valerie Walkerdine poses with other entrants. 'Children waiting for the judging of the fancy dress parade at Mickleover branch of the British Legion Carnival Sports', runs the caption. The first photograph singles Valerie Walkerdine out from the other entrants, to be photographed alone. It does not mention that she won the competition. There are numerous other photographs of the bluebell fairy. Some appear to have been taken by the same press photographer, others are amateur photographs, posed in the front and

Valerie Walkerdine as Tinkerbell.

back of Valerie Walkerdine's home. In addition to this extraordinary and multiple validation of a single image, the bluebell fairy, we could add other dimensions to the creation of the fictional representation. Clearly the costume itself is a construction, made by a neighbour from, I assume, a store-bought paper pattern. My father, who was at that time a semi-skilled worker in the machine shop at Rolls Royce aero-engine division in Derby, made the metal wand at work. Relatedly, as with the representations of

Elizabeth Siddall, my father had a nickname for me, itself clearly related to the fairy fantasy. This was 'Tinky', abbreviated from Tinkerbell. It is perhaps relevant that, out of the female characters in *Peter Pan*, it is Tinkerbell and not Wendy, which was chosen. By examining the regime of representations in which Tinkerbell enters as a relation, we can therefore begin to understand the constitution of Tinky and the bluebell fairy as fictions, representations constructed in the fantasied image of the Other. 'Valerie Walkerdine' was, in this guise, to be gazed at, dressed up to look like this and designated, in naming, its object.

In *Peter Pan*, Tinkerbell is certainly not the mother, this ascription being given to Wendy. She appears therefore to be another and opposite designation of the feminine. Perhaps then she is, in Juliet Mitchell's terminology, the hysteric.[12] That is, Tinkerbell is tiny, childlike, even smaller than the children in the story, much smaller than the eternal child Peter Pan. She is charming, mischievous, constantly comes between Peter and Wendy, and works magic. She is a fairy who, at one point, saves Peter's life by risking her own, and who is saved only by the audience's being told to believe in fairies to keep her alive. Wishes, wish-fulfilment then keep this representation a living symbol. But of what?

A fairy is not a human woman. She is tiny. She works magic, casts spells, charms, is not quite of this world. She does not grow up to be a woman. There are several similarities here with Elizabeth Siddall. Tinkerbell is feminine, but she is safe – the perpetrator of childhood charm, magic. She is a sexual object and yet totally safe. She is *not* a woman and not quite human. She seems to be the opposite of the mother. Feminine and powerless, the object of the male gaze, she is that Other created in his image, which is not the mother or the wife, but the one which he has power to construct, his Other, his forbidden femininity, the powerless child, object of his protection and wardship. The child who 'casts a spell' is magic, does not grow up, is doing the magic herself and yet is all dressed up to *be* charming, the construction and representation of a fantasy. However, this archetypical femininity, this object constructed in the male gaze, as femininity, is rather strange. It is a sexualized childhood certainly, but it seems to be a narcissistic image of the femininity of man, the hysteric, denying castration, the female constructed in man's narcissistic image. The representations of Elizabeth Siddall, the 'Guggums' created by Rossetti, were said to resemble the artist. When I examine these representations of myself, they are the site of an anxiety that I closely resemble my father. But is not the bluebell fairy saved by her feminine charms? The fairy is unattainable, not quite human, charming. Desire, passion and incest are thereby displaced and hidden.

Clearly this vision and creation of 3-year-old Valerie Walkerdine was much admired. There are *so many* photographs. The problem for me, in relation to these representations, comes in precisely what Cherry and Pollock invest in the historical individual. Although the point that they are making is crucial and well taken – that it is a fiction which is constructed – nevertheless, we cannot simply displace the 'historical individual' as though she were no part of, or in no way related to, this régime of representations. How did Guggums become one aspect of her fractured subjectivity? How did she become inserted as a subject into particular sexual and artistic practices such that these representations were produced? It seems to me necessary to move towards an investment of desire, in which Elizabeth Siddall, like myself as the bluebell fairy, *wants* to live that fiction, basking in the gaze of the Other who constitutes it. Similarly we cannot set Rossetti, nor my father, or those other Others, outside the fictions in which their own desire is created. The phallus too is a fraud.

The fantasy of Tinky and the bluebell fairy designate me, and I want to be there, to *be* that fairy – small, protected, adored and never growing up. Therefore to enter that fantasy. At what cost, though? The gaze is to be returned. To this day I can feel surging through my body the effect of the smile necessary to pose for such a gaze. Still, statuesque, frozen in the look, the light shining in the eyes of the Other. Only recently have I been able to understand its incredible investment of a fantasy in me, and to wonder what is hoped for in that image, to go beyond the safety of that gaze to anger at its patronage. A fantasy of childhood charms forever, remembered as I searched that book treasured by so many little girls, called *Flower Fairies*,[13] each ethereal little fairy painted, dressed like a flower in delicate watercolours. Such representations form an important site for the investment and creation of my desire. Tinky was not all I became, but it related to a mutually lived-out fantasy. I wanted to be and to remain Tinky. The affirmatory gaze in its narcissistic reflection confirmed the positivity of that site of subjugation. Let me elaborate simply then: certain aspects of this fiction seem relevant and salient to the constitution of the feminine as the hysteric in these two examples. First, it may be relevant that it was my father who manufactured the wand, precisely that which is waved to cast a spell – a fairy with a phallus?[14] Secondly, this gaze, this representation crystallizes wardship. As in Lacan's 'God and the *jouissance* of The Woman', the gazing, watching Other provides safety – the child who never grows up and, as in Lacan's vision, the moment of jouissance is the moment of death.[15]

For the safe place is an impossible location. In both the Tinky and Guggums representations, the child-woman is given a baby-name. In my case illness was a central trope. I was constantly ill with tonsillitis (passivity, diminutive size, not quite of this world). Elizabeth Siddall was more than a sickly child. She was a consumptive: she died, playing out the sadomasochistic regimes. The haunting, ethereal quality of the pale femininity of the Rossetti paintings, the romanticization of death, celebrate the production of a femininity whose goal is death. And who, in those representations, lives on as in Rossetti's fantasy? Not a strong and healthy Elizabeth Siddall, capable of moving beyond the artist's protection, which also effected her rags-to-riches transformation from working-class girlhood to artist's model. However, such death-inducing representations are central to our culture of the child-woman, where slimming and anorexia retain the hysteric with the phallus in the protection of the father.

The important point is that such fantasies have a psychical reality which has positive and material effects when its significations are inscribed in actual practices. When Mr Cole calls his daughter 'Dodo', for example, that suggests not only his desire to infantilize his daughter, but also his identification of himself as a 'fighter' for her and on her behalf. He becomes her Other – the big man, the protector. This is then inscribed in the semiotics of their relating and their positioning within practices. But Joanne is not only infantilized as Dodo. She is also positioned, in contradiction as a 'fighter' like her father – Dodo and yet a 'tomboy'. This reveals the complexity of his identification with, and investment in, her as he makes her simultaneously his feminine ward to be protected and later 'married off' and his masculinized working-class fighter, like her brothers. Joanne's fractured subjectivity is therefore lived not without some pain produced by this splitting.

### Recognition and latent content

I argued at the beginning of this article that psychoanalytically oriented film theory, despite its many strengths, still elides certain problems about subjectivity when it implies that subject-positions are produced *within* the discourses of filmic representations. To some extent that should be read as a self-criticism too. Like many other people, I have drawn on the work of Althusser, Lacan and Foucault to understand the relation between 'positioning in discourse', 'modes of signification' and the 'semiotics of the psyche'.[16] Although the centrality of plays of signification to the formation of subjectivity has been emphasized within such modes of analysis, very little empirical work has been done on how the process actually works in the regulative practices of daily life. As a result of concentrating on the dynamics within regimes of representation, we risk ending up with a sense of the determined and passive subject we had hoped to avoid. Hence the question I have tackled here: how do we reassert the importance of the creation of subjectivity as active, even if the subject is caught at an intersection of discourses and practices?

The subject is positioned or produced in multiple sites. These are not all-embracing, but may work with or against each other. The person watching a film, for example, will always be already inscribed in practices which have multiple significations. That is why the film cannot in and of itself produce a reading which 'fixes' the subject. Rather the viewing constitutes a point of dynamic intersection, the production of a new sign articulated through the plays of significance of the film and those which already articulate the subject. This sort of approach should make it possible to deal with the issue of specific readings, and the location of readers/viewers, without collapsing into essentialism. Thus Claire Johnston has argued for:

> a move away from a notion of the text as an autonomous object of study and towards the more complex question of subjectivity seen in historical/social terms. Feminist film practice can no longer be seen simply in terms of the effectivity of a system of representation, but rather as a production of and by subjects already in social practices, which always involve heterogeneous and often contradictory positions in ideologies.[17]

As I say, though, the problem has been that, however clearly this agenda has been set, there has been little empirical work to back it up so far. My account of how the Coles (and I) watched *Rocky II* is an attempt to show the effectivity of filmic representations within the lived relations of domestic practices – signifying and discursive practices which are historically constituted and regulated.[18]

This means attempting to examine the relations between domestic practices (and other practices and discourses) in a number of ways. We need to understand how these 'lived relations' are formed through régimes of meanings which position the participants and which 'lock into' relations of signification in the media. But more than this, we need to go beyond the present use of psychoanalysis. That is, by using psychoanalysis to understand relations *within* a film and then using voyeurism to understand the viewer, we are left in a sterile situation which assumes that all viewers 'take on' the psycho-dynamic of the film as far as it relates to the Oedipal conflict. As Laura Mulvey and others have pointed out, this leaves women as viewers in a difficult position. As ethnographic studies such as those of Janice Radway have shown, it also imposes universalistic meanings on particularistic viewing situations.[19] Radway and others, however, are almost forced back on to an 'effects' model because they end up having to understand readers and viewers as pre-located and pre-determined. Cathy Urwin has pointed out that children's use of figures from the popular media in their therapy is not necessarily Oedipal.[20] Using a Kleinian framework she finds pre-Oedipal struggles. Importantly she suggests that the use made by the children of these figures, although it relates in some ways to the dynamic in the film or television programme, particularly relates to their own struggles in therapy. Hence a young boy can use the figure of Superman, not in relation to an Oedipal resolution, but as a carrier for his fantasies of omnipotent power. This suggests that different readers will 'read' films, not in terms of a pre-existing set of relations of signification or through a pathology of scopophilia, but by what those relations *mean to them*.

Although we have to understand the dynamics within which the viewer is already inscribed in order to engage with viewing, I do not wish to resort to an essentialistic reading, nor to a notion of a preformed subject. It is important not to reduce each viewer to some 'stage' in the analytic move from infancy to maturity. Rather the viewers are themselves created in dynamics which are understood through, and inscribed in, historically specific practices and relations of power and oppression. The fantasies, anxieties and psychical states cannot be understood outside that history.

This, as I have stressed throughout this article, applies as much to the position of the researcher as to the families or viewers being observed. I have already considered my own relation to *Rocky II* and to fathers' infantilization of girl children. But what of my position as researcher? As I suggested in the introduction, this itself constitutes part of the dynamic I was studying. It has to be understood not as a problem of 'intrusiveness', but in terms of the power/knowledge couplet.

As observer, I became a 'Surveillant Other' not only watching but also producing a knowledge that feeds into the discursive practices regulating families. The 'social scientist' is the producer of a 'truth' which claims to 'know' those whom it describes. Together, observer and observed constitute a couple in the play of power and desire. We therefore need to examine the response of the observed to their experience of surveillance. Equally important, however, is the theorist's 'desire to know', for this contains both a fantasy of power and also a fear of the observed. (Scientific objectivity might therefore be seen as the suppression or disavowal of this desire.)

Humanistic forms of social science often attempt to escape this inevitable power dynamic by reducing 'power-differentials' or by 'putting subjects at ease'. Despite these patronizing attempts to get 'beyond power', I would argue that most therapeutically and psychoanalytically oriented work on families and films or television clearly remains normative and regulative.[21]

However disguised, the observer's account is a *regulative* reading which pathologizes the participants' actions. The knowledge it produces will inevitably differ from the meanings ascribed to them by the participants – meanings they produce as they live out the practices in which they are formed. But the struggle between them is not simply about the 'values' attached to meanings. Nor is it about validating people's interpretations. It is a struggle about power with a clear material effectivity. One might therefore ask how far it is possible for the observer to 'speak for' the observed.

The families I was studying in my research (which, as I have noted, concerned the education of 6-year-old girls rather than film or television watching) clearly indicated on many occasions that they experienced me as surveillant Other. Their responses to my presence cannot be understood without taking this into consideration. Equally I was struck by the fantasies, anxieties and pain triggered in me by being perceived as a middle-class academic confronting a working-class family. Although I invested considerable desire into wanting to 'be one of them' at the same time as 'being different', no amount of humanistic seeking for the 'beyond ideology' would get them to see in me a working-class girl 'like them'. Rather than disavow that dynamic, therefore, it became necessary to work *with* it and to acknowledge the clear effectivity of their reading of me as middle class in the data I collected.

But I also wanted to examine my multiple positioning as both middle-class academic *and* working-class child, to use my own fantasies in exploring how the participants perceived me and how they understood their experience. In this work I developed the term *recognition* as a reworking of Althusser's concept of 'mis-recognition'. Rather than engage with its negative connotations for the study of ideological (i.e. always-already distorting) interpellation, I wanted to use the idea of recognition *positively* in my work on domestic practices. Recognition is what places the subject in the historical moment. It is achieved through the circulation of the signifier as a relation in present discursive practices. Like Lacan's *point de capiton*, recognition acts as a nodal point (involving also forgetting and the repression of what went before): it provides the post-structure. In my own research, therefore, I wanted to use my own fantasied positions within those practices as a way of engaging with their unconscious and conscious relations of desire and the plays of anxiety and meaning. Often when interviewing the participants I felt that I 'knew what they meant', that I recognized how the practices were regulated or that I understood what it was like to be a participant.[22] Using this 'recognition' to explore the positivity of how domestic relations are lived seems to me an important step beyond assertions that academics should side with the oppressed, that film-makers should see themselves as workers or that teachers should side with pupils. Such rhetoric may represent *our* wish-fulfilling denial of power and responsibility – a way of disavowing our position instead of accounting for it.

To take a rather mischievous example, Paul Willis's *Learning to*

*Labour* could be interpreted from this perspective as the story of an "earole' who wants to become a 'lad', a male academic vicariously becoming one of the boys. What is missing from such work is any account of the ethnographer's own position in the web of power/knowledge/desire. Another problem with much ethnographic work (my own included) has been the way it takes discourse at face value. In working with a transcript, for example, of what can we take it as evidence? Ethnographic interviews with adolescent working-class girls are often used to justify theories of girls' resistance, as is their anti-school behaviour and taking on of femininity (through using make-up or subverting uniform). Yet could these discourses and actions not equally well hide pain and anxiety in relation to academic failure? The problem of ethnographic work is how to take adequate account of the psychical reality of both observer and observed.

This means disrupting the commonsense split between 'fantasy' and 'reality'. Fantasy is invested in domestic relations just as much as it is in films – that is the point I have been making in drawing out the intersection between the fantasy-structure of *Rocky II* and the domestic dynamics of the Cole family. The fiction, the fantasy is created in this interaction, not only in the projection and introjection between the voyeuristic observer and the observed.[23] This emphasis on the inscription of fantasies within family practices raises the question of the power relations within those practices and their regulation. Power, however, as Cathy Urwin has demonstrated,[24] is inextricably intertwined with desire. If positions created within the regulation of domestic practices also generate fantasy and desire, it becomes necessary to dig beneath the surface of the discourse – its manifest content – to find the latent content behind it.

Here, for example, I have attempted to analyse the constitution of subjectivity within a variety of cultural practices, of which watching videos is one. I have tried to avoid either essentializing social differences between viewers or reducing the relations of fantasy and desire inscribed within a film to any one reading without engaging with the family relations and domestic practices into which the video is inserted. Instead, I have asked how people make sense of what they watch and how this sense is incorporated into an existing fantasy-structure.

The basis for this approach is to be found in Freud's analysis of dreaming, where he explores the relationship between dreams as fantasy-scenarios and the inscription of those fantasies in everyday life. He takes their manifest content, as consciously described by the patient, and then focuses on the dream-work – the chains of associations, the changing patterns of condensation and displacement – to discover their latent content. Just as Freud drew on associations made by the patient and also on issues which had previously surfaced in the analysis, I have taken certain key signifiers which feature both in the film and in the domestic practices and examined how associations, either of equation or opposition, are made by the participants at various points in the dialogue.

Although this mode of analysis remains to be developed, I would like to stress two kinds of movement within these relations of signification. One, which I call the forwards movement, anchors and fixes the signifier within current practices, producing the regulative effectivity of the term as it operates as a relation within a régime of representation and truth. The other is a backwards movement which traces the associations of the signifier into the unconscious. This may relate not only to the history of the subject, but also to the forgotten relations inside the practice itself. (Some working-class domestic practices, for example, may have developed in relation to defences against poverty, and yet they may persist as cultural practices even when there is no threat of poverty.) By focusing on the relation between these two movements, it is possible to identify latent content without implying (as happens in certain forms of psychoanalysis) that there must be a psychical Originary Moment which is not also social-historical. Equally my approach acknowledges the effectivity of the manifest content: manifest/latent is not the same as phenomenal/real. It therefore engages with the positivity of recognition as it is lived. The signifiers generate their meanings from the living out of historically specific relations, not from the internal rules of a Saussurian sign system. Meanings inscribed within power/knowledge relations provide a basis for surveillant and regulative practices; other meanings are produced in opposition to them from people's lived historicity. Meaning thus becomes a site of oppression, contestation and political struggle. The subject therefore cannot be positioned in a single textual location which can be put under erasure to reveal the infinity of traces. As Derrida remarks, this activity contains a fiction of mastery over the process of uncovering, the deconstructing of the truth beyond the telling of the truth.

The examination of latent content would involve an infinite historical regression, were it not for the forwards movement which anchors the subject in history. We might make our own history, but in conditions which are not of our choosing – that is, in relations of domination and subordination/subjectification. Derrida accuses Foucault of forgetting that the subject is to be put under erasure. But if we are to produce a history of reading of *the present* and a political practice that is adequate to it, then we need to understand how surveillance functions, how power works, where the buck stops. We need to examine how existing discursive régimes function 'in truth' and have a positive effectivity in positioning the subject. The quasi-Foucauldian approach to how the truth operates is an attempt to produce the forwards movement of which I have spoken.

## Fantasy and intellectualization

How finally are we to come to terms with the voyeuristic social scientist? The 'space' of observation, I would argue, like that of watching videos, is a fantasy space in which certain fictions are produced. One effect of these fictions is to constitute a knowledge, a truth that is incorporated into the regulation of families. At the same time, the 'claim to truth' designates the social scientist as an expert in the bourgeois order which produces this intellectuality. But it also, I have suggested, hides the fear that motivates it. The masses must be known because they represent a threat to the moral and political order; the theorist/voyeur expresses shame and disgust at the 'animal passions' which have to be monitored and regulated – and which she cannot enjoy. This logic of intellectualization is evident in many studies of audiences. I therefore want to consider how the fantasies and fictions embodied in academic accounts as well as in films are inscribed in the daily lives of ordinary people.

Modern apparatuses of social regulation, along with other social and cultural practices, produce knowledges which claim to 'identify' individuals. These knowledges create the possibility of multiple practices, multiple positions. To be a 'clever child' or a 'good mother', for example, only makes sense in the terms given by pedagogic, welfare, medical, legal and other discourses and practices. These observe, sanction and correct how we act; they attempt to define who and what we are. They are, however, criss-crossed by other discourses and practices – including those of popular entertainment, for example. This multiplicity means that the practices which position us may often be mutually contradictory. They are also sites of contestation and struggle. We never quite fit the 'positions' provided for us in these regulatory practices. That failure is, in Freudian psychoanalysis, both the point of pain and the point of struggle. It shows repeatedly that the imposition of fictional identities – or socialization – does not work.[25]

What I am proposing here is a model of how subjectification is produced: how we struggle to become subjects and how we resist provided subjectivities in relation to the regulative power of modern social apparatuses. This model rejects the old image of the masses trapped in false consciousness, waiting to be led out of ideology by radical intellectuals. Rather, I would argue, these two categories form a couple defined and produced in relation to each other. The modern bourgeois order depends upon a professional intellectual élite which 'knows' and regulates the proletariat.[26] One side effect of the creation of this 'new middle class' has been that some of its radical members, having themselves achieved social mobility through the route of higher education, claim that it is *only* through rationality and intellectualization that the masses can see through the workings of ideology and so escape its snares.

The audience for popular entertainment, for example, is often presented as sick (voyeuristic, scopophilic) or as trapped within a given subjectivity (whether defined by the social categories of class, race and gender or by a universalized Oedipal scenario). What is disavowed in such approaches is the complex relation of 'intellectuals' to 'the masses': 'our' project of analysing 'them' is itself one of the regulative practices which produce *our* subjectivity as well as theirs. We are each Other's Other – but not on equal terms. Our fantasy investment often seems to consist in believing that we can 'make them see' or that we can see or speak *for* them. If we do assume that, then we continue to dismiss fantasy and the Imaginary as snares and delusions. We fail to acknowledge how the insistent demand to see through ideology colludes in the process of intellectualizing bodily and other pleasures.

It was in opposition to that approach that I tried to make sense of Mr Cole's self-identification as a fighter. I argued that fighting relates not only to masculinity, but also to lived oppression, to the experience of powerlessness and the fear of it. The implication is that we should stop being obsessed by the illusory tropes of an oppressive ideology, and that we should start to look at fantasy spaces as places for hope and for escape from oppression as well.

Asked why they read romantic fiction, the women Janice Radway spoke to said that it helped them to escape from the drudgery of servicing their families – and thus to cope with it. They read at quiet moments (in bed, in the bath) when they could recall the tattered dreams of their youth and long for someone to love them as they wanted to be loved. Their reading was therefore double-edged: not only a way of coming to terms with their daily lives, but also an act of resistance and hope. It is this question of the hope and pleasure that women invest in romantic fiction, which Radway brings out very clearly, that I want to dwell on. But I depart from Radway's analysis, because she remains caught up with the idea that these readers might move 'beyond' such romantic notions; she also rejects psychoanalytic explanations for failing to engage with the specificity of readers' lives.[27] That seems to underestimate both the material *and* the psychical reality of these women's servitude and the pain of their longing for something else.

The danger with such approaches to the study of the audience, however radical in intent, is that their insistence on the transcendence of ideology through the intellectualization of pleasure(s) can itself become part of a broader regulatory project of intellectualization. This seems to be implicit, for example, in the description of a course for women about women and/in the cinema.[28] When the students were encouraged to deconstruct the codes of representation in various types of film, some found it difficult because it meant giving up, or supplanting, the pleasure they had previously felt in watching movies. Similarly, in many media studies courses in schools, children are asked to analyse popular television programmes. What concerns me is how these women, children, whoever, are being asked to deal with their previous enjoyment of such things – a pleasure shared with family, friends and their general social and cultural environment. It seems that they are being left little room for any response other than feeling stupid, or despising those who are still enjoying these 'perverse' pleasures.

What this typically academic emphasis on rationality and intellectualization can overlook are the specific conditions of the formation of pleasures for particular groups at a given historical moment. Rather than seeing the pleasures of 'the masses' as perverse, perhaps we should acknowledge that it is the bourgeois 'will to truth' that is perverse in its desire for knowledge, certainty and mastery. This is the proper context in which to understand the *desire* to know the masses, the voyeurism of the (social) scientist. The crusade to save the masses from the ideology that dupes them can obscure the real social significance of their pleasures and, at the same time, blind us to the perversity of radical intellectual pleasures. The alternative is not a populist defence of Hollywood, but a reassessment of what is involved in watching films. This becomes part of the experience of oppression, pain and desire. Watching a Hollywood movie is not simply an escape from drudgery into dreaming: it is a place of desperate dreaming, of hope for transformation.

Popular pleasures produced in/under oppression can be contrasted with the more cerebral pleasures of discrimination or deconstruction. These ultimately derive from the scientific project of intellectualization, the Cogito, which culminates in the scientific management of populations, the power/knowledge of the modern social order. The intellectualization of pleasures, in other words, is linked not just to the desire to know but also to the project of controlling nature. This has had as its other and opposite a fear of the powers of the unknown, the animal, the unlawful, the insane, the masses, women, blacks. These 'others' became objects to be known and thus civilized and regulated. There exists among the bourgeoisie a terror of the pleasures of the flesh, of the body, of the animal passions seen to be burning darkly in sexuality and also in violent uprisings. No surprise then that the regulation of children's consumption of the modern media focuses so obsessively on sex and violence.

In the end then the 'problem' of popular pleasures – the Coles' enjoyment of *Rocky II* – turns out to lie not (only) with 'the masses' but (also) with the fears and desires of the bourgeois intellectual. The desire to know and to master conceals the terror of a lack of control, a paranoia which is the opposite of omnipotent fantasy, a megalomania. These I have called perversions to point up the way in which they project their own terror of the masses on to the masses themselves. It is this projection that motivates the desire to rationalize the pleasures of the body, to transform them into pleasures of the mind. This body/mind dualism valorizes mental labour as genius or creativity and denigrates the servicing and manual work which make them possible – the labour of the masses and their terrifying physicality. It is in this context of the mental/manual division that the physicality of *Rocky*, expressed so clearly in its violence, should be placed.

I have tried to establish the difference between the 'cold' aesthetic of high culture, with its cerebral and intellectualized appreciation, and the bodily and sensuous pleasures of 'low' cultures.[29] What is most important is to understand the different conditions in which these pleasures – and their associated pains and hopes – are produced. In the oppressive conditions of the bourgeois order 'animal passions' are regulated, the 'rising of the masses' is feared, the individual is defined in terms of brain or brawn, the only way out offered is through cleverness, guile, making it, working, trying. And so embourgeoisement is the only dream left in all those desires for, and dreams of, difference . . .

## Notes

This analysis would not have been possible without the work and insights of Helen Lucey and Diana Watson of the Girls and Mathematics Unit, University of London Institute of Education. Many of the arguments are developed in my 'On the regulation of speaking and silence', in C. Steedman, C. Urwin and V. Walkerdine (eds.), *Language, Gender and Childhood*, London, Routledge & Kegan Paul, 1985; V. Walkerdine *Surveillance, Subjectivity and Struggle*, Minneapolis, University of Minnesota Press, 1986; and *The Mastery of Reason*, in press; V. Walkerdine and H. Lucey, *Final Report of Grant No.C/00/23/033/1 to the Economic and Social Research Council*, 1985; and V. Walkerdine, H. Lucey and D. Watson, *The Regulation of Mothering* (working title), Cambridge, Polity Press, forthcoming. I would also like to thank Philip Corrigan, Dick Hebdige and David Morley for helpful comments and criticism.

1. Foucault has documented this in relation to a 'will to truth' in which the production of a knowledge has real effects in the surveillance and regulation of the Other. I add the dimension of *voyeurism* to this perverse will to truth because it allows us to explore the fears and fantasies present in this watching, classifying surveillance – the desire to *know* the Other and therefore to have power over, to control, to explain, to regulate it. This claim to certainty and truth becomes not normal, but profoundly perverse. It is linked both with disgust and with shame: shame at watching – desire to see how 'the other half lives' – and the vicarious excitement in that which is forbidden to the bourgeois researcher and in which s/he profoundly desires to engage but must only monitor, watch, describe and moralistically criticize and prevent. (Cf. S. Freud, *SE*, vol.VII, pp.156–7.)

2. In that sense I shall argue that the 'truths' which create the modern form of sociality are

fictions and therefore themselves invented in fantasy. 'The real' therefore becomes a problematic category which I shall deal with only by reference to 'veridicality', on the one hand, and cultural forms and practices, on the other. That is, both scientific and cultural practices produce régimes of meaning, truth, representation in which there are particular relations of signification. What is important in respect of these is the production of a *sign* – i.e. how we enter as 'a relation' and how in actual social practices and cultural forms we become 'positioned'. The concept of positioning relies upon the importance attached to signifier/signified relations. In addition, we can utilize the concept of fantasy to understand our insertion within other 'dramas'. In this respect then the mode of analysis is similar, and also potentially allows an examination of fantasies inscribed in *both* the imaginary and the symbolic.

3. Freeway is the name of an extremely small dog in the television series *Hart to Hart*. Using it as the Alsatian's name is therefore something of a joke.

4. That pain of becoming bourgeois through work: a route opened to working-class women, perhaps for the first time, in the post-war educational expansion. See my 'Dreams from an ordinary childhood', in L. Heron (ed.), *Truth, Dare or Promise*, London, Virago, 1985.

5. The dramatic butchery of the fights in the *Rocky* films would be impossible under the existing laws of amateur and professional boxing. Kathryn Kalinak makes a similar point about the impossibility of the escape route though dance presented in *Flashdance*; the heroine is simply much too old to take up a classical ballet career. See '*Flashdance*: the Dead End Kind', in *Jump Cut*, no.29 (1984), pp.3–4.

6. See, for example, S. Neale, 'Masculinity as spectacle', *Screen*, vol.24, no.6 (1983).

7. The term 'pencil-pusher' for a man with a clerical job was (at least in my family) a term of both abuse and envy. It was what everyone wanted, because it was easy, but it could not count as real work because it did not involve heavy manual labour.

8. This reading reflects my own identifications with *Rocky II*, but it is also evident in an account of reactions to the film among members of CSE Media Studies class, who were mostly male, white and working-class; see A. Brookfield, 'Reading *Rocky* films: versions of masculinity', in *Working Papers for 16+ Media Studies*, Clwyd County Council, 1985. Brookfield describes the working class youths' identification with Rocky but, 'although the narrative framework was structured around a "success story", the group challenged some aspects of the representation of success. In discussions of aspects of social class within the film the boys tended to adopt an oppositional stance towards the "American Dream" ideology. In doing so they picked up as relevant to their lives an element present in the lyrics of the theme music to the film. These suggest that poverty brutalises and makes it necessary to take to the streets and kill to survive' (p.88). I would take issue with Brookfield's assumption that 'the [Rocky] films address a wide and differentiated audience, who will bring a variety of readings to them; these different readings are based on different assumptions about "masculinity"; in general students' readings of the films remained within a dominant framework' (p.85). This implies precisely the notion that I have criticized, namely that working-class masculinity is a sexist, stereotyped version which certain views 'bring to' the film. Rather, I would suggest that masculinity is always lived as class specific, in relation to the body and the mental/manual division of labour. These are not therefore in any simple sense 'different assumptions about masculinity'.

9. The numbers refer to the counter on the tape recorder, and therefore provide a record of the passage of time during the recording. 'Untranscribed' refers to utterances which were inaudible and could therefore not be transcribed.

10. See Walkerdine (1985) op.cit.

11. D. Cherry and G. Pollock, 'Women as sign: the representation of Elizabeth Siddall in Pre-Raphaelite literature', *Art History*, vol.7, no.2 (1984). This analysis owes much to the work of Diane Watson: *Woman as Sign in Educational Discourse*, MSc Dissertation, University of London, 1984.

12. J. Mitchell, *Women: The Longest Revolution*, London, Virago, 1983, pp.115–24.

13. Flower fairies: see Cicely Mary Baker, *A Flower Fairy Alphabet*, London, Blackie, (date not

given: the edition I read must have been produced in the 1950s and it is still available in paperback).

14. To take this analysis further, this fiction inscribed me in a fantasy scenario in which the desire of the Other provided me with a fantasy of omnipotence – the power to do magic. This necessitated a bodily fragility; I was always sickly. Such a fantasy inscribes me therefore at various levels which cannot be equated with a fantasy/reality distinction. They are both adults' fantasies of their own suppressed desires directed *at* children (see J. Rose, *The Case of Peter Pan or, The Impossibility of Children's Fiction*, London, Macmillan, 1984) and the positions for the children to enter. Cicely Mary Baker's fictional child-fairies, the paper-pattern manufacturers of the blue-bell costume, the neighbour who made it, my parents, the press photographer, the amateur snapshots, etc., become a place where I can be gazed at and therefore create for me an enormous power. They provide the stuff of fantasy therefore in its widest possible sense: unconscious fantasies, daydreams of *being* a fairy and the acting out and living through this in the family relations themselves, viz 'Tinky'.

15. J. Lacan, 'God and the *jouissance* of ~~The~~ Woman', in J. Mitchell and J. Rose (eds.) *Feminine Sexuality*, London, Macmillan, 1982.

16. See J. Henriques, W. Hollway, C. Urwin, C. Venn and V. Walkerdine, *Changing the Subject: Psychology, Social Regulation and Subjectivity*, London, Methuen, 1984.

17. C. Johnston, *Edinburgh Television Papers, 1979*. For elaboration on this issue, see D. Morley, 'Texts, readers, subjects', in S. Hall, D. Hobson, A. Lowe and P. Willis (eds.), *Culture, Media, Language*, London, Hutchinson, 1980.

18. For further discussions of families watching television, see D. Morley, *Family Television*, London, Comedia, 1986, and A. Gray, 'Women and video: subject–text–context', in D. Phillips and M. Marshment. (eds.), *Women and Popular Culture*, London, Croom Helm (in press).

19. L. Mulvey, 'Visual pleasure and narrative cinema', in *Screen*, vol.16, no.3 (1975), J. Radway, 'Women read the romance: the interaction of text and context', *Feminist Studies*, vol.9, no.1 (1983).

20. C. Urwin, (1985), 'Wonder People', BPS Developmental Psychology Conference, Belfast.

21. For examples of current work on family dynamics and television which use various therapeutic models to identify normal and pathological viewing, see Goodman 'Television's role in family interaction', *Journal of Family Issues*, vol.14, no.2 (1983), pp.405–24.

22. It is here that a struggle must be located. This takes us away from the implied determinism and fixity of 'interpellation' to the possibility of a struggle over meaning.

23. Rather than analysing fantasy and reality as dichotomous, I approach *positions* and *meanings* as fictional spaces in which fantasy is lived out. The actual operations of fantasy are complex: they are inscribed not only in the lived relations of the family, I am suggesting, but also in the relations between observer and observed, in transference and counter-transference. Such relations are characterized by power.

24. C. Urwin, 'Power relations and the emergence of language', in Henriques, Urwin, Venn and Walkerdine, op.cit.

25. J. Rose, 'Femininity and its discontents', *Feminist Review*, no.14 (1983), p.9.

26. For a discussion of intellectuals, see P. Schlesinger, 'In search of the intellectuals: some comments on recent theory', *Media, Culture and Society*, no.4 (1982).

27. Radway's rejection seems to rest on an equation between psychoanalysis and a purely formalist account of how texts 'position' subjects. Although there have been occasional attempts at just such a synthesis, at a theoretical level the equation is misleading. It seems to me that psychoanalysis might open up a way of engaging with the reality of women's fantasies, pleasures and desires as they read the novels – see, for example, Cora Kaplan's article in this volume.

28. S. Clayton, 'Notes on teaching film', *Feminist Review*, no.14 (1983).

29. P. Bourdieu, *Distinction: A Social Critique of the Judgement of Taste*, London, Routledge & Kegan Paul, 1984, ch.1.

Chris Turner and Erica Carter

# POLITICAL SOMATICS:
## notes on Klaus Theweleit's
## *Male Fantasies*

Klaus Theweleit's book *Männerphantasien* (*Male Fantasies*)[1] was first
published in West Germany in 1977. One English reviewer has described
it as an attempt to 'understand Fascism through the Fascists . . . all the
little Nazis of [his] parents' generation'.[2] Yet, although he is himself
occasionally rather careless about the term, Nazism is not the immediate
object of Theweleit's study. Its actual pretext – in every sense – is an
ensemble of memoirs, diaries, letters and fictional writings produced by
men who were, in various locations, members of the *Freikorps*, the armed
counter-revolutionary groups that were made up largely of soldiers
demobilized in 1918 and other *déclassé* elements displaced by the war.
Across these writings he sets out to chart the textual landscape of fascist
fantasies, the 'territories' of a fascistic male desire.

The most immediately disarming feature of the book is that it does
not begin with a discussion of any phenomenon directly related to Nazism
or pre-fascism. We first encounter Theweleit in contemplation of a
postcard of the Hindenburg dam, which runs from the mainland to the
island of Sylt off the north coast of Germany. The image, retrieved from his
mother's photograph album, is the final link in an associative chain which
he will trace back to its rooting within German fascism.

> The picture postcard was loosely inserted in the album, among the
> pictures of the immediate family. A photo of Hindenburg, one of my
> earliest heroes, hung above the desk of my father, the railroad man,
> with a facsimile signature I had long considered genuine . . . my
> father . . . was primarily a railroad man (body and soul, as he put it)
> and only secondarily a man. He was a good man, too, and a pretty
> good fascist. The blows he brutally lavished . . . were the first lessons
> I would one day come to recognise as lessons in fascism.

The family narrative unfolds further: the birth of older brothers and
sisters, then of younger siblings: the adult Klaus Theweleit's meeting and
partnership with Monika Kubale: Monika, a clinical psychiatrist through
whom he will come to know the possibility of a resistance to fascism

enshrined, not in the writings of university historians, but in the symbolic and bodily practices of psychotic children.

> When she tells me of contact, true contact with lightning and rolling thunder, of the production of an intimacy through the feeling and exploration of distances – an intimacy that is not consuming, distance that is not far away – a place where caution is a beautiful word, related to foresight and to a feeling for the reality of a suffering which wishes for change but is caught in impasse and double-bind, I think then of the studied or hectic nonchalance of all those (myself included) who are striving to combat fascism here and now, but are blind to the experience of the non-fascist.

This introduction of fragments of autobiography, splintered images and narratives, is more than a ploy to disrupt the formal conventions of academic historiography. More forcefully, those textual elements are deployed as connotative links between a fascism which is past, and a present reality which always contains the incipient possibility of fascism. The task which Theweleit sets himself is not to 'cement' those links into a single, structurally stable historical discourse (a 'solid' piece of history-writing): his project, as we shall later see, is more 'fluid' than this. Instead, he will feel his way towards a mode of writing which both countenances and in its turn generates links between bodily resistance to fascism here and now – 'the reality of a suffering which wishes for change but is caught in impasse and double-bind' – and discourses of 'political' opposition.

How then does Theweleit's analysis unfold in the remainder of the first volume? In the first instance, it is not the literary text *as object* with which the author is concerned, but the process of production of fascist discourse. According to what dynamics, he asks, does the autobiographical or fictional text become the terrain of what he calls, after Deleuze and Guattari, a fascist 'desiring-production'? What he will insist upon in response to that question is that a materialist account of (fascist) fantasy demands the reinstatement of the human body as a force of textual production – the body which is itself produced within language, and is at the same time generative of it.

> We will look at the nature of the 'white terror', and one element within it, the language of the soldier males. The question here is not so much what such language 'expresses' or 'signifies', as how it functions, its role in the man's relationship to external reality and its bodily location.

Theweleit proposes then to investigate the perpetrators of the 'white terror', not formalistically, in discussions of their positioning within strategic fields of political and economic force in the Weimar Republic, but as physical formations, bodies of men moulded steely-hard: men whose bodily practices produced specific effects on other bodies, bleeding wounds on the social 'body' of the Republic. Most significantly, he demands that the socio-political and military formations of pre-fascism and Nazism be recognized as historically specific, yet reproducible formations of masculinity and the male body.

## Sexual difference, the body and fascist desiring-production

Theweleit's point of departure is the argument – a familiar one by now – that the subject is produced in language, in difference from and in opposition to a range of signified 'others'. He takes seriously the contention that it is *male* desire which is signified in the 'I' which surfaces into the symbolic systems of Western patriarchal culture; thus that language under patriarchy is founded on and endlessly reproduces fundamentally dichotomous relations between the sexes, in which women are placed as object, as 'other', subordinated to the 'universal subject', man.[3] Theweleit both gives credibility to that thesis and, drawing on Deleuze and Guattari's *Anti-Oedipus*, relocates it within an analytics which does not accord to desire a pre-social content: desire is 'in essence' neither masculine nor feminine, but becomes so only through its synthesis with (partial) objects in the external world.[4] The first section of *Male Fantasies*, entitled simply 'Men and Women', explores the recording of the productive force of desire through representations of femininity in the writings of the 'soldier males': woman as bride, mother or beloved: woman as aggressor (the *Flintenweib*, or 'rifle-woman'), as Bolshevist, Red nurse, White nurse, the 'Lady with the Lamp'. The linguistic process is understood here as a process of production, appropriation and trans-formation of reality; and what is striking about the language of these men is that

> the particles of reality taken up in their language lose any life of their own. They are de-vivified and turned into dying matter. They are forced to relinquish their life to a parasitic, linguistic onslaught, which seems to find pleasure in the annihilation of reality. Reality is invaded and 'occupied' in that onslaught.

What is more, it is above all the 'living movement of women', their 'emotional force' and 'sexual intensity' which seem unbearable to these men: thus their language

> either screens itself against their existence (e.g. wives, white mothers and sisters), or destroys them (e.g. proletarian women, 'rifle-women' and erotic sisters or mothers).

The initial chapter culminates in a section on attacks on women who have dared to come too close: Communists, proletarian women, the wives and mothers of male victims of the white terror. Theweleit quotes from Edwin Erich Dwinger's 1939 novel *Auf halbem Wege*:

'Take aim!' says Truchs.

'Right into them this time,' thinks Donat. . . . The human wall presses forward, as if itself about to attack. A rain of spittle hits the soldiers, hitting Truchs too in his long horse-face, dripping stickily down. . . .

The spitting woman, an image of the megaera, stands before the barrel of his gun – his sight is pointing straight into her mouth, into the centre of that slobbering hole, so wide open with hysteria that he can hardly even see the gums. 'Get away!' he screams again, as if afraid of himself. It's really her. Now he recognizes her.

'Fire!' roars Truchs. . . .

Everything turns suddenly to frenzied flight. Yet Donat sees nothing of this. He sees only the woman who was standing there before him a moment ago. It threw her onto her back, as if she had been blown over by some gigantic wind. Is that thing at his feet really her? That person without a face? The head isn't really a head any more, just a monstrous bloody throat. 'I warned her,' Donat thinks to himself, trembling. 'I warned her.'

The 'concrete' (and not 'merely' fantasized) bodily flows of the proletarian woman – the spittle which spurts from her open mouth, the scream which pierces the air around him – are the source of antagonistic currents of pleasure and unpleasure across the body of the soldier male. In the following pivotal section, where the author presents a set of preliminary theoretical conclusions, he looks first to psychoanalysis to locate the psychic origins of those currents of affect. He has found the relations of the soldier male to a represented femininity consistently resistant to analysis within the triangular categories of Oedipus. The men

want something other than incest, which is a relationship involving persons, names and families. They want to wade in blood, they want an intoxicant that will 'cause both sight and hearing to fade away'. They want a contact with the opposite sex – or perhaps simply access to sexuality itself – which cannot be *named*: a contact in which they can dissolve themselves while forcibly dissolving the other sex. They want to penetrate into its life, its warmth, its blood. It seems to me that they aren't just more intemperate, dangerous and cruel than Freud's harmless 'motherfucker' Oedipus; they are of an entirely other order. And if, in spite of everything, they have a desire for incest, it is, at the very least, with the earth itself ('Mother Earth').

They are far more likely to wish to penetrate 'her' in some violent act of 'incest', to explode into and with her, than wish themselves in the beds of their flesh-and-blood mothers.

The object relations assumed within Freud's categories of Oedipus cannot be identified in these texts. What we have instead are states of perception, 'affective intensities', hallucinatory moments of fear/pleasure and delirium. What these men seem both to fear and to desire is an explosive fusion with an 'other', a dissolution of ego-boundaries which they fear will destroy them. Drawing on pre-Oedipal psychoanalysis – especially the work of Melanie Klein, Margaret Mahler and Michael Balint – Theweleit suggests that it is in order to evade such a fusion that the female body is produced in the texts as a guarantor that there *is* difference, a marker of the other through whose body flow the desires which have been brutally expunged from the body of the soldier male: 'Desire, if it flows at all, flows in a certain sense *through women.*'

At this point, Theweleit's line of argument takes an unprecedented turn. In the first instance, he follows Deleuze and Guattari in contesting the traditional logic on which conceptions of desire are founded.

> From the very first step, the Platonic logic of desire (makes us) choose between *production* and *acquisition*. From the moment that we place desire on the side of acquisition, we make desire an idealistic (dialectical, nihlistic) conception, which causes us to look upon it primarily as lack: a lack of an object, a lack of the real object.[5]

Desire is accorded a productivity within occidental traditions of thought only in so far as it produces fantasized representations of the concrete objects we lack 'in reality'; fantasy thus gains only secondary status, as a substitute for an unattainable 'real' object of desire. What Deleuze and Guattari propose is that that lack and the split which its introduction into culture engenders between fantasy and the real be understood as themselves socially produced. Lack is no longer to be seen as the universal prerequisite of desire; instead, it is produced as such within specific historical configurations. Thus in contemporary capitalism, for example, consumer desires are awakened and new markets prised open through the 'implantation' of lack in the signifying system of advertising. The visual fantasies offered by advertisements do not accompany, oppose or even supplant 'real' needs: they hold a position in modern market economies as the dominant manifestations of a socially legitimated desire.

The concept of lack is central to the analysis of femininity within Oedipal psychoanalysis. Women occupy an inferior position in the tripartite relations of Oedipus because they lack the 'envied and valued penis and phallic power'.[6] What, however, are the consequences for the conceptualization of femininity if, first, Oedipus itself is viewed as one only of a number of possible historical productions of desire and, second, if (as Theweleit proposes) there *is* a desiring-production which takes concrete form in known cultural realities, *despite* the fact that it does not bear the stamp of Oedipus?

In his response to this question – in situating the real and the fantasized bodies of women as the channels through which all the desires of fascist 'soldier males' are made to flow – Theweleit invests femininity with a fullness which it cannot attain within the Freudo-Lacanian organization of culture around the law of the phallus. In the two-thirds of the book which follow this first chapter on 'men and women', he charts the flowing of desire through 'floods' (the 'Red flood' of Bolshevism, 'streets of blood', 'exploding earth' and 'lava', the turmoil of war), through 'bodies' (the fragmenting, exploding body of the soldier male) and, mediated by those two elements, finally through history. In the cultural constructions, artefacts and images of bourgeois history from the early Renaissance, he records the ebb and flow of desire through and beyond the body of woman across the rest of hitherto unsocialized Nature. Writing in the tradition of materialist historiography, in so far as he maintains the concept of production at the centre of his historical analysis, Theweleit scrutinizes the phenomena of bourgeois history as the effects of a desiring-production which streams out across 'bodies and the world', producing, colonizing and transforming the material of history in accordance with its own fluctuating currents. Inscribed within those historical processes is a fundamental contradiction; as the terrain of Nature is 'deterritorialized' under capitalism[7] – as productive potential is unleashed through technological and economic advances, 'pathbreaking' discoveries in the natural sciences, the opening up of frontiers towards foreign lands, the appropriation of their productions and the colonization of their peoples – so also, Theweleit proposes, there is a cruel strait-jacketing of the human pleasures liberated through that release and transformation of cultural energy. Capitalism is revealed as profoundly duplicitous from its inception: in an early instance of 'deterritorialization', the opening-up of new trade routes to the non-European world generates in turn new bodily pleasures for the European aristocracy and the emergent bourgeoisie.

> Every new trade route disclosed a novel pleasure; every new object from some foreign land held the possibility of a new sensation. Pepper took its place alongside the salt of the earth. Paprika and silk: those were once words for new (bodily) feelings.

Then 'reterritorialization': money becomes the universal unit of economic (and, later, social exchange); through the rise of the guilds, expanding economic processes – artisanal production and trade – are contained anew within bureaucratic and juridical discourses; even at this early stage, merchant capital begins its 'work of oppression' with the codification of restrictions on the movement of runaway serfs – the early forerunners of the industrial proletariat – in their passage from country to city and town.

At every stage in Theweleit's vastly ambitious work of historical reconstruction, through minute to macrocosmic accounts of kaleidoscopic transformations in class and sexual relations from the sixteenth century to the present day, the narratives of history are traced through the imprints they have left on the bodies of human subjects – above all, on the bodies of women. There is, asserts Theweleit, a productive force of femininity, through which women gain access to history. Women are, as it were, 'reinserted' into history, not as a force of production in the (Marxian) economic sense, but as a force for the absorption of the desiring-production which engenders capitalist patriarchy. It is this which creates and sustains the fiction of a femininity which is not defined either as the absence or lack of a phallus, but as a certain abundant presence, an infinite plenitude of 'de-vivified' images of women, and a multitude of living bodies on which are inflicted patriarchy's violent wounds.

> It seems to me that women's productive potential, still relatively unformed [in early bourgeois society] must have been admitted into areas of social production whose products served to uphold the system of dominance. They were allowed to enter here as representations of a fiction of abundance ('Paradise regained in the body of high-born woman') which arose out of the encoding of the body of the Earth, 'unproduced' Nature, with the fiction of a boundless and all-fulfilling female body. . . . The *fictive* body of woman has become an imaginary arena for phantasies of deterritorializations, while actual male–female relations have continued to serve, and have been actively maintained, as focal points for the implementation of massive reterritorializations.

## Feminist historiography and the 'body politic'

To attempt to extrapolate a single historical theory from *Male Fantasies* would be to work against the grain of a text which persistently refuses the systematizing order of the scientific discourses on which it draws. For Theweleit 'theory' is a treasure-chest of heuristic implements: sociology and social history (centrally, Norbert Elias's socio-history of European civilisation), Marxist historiography (including the excellent Weimar working-class histories of his own mentor, Erhard Lucas), anthropology (with a circuitous ramble through the controversial work of the feminist

Elaine Morgan), materialist philosophy, the psychoanalysis of Freud and the post-Freudians, the materialist psychiatries of Reich, Reiche and, most crucially, Deleuze and Guattari. Yet any theoretical system assembled by Klaus Theweleit itself fragments in the process of its own construction. Each chapter, even the last, ends on a question:

> only the multiple, the partial, the segmentary, the replicated, the chaotic, microanarchy, is to be . . . well, what then?

> whatever the outcome, it is not to be raised to the pinnacle of theory, nor lowered to the level of the profoundest of truths. Or is it?

Is it indeed? How are we to assess Theweleit's plea for a historiography which prioritizes male–female relations within its reconstructions of capitalism and fascism, yet refuses to answer its own questions as to the universality – or otherwise – of those relations? Early in the first chapter, he asks, with feminist hypotheses in mind, whether fascism is 'simply the norm' for men under capitalist patriarchy. In a footnote, he delivers the question into the hands of the women who first raised it.

> I wish to cite no bibliographical evidence here: any reader interested in pursuing the point further should enter into those discussions currently being conducted by women.

This evasion – principled though it may be – registers a distance between Theweleit's theoretical strategy and lines of enquiry developed within feminism. Michèle Montrelay has suggested that psychoanalysis may have been 'articulated precisely in order to repress femininity (in the sense of producing its symbolic representations).'[8] There is perhaps a similar problem with Theweleit's reconstruction of the psycho-sexual histories of *Freikorps* males; for, in multiplying the possible significations of femininity, he may run the danger of obliterating the feminine body as it is felt, spoken and culturally deployed by women. For feminist historians, though they may share the author's interest in fascism as the key to a new 'cultural' historiography,[9] the central problem of German fascism is not that of how men's support could have been enlisted for the transmutation of their desiring-production into a 'murdering-production' recorded on the bodies of Jews, Communists, women, homosexuals and other groups. Instead, feminists have asked how Nazism could apparently have excluded women so entirely from *any* historical production. Theweleit's work has certainly been taken up by feminist historians;[10] but investigations into female 'desiring-production' are necessarily conducted from a different vantage point. The body of woman is not inactive in its 'absorption' of a masculine desiring-production; through their own work on themselves and their bodies, women have traditionally produced themselves as the terrain on which sexuality (male *and* female) can be engendered. One possible response to Theweleit from within feminism may then consist, not in a return to the pure female body untouched and unadulterated by fascist fantasy, but instead in a reworking of the multiple fragments identified within *Male Fantasies*, a dismantling and reassemblage which restores cultural power to the hitherto subordinated body of woman.

> 'The body doesn't incorporate ideas; it generates them,' Frieda Grafe wrote in an article on the paintings of Frederike Pezold, whose work begins to reconstruct the female body (her body) by dismantling it into partial fragments – 'corporeal signs' that represent nothing at all, but that permit the body to regenerate itself through the contemplation of its own components.

### The anti-subjectivist reflex

It would be difficult to discuss Theweleit's work in an English context without considering some of the rather negative responses his approach has generated among those British Left historians who have examined it seriously. An early review by Richard J. Evans, which appeared in Germany, characterized *Male Fantasies* as 'psychohistory', as – and this seems somewhat eccentric – an application of 'Freudian' concepts to history and, with reference to Geoffrey Barraclough's article, 'Psychohistory is bunk', rehearsed the familiar arguments against 'psychologizing' explanation. More recently, an account by Jane Caplan of Theweleit's contribution to the Ohio State University 'Women, fascism and everyday life' conference in April 1983 refers to 'Theweleit's unusual and extremely subjectivist approach to the problems of effective consciousness'.[11] She goes on to accuse him of 'solipsism'.

Now we were not at Ohio State and we have no means of knowing what Theweleit may have said there, but the charge of subjectivism common to both reviews is the index of a problem. Whether this is in fact a problem within Theweleit's conceptualization or in the presuppositions of the reviewers seems to us at least an open question. Certainly for Theweleit, a particular style of thinking in terms of oppositions between 'rational' and 'irrational' or 'objective' and 'subjective' represents a complicity with unacceptable forms of economist reductionism and functions only to exclude certain questions from the purview of historiography and political theory.

> In its crudest and most widespread form, this line of thinking calls anything related to social production 'objective', 'rational', 'real'. 'Subjective', 'irrational' and 'unreal' are the labels reserved for

anything that merely occurs in human beings, in the 'psyche', impeding the victory of the rational and 'objective' process which of course leads inexorably towards socialism.

In truth, these bi-polar opposites are related to another opposition – that of negative and positive – and to the distinction between 'right' and 'wrong'. They are evaluative terms, for the most part negative judgments. It is systems, not knowledges which they sustain. And the systems they come from are obsolete. Like some glacial deposit from the European Enlightenment, they lie scattered in the conceptual landscape of science, blocking reality from view, preventing the development of new concepts which might correspond better to processes in the real, and serving as barricades in the struggle waged by ideologues and defenders of the bourgeois ego (including the unwitting variety) to stave off their own demise.

Whilst on the one hand, Theweleit's evident distaste for the more dogmatic Marxist theorists amongst his compatriots emerges in the tone of this passage and its tendency to bold generalization, there is arguably an element of over-generous reticence in the paragraph which follows, where he exempts Marx from any part in this objective/subjective thinking. It is, to say the least, quite possible to locate a certain 'closure' within Marxism that ascribes objectivity quite arbitrarily to certain theoretical entities. As Marshall Sahlins points out,

> Marx ... reserved the symbolic quality to the object in its commodity-form (fetishism). Assuming that use-values transparently serve human needs, that is, by virtue of their evident properties, he gave away the meaningful relations between men and objects essential to the comprehension of production in any historical form. ... Use-value is not less symbolic or less arbitrary than commodity-value. For 'utility' is not a quality of the object but a significance of the objective qualities. The reason Americans deem dogs inedible and cattle 'food' is no more perceptible to the senses than the price of meat.[12]

The example may seem trivial but, if we refer not simply to the meaningful relations between men and objects but to the whole complex of relations between men and objects, women and objects and men and women, we begin to appreciate, however imprecisely, the existence of a 'cultural' field that is not addressed by the 'empty subject' presuppositions of Marxian philosophical anthropology. The subjects of social action are not simply *Träger* (bearers) of economic relations in capitalism, in spite of the fact that capitalism may seem to have ushered in a world of rationally calculating individuals. As Sahlins goes on to argue, everything in capitalism conspires to conceal the symbolic ordering of the system. . . . A praxis theory based on pragmatic interests and 'objective' conditions is the secondary form of a cultural illusion.[13]

Theweleit attempts to overcome that illusion and to get back beyond the point where orthodox socio-political analyses normally cleave reality into the two realms of 'objective' material production and 'subjective' cultural representation (or fantasy). This is the purpose of his appropriation of the reconceptualization of the social proposed in Deleuze and Guattari's *Anti-Oedipus*, which both reinjects into that field the productive force of the unconscious and reasserts the cultural – desiring – dimensions of all social production, which Marxism initially segments off and then adds back later, in sanitized form, as 'ideology'.

Mobilizing and filling out Deleuze and Guattari's conception of desiring-production and its vicissitudes (with all the dialectic of de- and reterritorializations), his analysis seeks to locate points at which cultural signifiers can be made to yield up the part played by phantasy – in its strongest, constitutive sense – in the (re)production of material reality. Rejecting a decultured and delibidinized 'materialism', safely insulated from the troubling flow of desire, he comes at the nature of a Western European 'cultural order' (though he does not call it that) by focusing on two materialities repressed within conventional Marxism, the body and the word.

Now this would be of little interest and could indeed be consigned to the margins of historiography, either as vague theoretical speculation or as a merely 'local' study of cultural aspects, were it not that Theweleit's method is enormously *productive*. And it is not so merely in regard to historically past material, but in its negotiations with the present, to the point indeed that one reviewer has written that 'Theweleit's work gives us a new *tradition* for the historical conception of our psychology and our sexuality'[14] (our emphasis).

The productivity to which such an assessment pays tribute comes about as a result of the high degree of psychic coherence Theweleit is able to demonstrate in the various, often bizarre (but equally often only too normal) productions of the *Freikorps* 'soldier males'. If these men's writings had simply represented a delirium that could be dismissed as chaotic irrationalism, as the eclipse or destruction of reason, it would have been well to seek some external mechanism outside and prior to that delirium to provide a historical exploration of the 'breakdown' that produced it. Equally, if they merely re-presented economic 'interests' constituted elsewhere, the task would merely have been one of decoding, of translation. What Theweleit's analysis suggests, however, is that the internal structuring of the pre-fascist delirium points to a range of material processes that cannot be reduced to the truncated 'materialism' of economistic explanation. The production of fascist reality is a process which has a whole array of sites, not the least important of which is the relation between the sexes 'which is a relation of production'.

## A 'new politics'?

What political consequences now flow from a recognition that sociopolitical formations always intersect with particular formations of phantasy and the body? If Klaus Theweleit has placed the body at the core of his political problematic, he cannot by extension be understood to be offering an uncomplicated version of body politics as a revised blueprint for a socialist-feminist future. The politics of *Male Fantasies* have recognizable correspondences, affinities and resonances within what have been termed the 'new social movements' in West Germany – and yet the very terminology which allows those correspondences to be identified must itself be called into question. In the broadest of terms, the body can indeed be seen to be mobilized in two ways within those movements as object of desire: first, as a site of coherence, around which political collectivities crystallize and are consolidated; and second, as a site for the marking of difference – tattoos on the body of the punk, or proliferating subcultural styles in dress. But it is precisely in this latter function that the 'oppositional body' militates against any explanation which seeks to replace it within the unified 'sphere' of a new politics, whose proponents may now realize socialist aspirations for the mobilization of a unitary mass of the people.

For Klaus Eder, writing in *Telos* in the summer of 1982, it is the ecology movement that seems to crystallize all the aspects of protest into a historically new social movement: one and one only.

> Both the (bourgeois) movement for political emancipation and the labour movement challenged cultural traditions and provided a normative direction to social development. Both sought to redirect social evolution and have created a new society, although they have not succeeded in transforming it. Thus, it is necessary to ask whether they prefigure a new social movement trying to rebuild society.[15]

It is not the theoretical purity, or otherwise, of Eder's arguments for a single solution to contemporary political dilemmas which is the crucial issue here. As Eder himself suggests, what is at stake is the 'historical adequacy' of his argument. Having identified a particular logic of linear development within what he terms 'the new social movements', he finds himself confronted with the uncomfortable historical realities of movements, whose trajectories are insistently multidirectional, their forms and practices diverse. The solution he proposes reveals, precisely, the inadequacy of his own historical analysis.

> Our answer is to intervene in those collective actions and crystallize them into a new social movement . . . it is difficult to refrain from the learning processes constituting a new social movement.[16]

Difficult, we might ask, for whom? To the extent that Eder sets himself the task of deriving logically the actual behaviour of individuals from (their) concrete actions and behaviour, and of formulating a revolutionary theory deriving from that logic, he is writing in the tradition of a Marxian Critical Theory passed on and developed within 'the institutions' by the new young professors of 1968 and after. What distinguishes the movements of the late 1970s – out of which, we would suggest, the Theweleitian problematic emerges – from the earlier New Left in Germany is, however, precisely the rise of autonomous organizations beyond the institutions: organizations whose internal logics deny the very gap between scholarly theory and socially emancipatory praxis on which Critical Theory is predicated.[17]

The political question which it is appropriate to pose in relation to *Male Fantasies* is then not that of how it might 'crystallize', 'systematize' or invest with an external logic the purportedly 'illogically' conceived politics of the new social movements. Any forced coalition of, say, feminism, with other subcultural and countercultural movements denies the very assertion of difference by which those movements are constituted. A text which, like Theweleit's, acknowledges the materiality (in both senses of that word) of the body, and the significance of that 'micropolitical force' which, for Guattari, 'constitutes the true fabric of history', acquires effectivity, not through the objectification and mastery of its objects in scientific discourse, but through its associative coupling with already existing objects of desire in the socio-political field. The 'political test' for the text will not be what it claims to 'know' of politics, but rather, through what channels and by means of what *agencements*[18] it can connect with that fabric.

## Notes

1. K. Theweleit, *Männerphantasien*, Frankfurt-am-Main, Verlag Roter Stern, 1977 (vol.1), 1978 (vol.2). Translations here are by the authors, who also revised the American English translation of vol.1. The translation, *Male Fantasies*, is being published by Polity Press and University of Minnesota Press in spring 1987.
2. P. Franks, '*Male Fantasies*: capitalism–sexism–fascism', *Radical Philosophy*, no.26 (autumn 1980), p.35.
3. For a placing of these debates within a critique of the so-called 'great discourses' of German philosophy and literature, see S. Bovenschen, *Die imaginierte Weiblichkeit. Exemplarische Untersuchungen zu kulturgeschichtlichen und literarischen Präsentationsfor-*

*men des Weiblichen*, Frankfurt-am-Main, Suhrkamp Verlag 1979 (particularly ch.1: 'Schattenexistenz und Bilderreichtum', pp.17–62); also B. Wartmann, *'Verdrängungen der Weiblichkeit aus der Geschichte. Bemerkungen zu einer 'anderen' Produktivität der Frau'*, in *Weiblich-männlich. Kulturgeschichtliche Spuren einer verdrängten Weiblichkeit*, Brigitte Wartmann/Ästhetik und Kommunikation (eds.), Berlin, 1980, pp.7–33.

4.  See G. Deleuze and F. Guattari, *Anti-Oedipus: Capitalism and Schizophrenia*, Minneapolis, University of Minnesota Press, 1983, pp.1–8.

5.  G. Deleuze and F. Guattari, op.cit., p.25.

6.  S. Lipshitz, 'Introduction to British edition', in J. Chasseguet-Smirgel, *Female Sexuality: New Psychoanalytic Views*, London, Virago, 1981, p.xii.

7.  For a fuller account of processes of 'deterritorialization' and 'reterritorialization', see Deleuze and Guattari, op.cit., pp.240–62.

8.  Cit. C. Owens, 'The discourse of others: feminists and postmodernism', in H. Foster (ed.), *Postmodern Culture*, London, Pluto, 1985, p.63.

9.  As one writer has put it, 'any investigation into Nazism/fascism necessarily demands a problematizing of the whole of Western historiography as it is presently constituted; a problematization, that is, from the perspective of cultural revolution, in the absence of which any study of the cultural character of woman, and the mechanisms of domination which are both programmed into this, and at the same time transcend it, must remain irrelevant', G. Treusch-Dieter, 'Ferner als die Antike . . . Machtform und Mythisierung der Frau im Nationalsozialismus und Faschismus', *Konkursbuch*, 12, Tübingen, 1984.

10. See G. Treusch-Dieter, op.cit. Atina Grossman also pays tribute to *Male Fantasies* when she writes of the dread which haunted right-wing sexual conservatives in Weimar Germany of a female sexuality conceived in terms of an 'uncontrollable streaming forth, breaking through and invading boundaries', A. Grossman, 'The new woman and the rationalization of sexuality in Weimar Germany', in A. Snitow, C. Stansall and S. Thompson (eds.), *The Powers of Desire – The Politics of Sexuality*, New York, Virago, 1983. p.166.

11. J. Caplan, 'Women, fascism and everyday life conference', *History Workshop Journal* (spring, 1984), p.198.

12. M. Sahlins, *Culture and Practical Reason*, Chicago and London, Chicago University Press, 1976, pp.169–70.

13. ibid., p.220.

14. P. Franks, op.cit., p.37.

15. K. Eder, 'A new social movement?', *Telos* 52 (summer, 1982), pp.10–11.

16. ibid., p.20.

17. See M. Krüger, 'Notes on Critical Theory in Germany', *Semiotext(e)*, vol.IV, no.2, pp.130–1.

18. For a discussion of the term 'agencement', see David Cooper's introduction to the English translation of Felix Guattari's *Molecular Revolution* (Harmondsworth, Penguin, 1984), where Cooper also refers the reader to G. Deleuze and C. Parnet, *Dialogue* (Paris, Flammarion, 1977, pp.84–91).

# INDEX

# NEW FORMATIONS

Routledge publishes *New Formations* as a journal three times a year. *New Formations* continues the critical analysis of cultural practices, products and institutions developed in the three volumes of the *Formations* series. It engages with a wide range of current debates – about meaning and power, cultural and sexual difference, modernism and post-modernism, psychoanalysis and post-structuralism, popular culture and avant-gardes, democracy and civil society, national cultural policies and institutions – and questions their presuppositions, concepts and perspectives. It aims to be lively, polemical, international and diverse and to draw on a variety of contributors from within and beyond the academic world.

*New Formations* also includes more topical forms of writing – interviews and discussions, critical work on particular aesthetic practices and political commentaries – and a substantial reviews section.

If you would like to submit a proposal for *New Formations* or to receive more information about the journal, please write to:
The Managing Editor, *New Formations*, 41b Hornsey Lane Gardens, London N6 5NY, England